Memoirs of an Unfortunate Person

Memoirs of an Unfortunate Person

MOTY STROMER

YAD VASHEM AND
THE HOLOCAUST SURVIVORS' MEMOIRS PROJECT
New York • Jerusalem

This book is published by Yad Vashem, the Holocaust Martyrs' and Heroes' Remembrance Authority, c/o American Society for Yad Vashem, 500 Fifth Avenue, 42nd floor, New York, New York 10110-4299, and P.O.B. 3477, Jerusalem 91034, Israel

www.yadvashem.org

and

The Holocaust Survivors' Memoirs Project in association with the World Federation of Bergen-Belsen Associations, Inc.

The Holocaust Survivors' Memoirs Project, an initiative of Nobel Peace Prize laureate Elie Wiesel, was launched through a generous grant from Random House, Inc., New York, New York.

Cover photos and all other photographs courtesy of Moty Stromer

Library of Congress Cataloging-in-Publication Data

Stromer, Moty.
  Memoirs of an unfortunate person: the diary of Moty Stromer / by Moty Stromer.
      p. cm.
  ISBN 978-0-9814686-0-0 (alk. paper)
1. Jew--Persecutions--Ukraine. 2. Holocaust, Jewish (1939-1945)--Ukraine--Personal narratives. 3. Holocaust survivors--Personal narratives.
4. Stromer, Moty. 5. Ukraine--Ethnic relations. I. Title. II. Title: Diary of Moty Stromer.
DS135.U4S77 2008
940.53'18092--dc22
    [B]
2008000376

Typesetting: Judith Sternberg
Produced by Offset Nathan Shlomo Press
Printed in Jerusalem, Israel.

TABLE OF CONTENTS

Translated from the Yiddish by Elinor Robinson,
with assistance from an earlier translation by Stanley Bergman

Language Editor: Jeanette Friedman

DEDICATION

*To Abish and Elish
my sweet little nephews*

FOREWORD

~~~~~◇~~~~~

By David Silberklang

This gripping diary and memoir by Mordechai Moty Stromer was written while he was hiding in the home of his rescuers, the Streker family. The book is a combination of diary and memoir, containing elements of both styles of writing. Even Moty Stromer's daughter, Sue Talansky, goes back and forth between the two terms in her moving introduction below. Written in real time, the book provides insight into Stromer's daily concerns and fears. He hears the approaching Soviet army, its bombings and shellings, and he dreads the day that his *Volksdeutsche* protectors will need to leave before the incoming Soviets. What will he do then? And when his rescuer's relatives move into the house, he finds himself treated much more poorly, yet they continue to harbor him at great risk. At the same time, he shares with us his entire story, which he recorded so that the surviving family members abroad, his sister in particular, would know what had happened to their family.

Stromer's recall of detail is remarkable, and he opens before us every aspect of daily life, from the vicious, murderous beatings by his erstwhile Ukrainian countrymen and neighbors, to the organization of the ghetto apartment that he shared with his sister and her family and others. The two aspects to the writing — the present tense observations and concerns and the detailed account of all that he had experienced from the early part of the war — are interwoven into a riveting story that is difficult to put down.

The book also provides insight into Jews' experiences in small towns and villages during the Nazi occupation, as well as into daily life in the Lwow ghetto. One of the many fascinating aspects of the diary-memoir is the glimpse it affords into the Janówska Road camp, where tens of thousands of Jews were murdered. Yet, despite the horrific conditions of that camp, Stromer managed to help maintain his sister Zlateh and her children with goods that he found or bought in the camp or on the black market. When he was sent to work in a canning factory in the city, his daily living conditions actually improved considerably. This is one of the ironies of the Nazi camp system — for some Jews, their living conditions improved as most of the other Jews were killed and as their own sense of their imminent mortality increased.

Stromer also provides a rare and unexpected insight into the Bełżec death camp, when he quotes at length from what an escapee from that camp told him when he came to the ghetto. This was the death camp that murdered more than 500,000 Jews in 1942, including much of Moty Stromer's family, and from which there is only one written Jewish eyewitness account (by Rudolf Reder).

The fears, pain, anguish and trepidation of daily life are told in simple, yet poignant words, alongside the observations regarding determination, courage, and initiative in the struggle to live. His parting from his fiancée Pepe and from his sister Zlateh and her two little children, Abish and Elish, are told with a profound, present-tense pain that sears the reader and evokes a deep empathy. Stromer's anguish and guilt feelings following the liquidation of the ghetto and his inability to save his sister and nephews are palpable. They also highlight the Jews' collective helplessness before the Nazi onslaught, despite their resourcefulness.

Moty Stromer remained a religious man, always expressing his belief in God repeatedly and trying to pray regularly and observe the Sabbath as best he could under the circumstances, even while hiding. He informs us at one point that he does not write on the Sabbath. At the same time, Stromer was an avid admirer of the Soviet Union. During their occupation of his hometown of Kamionka-Strumilowa equality reigned — equal opportunity for all and fairness, he felt. This was a marked improvement from what he had experienced during the last years of the Polish republic and far better than what he suspected Jews could expect from the Germans.

The drama of the last chapters is engrossing, as Stromer tells of the end of the ghetto, the frantic search by many Jews for a way to save themselves, and the fleeting goodbyes that some did manage. And as he tells us how he escaped capture and got to his hiding place and prays to survive the war, his solitude, facing World War II and the Holocaust alone, are jarring. And he wonders: "[W]hen will I be able to be a free man? You can hardly imagine what freedom means. That can be understood only by someone who has lost his freedom."

Indeed, what he experienced is very difficult for any of us who was not there to understand, but this diary-memoir sheds light on aspects of the Holocaust that might otherwise remain obscure to later generations such as ours.

Moty Stromer wrote in Yiddish, in the most difficult circumstances, and he was aware that he was writing with grammatical errors. However, he did not want to write in Polish, in which he apparently could write better, so that no local people would be able to read his diary. However, he hoped one day to have an opportunity to correct his grammatical errors. "If God only helps me to live through this terrible period, I will, together with my brother-in-law in America, publish this whole experience as a separate work.... The book would be a memoir, the diary of an unfortunate person. Is it possible to describe everything I have lived through up to this very day? Can anyone understand what I have been going through in this place, ... in the attic, without seeing a living soul, and always in the dark?"

He wrote this in late May 1944. He did not get to correct and publish this in his lifetime. We are very pleased that we have been able to bring his wish to publish his fascinating diary-memoir to fruition. I invite you to enter the remarkable story of Moty Stromer.

INTRODUCTION

My father, Moty Stromer, was born on July 5, 1910 in a small town called Kamionka-Strumilowa (Kaminke in Yiddish) not far from the city of Lwow (Lemberg in Yiddish) in southeastern Poland. The town had a population of about 4000 Jews, and most of them knew one another.

Moty's Yiddish name was Mordechai and in Polish he was known as Marek. His parents, Shaul and Gittel Taksel Stromer, ran a prosperous wholesale and retail liquor business. Their home and store were located at 38 Third of May Street, and they had four children: Moty, Zlateh (b. 1913), Henia (b. 1915), and Meyer (b. 1919).

The extended Stromer family was a large one. Shaul was the only child of Reuven and Leah Stromer, who were first cousins. Moty was very close to these grandparents and to all the great uncles, aunts and cousins who lived in Kaminke, in Lemberg and in nearby Greiding.

Shabbos and the holidays were celebrated together and family *simchas* (life cycle events) were always well attended. The Stromers attended a synagogue not far from their home, a wooden synagogue that was so famous, visitors to town would often stop there to take photographs and view its magnificent *bima* (pulpit) and *Aron Kodesh* (Holy Ark).

Grandfather Reuven's home was damaged during a bombing in World War I, and in 1926, he was able to rebuild it. When it was done, he invited half the town to celebrate its rededication (see photo).

My father's formal education began and ended in a small *cheder* and a Polish primary school. He never was able to continue his studies, but the family was extremely proud of his younger sister, Henia who graduated from a Polish gymnasium (high school plus) and matriculated, no small achievement for a young Jewish girl in the Poland of the 1930s.

A voracious reader and autodidact, Moty was familiar with many western literary classics and especially loved works by Robert Louis Stevenson and Daniel Defoe that he read in Polish translation. In the chapter headings of his diary, one can see the influence of these authors. When cinema came to Poland, he also became a fan of American Westerns, which entertained him for the rest of his life.

Moty was inducted into the Polish Army in 1932 and served in an equestrian unit. This experience strengthened his knowledge of the Polish language and character and, no doubt, was of use to him during the war years. When he returned from his army stint, he worked in the family business alongside his parents, whom he adored.

Relations with the local non-Jewish population were good and a plentiful harvest brought happy customers to the liquor store. Conversely, when the farmers fell on hard times and needed a loan to tide them over, the Stromers were happy to oblige. The store was located near a church, and the locals always joked that Shaul Stromer made a living from the living and the dead — since customers would congregate at the tavern after funerals, weddings and christenings.

Every day, Gittel worked with Shaul and baked the delicious yeast cakes that were served with the customers' drinks. She was so industrious, that on Thursday nights she would go to bed wearing her apron, so that at sunrise on Friday she was ready to begin Shabbos preparations immediately. Though the work was hard, there was apparently time and money for annual vacations at the nearby spa of Krynicia and for ample dowries for the Stromer girls.

In 1935, Zlateh married Mechel Eisen, an intelligent and handsome young man — a student from the yeshiva of Bratislava. They moved to Lemberg and had two young children, Abish and Elish (Abraham and Elisha). In August of 1938, Henia married a scholar named Zalman Edelstein from Strelysk, and the pair left for America one year later, exactly one month before Germany invaded Poland.

According to his diary, my father enjoyed the period of time between

August 1939 and June 1941, when this part of Galicia was under Soviet rule. He writes of the benefits of the communist system — the plentiful food supply, ample leisure time, and the egalitarian spirit.

During this period he fell in love with his mother's cousin's daughter, a young woman named Pepe Haberkorn. In the spring of 1941 the family was busy planning the engagement and wedding, when everything turned into chaos and was destroyed forever on Sunday, June 22, 1941 — when German tanks and troops entered Kaminke.

Ten days later Moty's grandfather, Reuven Stromer, and his great uncle, Chaim-Hersh Stromer, were brutally murdered. Moty himself was savagely tortured by Ukrainian nationalists in nearby Remenow. His diary is a detailed account of his horrifying experiences in Remenow and in the Lemberg ghetto, where he remained until it was liquidated in June 1943.

In Lemberg, Moty shared living quarters with Zlateh and Mechel and his young nephews, and later with Pepe, her parents and brother. The group faced one crisis after another, and narrowly escaped deportation and death on several occasions. But the end was inevitable. When the Lemberg ghetto was liquidated, Moty lost the souls dearest to his heart — first Pepe, and then his beloved sister Zlateh and her two boys.

Soon after, revolver in hand, Moty abandoned his work detail and fled. Running towards Kaminke he decided to try to find shelter with people he knew before the war: Józef and Rozalie Streker, a *Volksdeutsche* (ethnic German) couple who had a farm in an area called Jagonia. The Strekers, at great risk, hid him in their attic for ten months, until the approaching Soviet armies and the implicit threat they posed to ethnic Germans forced them to abandon their home and its terrified, hidden tenant.

It is in the last two months of hiding, from April 6 to June 2, 1944, that my father wrote his memoir. Hungry, cold, heartsick and frightened, he asked for paper and pencil in order to write down his thoughts and memories. Józef Sztreker obliged by giving him a blank ledger book and some pencil stubs. Writing in Yiddish, in a painfully neat and tiny script, he recounted as best he could the fate of those he knew and loved.

At the beginning and at the end of his writings, he repeatedly requested that the memoir be sent to his sister Henia Edelstein and/or his great uncle, Max Stromer, both of them in Brooklyn, New York. There is a sense of urgency in these lines and the script became larger and larger, as if he were shouting these directions on paper with his last ounces of mental and physical strength. It was clear to him that despite all the dangers he survived, he still might not make it through the war alive. He needed to do everything in his power to insure this manuscript's survival, if not his own.

Whereas many a memoir is written for the perusal of a general readership, this memoir assumes a special reader from the very beginning. My father's dream was to have two very specific readers — his beloved sister in America and his beloved younger brother, Meyer Stromer, who was in the Soviet Union during the entire war. My father repeatedly states what a comfort it would be to him to have them read these lines and comprehend just what transpired in their little shtetl and its environs. Perhaps because he addressed his siblings from the start, the memoir assumes the readers' familiarity with the characters, relationships and place names that it describes.

For the general reader things can be confusing, unless the family tree we are including in this volume is consulted.

Many aspects of the memoir continue to amaze and astound me. First, is my father's incredibly strong imperative to bear witness, to account for the final destiny of each and every individual that he can think of. In the end, time is so short and the number of victims is so extensive, that he resorts to simply listing their names.

This imperative to chronicle details is fueled by the desire to give these souls their proper due as unique beings, to pull them from their mass graves and to set a *matzevah* (a tombstone) of remembrance upon each one — to give them a *yad vashem* (an everlasting monument). He was further inspired by his desire to bear witness against the Nazi murderers and their Ukrainian collaborators, whose savagery and bestiality he witnessed and experienced first hand nearly every day of the 1066 days since he left Kaminke.

He was careful to name those who murdered, looted, beat and mutilated his acquaintances, family and friends. He vows again and again that vengeance against the German nation must be exacted. (After my father's death, the United States Department of Justice requested a copy of this manuscript for its war crimes investigations.)

I am also impressed by my dad's remarkable memory. The dates and names that he remembers, the *Aktion[en]* he records in clear and chronological order, the street names and addresses that he kept straight are numerous indeed. His knowledge of general history is ample, and by reading newspapers discarded by the Strekers, he had a pretty up-to-date sense of how the war was progressing and how close at hand was its end. His knowledge of the fate of European Jewry was extensive despite the news blackouts, and underscores the ability of the Jews confined to the ghettos to get information from couriers, informants and rumor mills. There were those who soon deduced the true meaning of the work details and understood exactly what Hitler's final solution was.

The quality of my father's writing in Yiddish is extraordinary. The raw Yiddish has never been edited, though the translation has been adjusted for the modern English-language reader. The diary was written in cramped, dimly lit quarters and its author was under constant air attack, bombardment and fear of discovery, so his ability to maintain clarity and organization is incredible.

Some of the passages are achingly beautiful; particularly the poignantly bitter description of how the family sold off the little boy's toy wagon so there would be food to eat. My father considered this as more than a simple diary. It was a literary achievement, particularly for a self-educated man. This is evident from the chapter divisions, chapter titles and the fact that he very deliberately gave his work the title: *The Memoir of an Unfortunate Person.*

Much has been written about God's absence during the Shoah, but in my father's account of his personal Shoah, God is very much present and accountable. His faith in God's help — *"Got vet helfin"* — is evident on almost every page of the Yiddish work. Even in the darkness of the Streker attic, Moty recited *Kaddish* (prayer in memory of the dead) daily, as the service of a man dedicated to remembrance.

Mechel Eisen, Zlateh's husband, was instrumental in creating a modicum of religious observance in their poor little group. Mechel's Yom Kippur services, his Pesach Seder, and his sanctification of ritual sustained them even when it was nearly impossible to think of anything beyond survival. Their Judaism was a source of strength and hope for all those around him.

Zlateh was a paragon of *midot tovot* (good deeds) and conducted herself in a most selfless and generous manner. Through it all, she shared her food, money and supplies with anyone who needed help. She championed the rights of the typhoid sufferer when the others want to turn him out, and it was she who lifted the spirits of those who could bear their suffering no longer.

In my father's eyes, Mechel and Zlateh are the hero and heroine of this memoir for their righteousness, generosity and loving kindness.

My father certainly never thought of himself as a hero nor did he see his diary as a tale in which he played the role of chief protagonist. There is surprisingly little ego on these pages and this, too, sets Dad's memoir apart from so many others. I believe my father was driven to write his story in all its painful detail as an eyewitness testimony to events that were sublimely and essentially unbelievable. It is almost as if he sensed that someday the world would be filled with Holocaust deniers. Perhaps another person in his place would have despaired and concluded: "Why bother?"

It took Herculean fortitude and immeasurable optimism to maintain the hope that his words would someday find their intended readers. The very act of writing and recording his reality in the face of death was my dad's greatest act of heroism. And with all that said, when one closes the book, one walks away with the impression that if Moty Stromer wasn't a hero, he was certainly a man with unlimited reserves of strength, hope and ingenuity. His resource-fulness in procuring foodstuffs, creating hideouts and negotiating deals with locals are evidence of great courage and imagination.

I do not know how this manuscript survived — whether my father buried it in Jagonia and retrieved it later, or whether he took it with him when he left his hiding place.

I do know that soon after the last page was written, the war came to an end and Moty returned to Kaminke to find it *Judenrein* and dangerously un-welcoming. The family who appropriated his family's house and business shut the door in his face. (What bad luck! Their Jew had survived!) Moty turned towards Krakow without a backward glance. There he met my mother, Ruth Baumwald, whose father, Hirsh, was Mechel Eisen's cousin.

My mother was a beautiful young woman, twelve years my father's junior, and like his sister Henia, a graduate of a Polish gymnasium. Ruth, her sister Lusia, and her parents, Hersh and Sala, also survived the war by hiding in the Lemberg ghetto. My parents-to-be fell in love and were married in 1947 by the chief rabbi of Krakow, who years later, in New York, officiated at my wedding, as well as my sister's.

Eager to leave Poland for good, the Baumwalds and the Stromers headed west, for Antwerp, Belgium. Nina was born in 1948 and named Gittel in Yiddish after my father's mother, and I was born in 1953 and named Shulamith, after my father's father.

America, *"de goldene medina,"* still beckoned, and my father yearned to join his sister Henia in New York. His brother Meyer survived the war in the USSR and was already in New York. In March 1955 he married Gusta Katz, a young woman from Kaminke.

Antwerp proved too provincial for my dad, and despite my mother's tearful objections, the Stromer family sailed for America aboard the USS Queen Elizabeth in mid-1955. The family eventually settled on the Upper West Side of New York, where many other Holocaust survivors lived and socialized.

Dad went into the real estate business, first leasing, and then purchasing, brownstones in our neighborhood. Nina and I were enrolled in Manhattan Day School, a Jewish school that was then on Manhattan Avenue and West 104th Street. We joined Rabbi Bernard Bergman's congregation on West 103rd Street, which later became the *shtiebl* of Rabbi Menachem Mendel Zaks.

My parents' social life was simple and normal for their day. Shabbos afternoons were spent chatting with friends on the benches of Riverside Drive while the children played punch ball nearby. There were occasional movie nights and visiting a café at tea time on the West Side was fun. On special occasions, they would celebrate in The Palm Court at the Plaza Hotel.

Summers were spent in rented houses in Long Beach, where every evening the boardwalks hummed with conversations in Polish, Hungarian and Yiddish. On Sundays we visited family — Aunt Henia and Uncle Zalman and their daughters, Leah and Reva, still lived in Brooklyn, and Uncle Meyer and Aunt Gusta and their sons, Jackie and Saul, lived on West 86th Street in Manhattan. My father's great uncle Max was the family patriarch, though visits to his home in Brooklyn were rare. My maternal grandmother, Sala Baumwald, came for extended stays, and when she returned to Antwerp, Dad wrote to her daily. The little blue aerogram letters were written each morning, after his morning prayers.

Dad was a garrulous soul, a people-person who loved to tell a good joke or recount an anecdote. He often spoke of life in Kaminke, about the characters in his shtetl, the beauty of the Polish countryside, and of the walks near the Bug River. He was full of Yiddish witticisms and quips.

He loved America and the life that it afforded him but he always thought the typical American was somewhat naive when it came to understanding world politics and the nature of antisemitism. His English was thickly accented but he read the *New York Times* every morning without fail and watched Walter Cronkite's evening news each night.

My father spoke about the war quite a bit, in stark contrast to my mother, who tried never to mention it. He told many stories about his own family before, during, and after the war, and there were times when nightmares from the past woke him from sleep.

Since he believed that his sister was killed on a Thursday (June 3, 1943) he vowed that he would fast every Thursday. My father ate dinner on Wednesday nights and did not touch another morsel till after sundown on Thursday night. In his diary, he notes that he was already fasting on Thursdays and he kept this vow until his cardiologist made him stop in the 1970s.

For years he kept up a correspondence with Rozalie Streker, the woman who had saved his life by hiding him in her attic. I distinctly remember sitting at the kitchen table each Christmas and Easter season, as we flipped through Polish gift catalogues and helped him decide what to send the Strekers for the holidays. This sense of *"hakarat hatov,"* acknowledging goodness, was second nature to him.

The recognition that the Strekers will receive from Yad Vashem as "Righteous Among the Nations" as this book is being published would have made him very happy.

Moty kept up with fellow survivors and with members of the Kaminke Society in New York. Soon after my mother died, he attended The American Gathering of Holocaust Survivors in Washington, D.C. in April 1983. He was very moved by the conference and came home with a priceless anecdote. It seems that in the crowd was one particular man who seemed familiar to him — whether from the camps, the ghetto, the work detail, he wasn't clear. He just wasn't sure. Before the event ended he finally approached the fellow and asked him in Yiddish where he was from. The man replied, "Don't you recognize me, Mr. Stromer? I'm the guy from Zabar's who slices your lox!"

We found this story so special, we submitted it to the *New York Times*, and it was printed in the Metropolitan Diary column on May 4, 1983.

My parents dedicated their lives to their daughters and our achievements brought them their greatest joy. Parent-teacher conferences were occasions of enormous importance and graduation honors, report cards and transcripts were Xeroxed and passed around amongst my dad's friends and associates. Nina and I attended the Bronx High School of Science and then Barnard College, and whenever an academic honor was bestowed upon us, my father's pride was beyond measure. When my sister married Andrew Gaspar in 1971, and I married Arthur Talansky in 1975, these two young men became part of my dad's all-star team. He became quite an educational snob and when degrees were earned at Barnard, Columbia, Michigan, Yale, Harvard and Mt. Sinai School of Medicine, his cup of *nachas* (pride in his family) was filled to the brim.

The greatest blow came when my mother died suddenly of a brain tumor in her fifties, and my father was left bereft and grieving. He lived on for another twelve years, devoting much of his time to visiting Nina and me.

Dad slowly retired from his business and occupied himself with his newspapers, his nature programs and his grandchildren. He loved collating photographs of the past and present and sending them around the globe — so much so that some of my clever cousins nicknamed him "Photos — Do Not Bend." His seven grandchildren called him Grandpa Moty, and he loved to chat with the Polish women we hired to care for him in his final illness. My father died in his sleep on Shabbos morning the 23rd of Tevet, January 16, 1993.

For more than two decades, Dad hid this diary in a yellowed plastic bag, high on a shelf in our foyer closet. I don't think I saw it more than once or twice in my childhood. When my father died, I finally turned my attention to it and found that though my Yiddish was serviceable, I could not make out some of the handwriting and needed help reading and translating more than 200 pages of tightly packed Yiddish script.

I turned to Stanley Bergman, a brilliant archivist and librarian at the YIVO Institute, who spent a year translating the pages and finished in 1995. Mr. Bergman's translation was the key I needed to unlock my father's past.

Why did Dad hide the manuscript all those years? I have several theories. Dad came to America in the midst of the McCarthy era, and I am sure that he felt it would be unwise to publicize the great admiration he had for the

Soviet regime. He admired the way they occupied Kaminke and bestowed a form of equality on the Jews. During the German occupation, he prayed for Soviet victory over the Nazis.

Perhaps there was a more personal reason, as well. I think that out of respect for my mother, Dad did not want us to know that Pepe was his fiancée before the war and that he had had deep feelings for her. I never heard the name Pepe Haberkorn from him and discovered her existence only through the diary.

Finally, though my father told us dozens of stories about the war, he never mentioned the torture he underwent in Remenow. The details of how he was beaten, stabbed, burned and mutilated were hidden in these pages, and I think he felt it was better left buried. Like Daniel Mendelsohn, the author of the recently published *The Lost*, I regret that twenty years ago I did not ask the many questions that haunt and vex me today.

With the help of the brilliant and talented language editor, Jeanette Friedman, this memoir took the shape that you have before you. Her grasp of the material, editing skill and commitment to the task were extraordinary. *Sie veyst alles.*

Though my father called his diary *The Memoir of an Unfortunate Person*, I believe very strongly that he did not think of himself as anything but a very fortunate person for the remainder of his life. He had a beautiful, intelligent and elegant wife whom he adored. He had successful and loving children and grandchildren. He was happy with his lot, never complained about physical ailments, and always looked at life from an optimist's point of view. During his final illness, his visits to doctors were filled with picture taking and banter. When faced with a problem, he always quoted from *Tehilim* (Psalms): *"Hazorim bedimah, berinah yiktzoru"* (those who sow in tears will reap in joy). Every chance he got, he comforted and encouraged us with this phrase. It was so much a part of his philosophy of life, that we engraved it on his gravestone, directly beneath his name.

The publication of this memoir, more than sixty years after it was written, is the most poignant illustration of my father's philosophy of life. In his wildest dreams, as he filled these tear-soaked ledger pages, he could not have imagined the loving and beautiful family that he would someday establish.

With the publication of this diary, we honor our dear father and the *kedoshim* (holy martyrs) of his family, and celebrate his life, his spirit, and his legacy.

Daddy, we gather here in Jerusalem this winter of 2008, on your fifteenth *yahrzeit* to honor you.

Hazorim bedimah berinah yiktzoru.

Sue Stromer Talansky
Great Neck, New York, 2008

Editor's Note: The text has been edited for coherence, factual errors, continuity, syntax, clarity and grammar. The author's place names are used here as he used them.

June 1, 1944

With the help of God

Please inform my brother Meyer Stromer, who joined the Soviet army; my sister in America, Henia Edelstein, and my brother-in-law Zalman of Brooklyn, or my uncle Max Stromer, also in Brooklyn. If a Jew with a Jewish heart gets this to him, he will surely have performed one of the greatest human deeds, not only for my family, but also for the Jews who have suffered from Hitlerism.

Mordche Stromer

~~><~~

[Indicates a change in time]

With the help of God

I am writing these words on the night before I have to leave my place, this attic, where I have been more than — or exactly — 300 days and nights. The days in this place were no brighter than the nights; but what do I want? To be able to spend more time in this place — or to find one like it. May God help me! Please convey this to my brother Meyer Stromer, or my sister in America Henia Edelstein, to let them know.

Their brother, Mordechai Stromer
Kaminke Strumilowa

I request that this [diary] be forwarded to Henia Edelstein, or Meyer Stromer, or Max Stromer in America. His address is 1035 Washington Avenue, Brooklyn, America. My sister Henia Edelstein is also in Brooklyn. I do not remember her address. Or you can inform the Kaminker Society in Brooklyn. My cousin, Neshe Groskof, in London, 40 Gloucester Avenue, can also be informed about this. I am not sure whether these addresses are correct. Mordechai

Today is Thursday, April 6, 1944.

I had a difficult time trying to decide whether to write this or not, because I always hoped I would live through the greatest disaster — the one that goes under the name of Hitlerism. I would like personally and openly to tell my dear sister [Henia] and maybe my beloved brother [Meyer], how many days I struggled to decide whether to write — yes or no. And now that I am writing, I do not know if I will be able to finish. At any rate, I will try to write down part of my experiences, even though it is impossible to tell it all on paper — as the situation gets worse from day to day. The chances for survival are getting smaller from hour to hour because the Ukrainian bandits are murdering Poles and burning Polish villages. It happens that I am, at this moment, in a place that could also fall victim to this bunch.

Once everything is on paper, [will I find] the right person to hide the manuscript? God has helped me. As I write these words I hear exploding artillery shells. Is there a possibility that my memoirs will burn in a fire? I am writing with mistakes, and my Yiddish is very poor, but how can I write in another language, when that would mean that some Jews would not be able to read [these words] about the great upheaval and suffering?

The fact is that my personal tragedy is the tragedy of hundreds of thousands of Jews. It makes no difference how the story is told. I am sure there are worse and even more terrible stories than mine. I will write with mistakes. No one will intervene in my disaster or that of the Jewish people.

If the document survives and reaches the right hands, let it be in the hands of my only sister, Henia Edelstein in America — as a memento from me. I wish her to know how glad I would be to know that she will read my story. But be it as it may, I hope that I will survive long enough to see my remaining family. Then I will laugh at life, because on more than one occasion I have looked death in the eye.

Mordechai

CHAPTER 1

A Short Overview of Our Life During the Period of Soviet Rule

After the collapse of the Polish state, in a speech given in Moscow on September 17, 1939, Mr. [Vyacheslav] Molotov, the Foreign Minister, at the behest of Josef Stalin, ordered the Red Army to cross the former Polish borders and occupy the nations of Western Ukraine and Western Belorussia. Those of us who lived in those areas were very happy with the order, because if the German armies occupied us, we would quickly become victims of the Hitler government. After the Red Army marched in, many people were afraid of communism, especially the very rich people — the proprietors of mills and sawmills, the owners of small factories and the big store-owners.

I was not afraid, quite the opposite: I was overjoyed, because in the years just before the war, life was already difficult for the Polish Jewish middle class. The Polish government was antisemitic. [The Polish Prime Minister Felicjan Sławoj Składkowski (1936–1939) declared economic war on the Jews in 1936 by implementing boycotts and regulations aimed at reducing Jewish income.] There were antisemitic incidents everywhere and Jewish students were being murdered in Polish universities.

It seems to me that my dear sister [Zlateh] and brother-in-law were still living in Lemberg when those incidents occurred. Today all this seems trivial to me. Does it matter if, in the course of ten minutes, one person or five hundred people are shot? They are like a drop of water in the ocean.

29

In particular we, the Jewish Polish small businessmen, complained about being suffocated by the Polish tax system. I do not want to write too much about these matters. However, I must say one thing: the Soviet government turned many Jews into human beings. Personally I had worked hard all my life. I did not, as the saying goes, have a Shabbos or a holiday. It was always business and then more business.

When the Russians first came in they didn't order anyone around. Gradually they organized cooperatives. We joined one right away and met in the old beer saloon. We were all working — my father, my brother and I — when I realized that I no longer had to stay in the store all day and half the night. I became an employee instead of an owner. Every day they gave me merchandise and I would sell it within a few hours. After that I was free. I could wash up, dress up and go for a walk, read a newspaper, or listen to the radio. I was not interested in taxes or patents. I was a free spirit. After those few hours of work I had time for myself and for my beloved parents.

Now I cannot imagine that it is all in the past, that the happiest time of my life will not return, even if I live to see the Bolsheviks again. The most beautiful part of my life was torn out of me in a way that cannot even be compared to the way wild, horrible people destroy their enemies.

I seem to be straying from the subject. Believe me, all those events force themselves into my mind, and it is difficult for me to gather my thoughts.

According to the Soviet constitution, a person who does not work does not eat. After a time, we — my brother [Meyer] and I — went to a military restaurant and found work. We had one thing to worry about on the job: the commanders had to get their breakfasts, lunches and dinners on time; the food had to be excellent and the service efficient. I left for work every day at dawn, so that I could be there when breakfast was served. I was responsible for collecting the money for the food and drinks that we sold — and for the finances. I had horses, a wagon, a truck, and helpers at my disposal.

I would take the wagon to buy goods for the buffet: apples, pears, chocolate, various baked goods, eggs, butter, and cheeses. Chicken, geese and ducks were slaughtered and also prepared for the buffet. In short, all kinds of good things were available. The prices for these cooked meals were low. Breakfast and supper were two rubles, and dinner was three rubles. For breakfast you could get meat, potatoes or cereal, as much bread as you wanted, tea or milk — and for dinner, there was meat.

Considering that a commander received a monthly paycheck of five hundred to a thousand rubles, he could live very well. I got five hundred rubles a month and all I could eat and drink. My brother got only 250 rubles a month, plus food and drink. If I wanted to, I could live in the barracks. I washed my clothes in the military laundry and we even had a bathroom at our disposal. We made a living, and I did not let my mother [Gittel Taksel Stromer] lift a finger; she looked like a beautiful rose.

[Eventually] we rented a space and opened a [general] store for military personnel, where Father [Shaul Stromer] was our night watchman. All the military wives would come in to buy foodstuffs and household items. The soldier who worked with us always told me about the better items he bought, so that I was able to get the best quality and most attractive foods for the buffets we prepared and was also able to bring home the best of everything.

All this took place under the government of workers and peasants. A Soviet general was not ashamed to serve. Generals ate with those of lower rank, shook hands with others and bargained like the most ordinary people. In the beginning, I thought this was impossible because it was not how things were done when I served in the Polish Army. Russian officers, who were slightly lower in rank than the commander, regarded all workers as their equals — one worked at a job, the other at a military job.

Whenever my mother wanted to visit my sister Zlateh in Lemberg,[1] I would get a light car to take her there in just under one hour. My colonel's wife, my employer, or my colonel's wife's sister would travel with her. As it happened, the two women were Jewish, and one of the men was a Russian. The Colonel's wife and her sister knew how to read and write Yiddish and loved to visit my sister on Fridays to eat fish and challah and then return home. My mother would stay on for the Shabbos. Then, on Sunday or Monday, I would bring her back in my car.

On the second day of Pesach [Passover 1940] my brother was inducted into the [Soviet] army and sent to Bessarabia on a military mission. When the

---

1   The Yiddish name for the city, based on the city's name under the Austro-Hungarian empire. Lwów in Polish; Lvov in Russian. Today it is Lviv in Western Ukraine. Its Jewish population before the war was approximately 110,000, swelling to more than 200,000 by summer 1940 with the influx of refugees, most of whom were then transported to other parts of the USSR by the Soviet authorities.

war broke out between Russia and Germany, he was in Odes, Bessarabia and evacuated with everyone to Russia. That was the last piece of news we got about him. What information we had came from a fellow named Kruk, who was with my brother in Bessarabia. Later, Kruk returned to Kaminke.

The horror broke out on Sunday, June 22, 1941, and the warmest and most beloved part of life was destroyed for me and for hundreds and thousands of Jewish families in the most barbaric way. On the Sunday the war broke out, Mother was visiting Zlateh. They were discussing a wedding date with Pepe [Haberkorn, the author's fiancée] who was supposed to come back with Mother and stay with us for the summer.

From June 22 to 29, I continued working at my job, although the whole army was at Most Rawa and Zolkwia [a variation on Zholkwa, the Yiddish name for Żółkiew]. Some of us stayed and continued to slaughter cattle and pigs that we sent to the front lines.

I was asked to join the Russians and follow them to the interior of the Soviet Union. However, on that first Sunday, I did not have the heart to leave my dearest and most beloved ones. If we had thought at that time that such terrible events would take place, we would have run like small children into Russian territory.

By the second Sunday, [June 29] it was too late. My mother urged me: "Go! Run away! We will stay here." But there was no army left. Everybody ran to Bisk, and from there to Zloczów, Tarnopol and ultimately to Russia. I asked officers I knew to take me to friends of the cashiers where I worked, but they could not be found, and strangers did not want to take too many people with them.

People were not thinking about others. Their first concern was to save themselves. Everything was happening at lightning speed. I went home and lay down on a bench because my head was on fire. The moment Father entered the house with the news that the Germans were marching in and that they were already near the school, I walked out of the house and around the back of Moishe Mordechai Polak's house, to the home of my [paternal great] Uncle Chaim-Hersh. I stayed there for a few days, then left town. To this day, I never saw Kaminke again.

CHAPTER 2

Remenow

Chaim-Hersh's house was closed up. Everyone had gone to hide in the basement at Yitzchok Sztefer's house because it was built of bricks. They were afraid to stay in their own houses, which were made of timber, because they thought a single bomb would make a wooden house collapse. I entered the basement and called out the good news — that the Germans had arrived.[2]

Chaim-Hersh's daughter, Ruchele, and her husband and three children lived with him, and so did Chatsde, the wife of the late Chaim-Itshe [a first cousin] and her three children. Chatsde believed that things would be fine under German occupation. I stayed with my uncle on Sunday night [the 29th], all day and night Monday [the 30th], and all of Tuesday, July 1, when the alleyways were full of German soldiers. On Monday, when he went to draw water, my uncle was caught next to the well. A German held him by the beard and beat him while another German took photographs.

Even then, Chatsde was saying we would get along better with the Germans than with the Soviets because the Germans were a cultured people. She was upset at the Russians because they had taken away her status as a wealthy woman, and had ordered her to leave Lemberg. She had been issued a well-

---

2   The Soviets had restricted access and news to Lvov, so most of the Jews didn't know what had happened to their compatriots in Poland.

known Passport Eleven from the Russian government.[3] It is possible that after my uncle was beaten, she changed her mind about the Germans — I didn't ask her about it. However, I am sure that later on she changed her mind.

My blood was seething, but what could I do? I was like a lion a cage.

On Tuesday evening, July 1, we found Jews who had been murdered. A Jewish doctor, passing by the courthouse, was killed, and near Uncle Chaim-Hersh's house, the Germans caught Yankel Oksen's little boy and killed him on the spot. Also killed were Moishe Katz and little Chaimke, Itsele Berzaner's grandson. I can list dozens of people who were killed, but that is not part of what I want to say here. I just feel I should just mention, in particular, these two small children.

That same night, my mother came to me and said: "Dear child, you must run away from here because I am afraid of what tomorrow may bring."

On that same day, I talked it over with Shaya Gever [a cousin]. We decided to walk to Lemberg at dawn the next day, Wednesday. At daybreak, my mother woke me and said: "Go now, because Gever has already left." I quickly dressed, said goodbye, and walked out through Saboszanka, a suburb of Lemberg. I met Gever, who was with one of his little girls, in Saboszanka. He was carrying a milk can to make it look as if he was buying milk. We walked on together to Remenow and no one gave us any trouble. Some shepherds on the road asked us for cigars, and we gave them a few. By seven in the morning we were in Remenow.

There, before you entered the village, at the foot of a mountain on the left side of the road, stood a Jewish home. The woman who lived there was standing outside, weeping hysterically. She told us that their shepherd had taken her husband to work early in the morning, and after four hours they still had not returned. Many Jews were already shot to death in the village. The woman's daughter had been in Lemberg on Tuesday, and reported that Jewish blood was flowing in the streets. She said the whole village was bathed in Jewish blood; Jewish homes were being looted.

This was the first account we'd heard of what was happening in Lem-

---

3   The Soviets issued many "bourgeois" Jews so-called Paragraph 11 passports, which rendered them underprivileged, second-class citizens forbidden to live in larger cities or within 100 km of any border. They lost good jobs and their bank accounts were confiscated.

berg, where Gever and I were seeking refuge. We tried to comfort the woman before we left by telling her that her husband would certainly come home very soon. We said goodbye and went on our way. But we didn't get very far. When we reached the top of the hill, a big strapping Ukrainian Christian approached us and demanded to see our identification papers. Then he pushed us into a building on the right side of the road leading from Kaminke to Lemberg, right next to Remenow's saloon. Once inside, we showed him our passports, which we held in our hands. The man took them away and put them on the table.

Soon two more bandits came in. They searched us and took everything we had. I had a good few hundred rubles, a bottle of liquor, two pairs of socks, and handkerchiefs. Gever had money and a first-class watch. All these items were deposited on the table. Other Ukrainians came into the room and started beating us. The beating went on for hours and it was murderous. There was not a part of my body that was not black and blue or bleeding. We could no longer yell or groan. All the hair from the front of my scalp was torn out. Blood oozed from my head, nose, mouth and ears.

If the same men had beaten us all that time, they would have run out of strength in their arms and legs. Unfortunately for us, a fresh bunch of their fellows came in and the beatings continued without pause. They were yelling and accusing us of having killed many of their friends, saying that we were hurrying off to help our friends in Lemberg.

They also accused us of being Bolsheviks. They told us that Stalin ought to help us. They beat us with sticks, knives, rifle butts and revolvers. One of them even beat us with the sharp edge of a shovel. Gever fainted a few times. At one point I stopped screaming, but I did not faint, and that made my torturers very angry. So they found a brand new method of hurting me. One of them took an empty can and fetched small stones from the street — the gravel that is left when rocks are broken for road construction. They spread this sharp gravel on the floor and I was forced to kneel down on it, which caused my knees to bleed profusely. At the same time a few of the thugs stood or danced on my legs.

Everything turned black, but I still did not faint. Then they stretched me out on my back while one of them jumped on my chest. The pain was dreadful and I cannot understand how I lived through it. Gever was spared this beating because he had fainted and was lying unconscious on the floor. I was stabbed eleven times, and Gever had been knifed over and over in various parts of his body. He was lying on the floor and no longer looked like a human being. I was no different. They stripped us, took all our clothes and left us naked on the floor.

When I had turned completely black like coal, the door opened and a Ukrainian from Kaminke entered. He was the well-known Belahorek, and with him was his son, a young student. I thought for sure that they came from Lemberg. I spoke to Belahorek in a very weak voice, and asked him to order my execution and put an end to my torture. He did not recognize me. He could not recognize me. It was impossible, because I looked more like a wild animal than a human being. He smiled.

He was the son-in-law of Kodkodinski. You should know that during this whole time they were discussing whether to kill us on the spot or take us out into the field and kill us there. They had weapons that were left over from the period of Russian rule. After my entire body had become one large wound, they all left the room.

Soon afterward, one of them brought in a Jewish boy. Ten minutes later they brought in two more people I recognized. They were Baila Reher, Shishl Reher's daughter, and her husband, from Sokal, who had served with me in the Polish Army. His brother-in-law lived in Kaminke and was known as "The Fat One," a kettle-maker. The couple had met at a local cooperative and was married there. They were not beaten by the thieves, but they had their money, watches, and all their food taken away. The [Rehers] did not recognize me, or Gever, who was unconscious.

The thugs left the room, except for the one who had brought me and Gever into the room in the first place. He was the worst. He was the one who had torn all the hair out of my head and now continued to hit me on the head with his rifle butt. In a very weak voice I asked him to stop. I told him to take money from the table, and that I would say that I had less money to begin with. In reply, he struck me again on my already aching head and caused yet another wound. A moment later the rest of the gang returned and ordered us to get up from the floor.

We were all kneeling, facing the wall. The couple was still dressed, as was the boy. I was almost naked, wearing only short pants, and Gever wore only a pair of long pants. I could not stand on my own, so they ordered the boy and Baila's husband to support me. Baila said a prayer for Gever.

Then one of the men held up a piece of paper and declared that as a result of their deliberations, we were all sentenced to death by shooting. The sentence would be carried out immediately, outside, in the nearby field. One of them brought in a pair of old Austrian pants and a jacket taken from the garbage, and told me to put them on. A few men held Gever under his arms and quickly dressed him in similar old clothes. I could not move either my arms or my legs. Despite this, I somehow managed to get into the old clothes with the help of my two friends. As I did so, I envisioned the World to Come. My whole body was studded with embedded gravel.

I fell over a few times and it was hard to get up. I could not hold on to anything with my fingertips, because they were swollen, bleeding and burned. The murderers had taken a piece of wood, cut it into small pointed pieces, and pushed them under my nails. I think they also dipped the wood in gasoline because one of them had asked where the gasoline bottle was. You cannot imagine the pain I felt. It was so intense that I threw myself onto the floor, dragging with me many of the men who were holding onto me. Many times I and some of the men were lying on the floor. They punctured only six of my fingers: the fingers of my left hand and the little finger of my right hand. At that time I was also stabbed with a knife because two of the men got blood on their clothing.

When I managed to pull on the pants, one of the men picked up a brick, grabbed me from behind by the small amount of hair that remained — most of it had been pulled out — gave me another blow, and ordered me in jest to wash the blood off my scalp, where it was all bloody at the front, before I was killed. "You are going to your death," he said.

In my heart I felt that this would not be my end. Gever, though, told me that he would not live through the day. All the men left the room again, except for one who held a gun in his hand. He took the rags that passed for jackets and covered our heads. He ordered us to kneel on the floor and kiss the Ukrainian earth, which up to that day had carried us and fed us. We four men were now standing in the four corners of the room, facing the wall, while Baila was lying on the floor, in the middle of the room, face down. The room was full of our blood, as well as that of a young Christian they'd shot before we arrived. He'd been a young member of the Komsomol [communist youth organization] and a committed Soviet. A woman whose daughter had to wash floors at seven o'clock in the morning told me he was from the local village.

As we stood facing the wall, the bandit guarding us took money from the table and hurriedly stuffed it into his pocket because he didn't want the others to find out. By that time, they had finished the bottle of liquor. It was two o'clock.

After a while, the whole group came back into the room. It is possible that there were Jews in another room because we heard screaming. We were in a small room on the left side of the building and the room on the right side of the house was bigger.

One of the group — presumably the leader — ordered one of the men to load his gun with five bullets, told Gever to put on his jacket, and asked him if he wanted to go to Lemberg or Kaminke. Gever said that he wanted to go to Kaminke. The man said he would get an escort to Lemberg and ordered the man with the loaded gun to take him. Gever was given a pair of shoes because his good shoes were taken. The pants they gave him were tight, and there were no buttons on the jacket. As he was led outside, Gever looked back and said goodbye to me with his eyes. I could not bear it.

Ten minutes later I was ordered to put on my jacket. Two men helped me because I could not move a single limb of my body. Another man was ordered to load his gun with five bullets and take charge of me. I held on to the wall. At that moment I was more hopeful than at any time since the disaster began, maybe because I had not lost my courage. I showed the murderous Ukrainians that I could cope. I did not fall down. I overheard them saying that once I got to the street I would be free. So this did not have to be my end. Holding on to the wall, I was determined to reach the door.

They asked me where I wanted to go, Lemberg or Kaminke. When I did not respond immediately, a hail of blows descended all over my body, but I was beaten only by those who held something in their hands. They found it disgusting to touch us with their bare hands. However, no one spared me their kicks. Finally, half fainting, I found myself outside on the street. The pure air of summer soon revived me.

My ordeal had lasted from seven o'clock a.m. to three o'clock p.m. During that time, the windows to the room we were in were closed and the shutters were half closed, so that the people passing by would not hear our screams. Even while blood oozed from us, our tormentors muffled our mouths with rags. You must know that they were all dressed up for a holiday. The whole village was decorated with Ukrainian national flags. I had noticed that when Gever and I first entered the village early that morning.

The open air refreshed me. The man escorting me yelled at me to move faster in the direction of Lemberg. I noticed the forest on both sides of the road and half walking, half crawling, I dragged myself across the courtyard to the right side of the road. It is possible that it was too far for my escort to walk with me.

Further down the road, military trucks drove out into the road from the right side of the street leading to the main road to Lemberg. It was pouring and the soldiers looked at me as if there was something to look at. The non-Jewish women were screaming and singing to the troops, and it is possible that one of the screaming women was my escort's friend — she called out to him. From a distance, the woman called to him again and he said to me [in Ukrainian]: "You dirty Jew, I don't want to see you any more." I was running — if running and falling can be called running. Using my right hand, I washed my face and head with rainwater. My skin was burning to the touch. I walked along the side of the road and looked up at the mountain, and I saw Gever walking. A group of small brats was running after him. I haven't seen Gever since that moment.

Soldiers sat in their wagons under tarpaulins, sheltering from the rain. I crossed to the right side of the road, where the wagons were headed to where I wanted to go. The wagons on the left side of the road were going home to Kaminke. On the right side of the road, I was able to hold onto a wagon because the wagons and I both moved very slowly. One man with a wagon called me over. He asked me in German if I was a Jew. I pretended not to understand him, and told him in Russian, in the loudest voice I could muster: "I'm going to *Lwow*." Thank God, by the time I had repeated this twice, we were approaching the forest. Once we reached it, I jumped from the wagon and ran, slowly at first, then faster and faster into the woods like a lunatic. My mind may not have been functioning normally, but the pain reminded me that I was alive.

I ran until I reached a clearing, then looked back and realized that I had been running without a goal. The truth was that I couldn't run any more. I hadn't paid attention to what was around me or where I was going. Now I saw dead soldiers, horses lying on the ground, machine-guns, grenades, cannons and bullets. I did not examine anything. I had one thought in my battered head: keep going, keep going, further and further away from the terrible place called Remenow. What I report here was just a part of the troubles in that village.

CHAPTER 3

Kolodenki

I wanted to get to the road. The forest was small, so it didn't take me long. I followed the edge of the forest and began walking in the direction of Lemberg. When I reached Gredno, I turned left. Then, crawling a certain distance, I saw Remenow and recognized it by its tiled roofs. Instead of proceeding to Lemberg, I returned to the village for I had no strength left to continue to Lemberg. I was no longer afraid to pass through the village and consoled myself with the notion that if I was to be murdered, it would happen near home. I just wanted to die near my parents.

Again I crawled toward Lemberg. I cannot imagine, now, how it was possible to get there. I hoped to get a ride on a wagon, but none passed by. I saw Christians coming from Kaminke, but they did not recognize me. One of the men was headed to Lemberg, with a package under his arm and a bottle of tea in his hand. When I saw the bottle, I could not restrain myself — I crawled up to him and asked him for a drink. He did not recognize me, so I told him who I was. I knew him. He was from Jagonia, Jakopszei Eloidik by name, but called Jakobszej Filipkes. He was a railroad worker. With tears in my eyes, I asked if I could just wet my lips.

It is possible he felt disgusted, or that he felt like a German. At any rate, he refused to give me a sip. I told him that one day he might ask me for a drink. At that time I had no idea what the Germans were going to do to the Jews; but he did not know either, and so he handed me the bottle. I seized it with my right hand, as if the drink could put me back on my feet. This character walked away, and I continued to crawl along the road.

It wasn't long before I met Baila Reher and her husband as they headed back to Kaminke. They had come close to Lemberg, but some Jewish girls, students fleeing from Lemberg, who were returning to their homes in Radziechow and Stajanow, advised them to turn back. They described the situation in Lemberg and all the other towns as terrible. Blood was flowing like water.

We decided to go back to Kaminke. But I did not want to go through Remenow because Baila and her husband were told that if they were caught there they would be beaten as badly as Gever and I had been. The girls left immediately. Baila and her husband went with me. We went closer to the woods and kept bearing left, away from the road, to avoid the village. I did not want to go to the right because that was where the railroad was and the region was inhabited.

I did not know what was on the left. I supported myself on a stick I found and walked slowly. All my crawling up to that point made me feel as if I had stayed in one place. Now we shifted further to the left and kept a lookout to make sure the village stayed to the side of us. We crept along until we reached the road that led to Solimow, in the general direction of Zolkwia. We began walking toward Kaminke. We passed Remenow on the right and then we approached a ditch with water in it. With the help of my two friends, I washed myself in the water, and we crossed the ditch. Baila's husband jumped over it. I could not do it, so my friends helped me over, and we dragged ourselves toward the village of Zwertow.

We took some water from the ditch with us. I used Baila's husband's cap to cover my wounded head as much as possible. [The Ukrainians] hadn't had enough time completely to undress Baila and her husband because they were interrupted by the Germans' arrival, and they did not know the German position on the Jewish question. Maybe that was why the two of them were allowed to keep their clothes on. When they let the boy go, he decided to go to Lemberg.

As we walked along the road, we had many encounters, but the Ukrainians decided to let us go. At one point, one of them wanted to hit us, but his sister did not let him.

We finally reached the village of Kolodenki — Klodno-Zoltance

Kolodenki — a small village near Kaminke, next to a forest. It was about ten or eleven o'clock on a summer night. We met a Christian, and asked if we could spend the night at his house, promising him that at dawn we would proceed to Kaminke. He did not want to agree to the arrangement, but he told us about a house in the woods where a Polish person lived with his three sons. It was possible that one of them would shelter us for the night if we paid him for it, and they would be able to show us the way through the forest to Kaminke.

We had no choice but to go there, so we slowly dragged ourselves over. The peasant had given us the right information — we found what our informant had described. The place was easy to spot, because two or three houses stood at the edge of the forest.

I looked like someone who had been fished out of a river. I felt hot and cold, and my two companions would not let me sit on the ground. They said that if I sat down I would catch a cold. As I approached the house, I leaned on my companions. We climbed the stairs and saw a light inside. I did not like the fact that there was a light on inside the house so late at night. We noted that the proprietor of the house in the forest did not have first-class opinions, though his Polish family name was very attractive — Warszawski. Despite our misgivings, I had to have a place where I could rest my exhausted bones.

It became clear to us later that the man's two dogs woke him earlier to apprise him of our approach. He had guests who came in from the forest every night, especially since the Soviets were hiding in the forest. The Russians would come at night and ask him to exchange military uniforms for peasant clothing. It is possible that Warszawski hid guns and revolvers for the Russians. In any event, we were sure that he had weapons even in ordinary times, yet nothing bad happened to us in his home.

If God lets us live, I would personally like to thank that Polish man for everything he did for me.

I am writing about this event three years after it happened. Today is April 18 [1944], and we can hear artillery fire. The fire comes from the region near

Brody. It is hard to wait for the moment when we will see the Red Star. It is true that we sinned against the Russian government, but personally I had done nothing [wrong] and felt no guilt. I lived with the Russians as one does with brothers, and when they left, it hit me like lightning on a clear day.

When I entered the house in the forest, I could hardly stand on my feet and collapsed on the floor. In spite of the pain, I looked around and saw the Pole and his wife in one bed, a child lying on the floor, and two people lying on some straw. It was a small room, one that served as bedroom, dining-room and kitchen. The windows were shut tight, as if there was a [minus] thirty-degree frost outside. I asked the Pole to let us rest for a while, and wondered if at daybreak he would show us the way through the forest to Kaminke.

I asked him to step outside into the fresh air with me because I felt very unwell. He pulled on a pair of pants and went out with us. I sat down on a woodpile next to the house, and told him that we did not have a penny because everything had been stolen. However, if he escorted us to Kaminke he would be well compensated for his deed.

To make sure that we were from Kaminke, Warszawski questioned us about some dubious characters from town that I happened to know because I used to run a liquor store there. The man's wife and his oldest son, aged about twenty, were present at this conference. As it happened, I knew most of the man's friends and acquaintances in Kaminke. I at once won over the whole family. The lady of the house brought out a bucket of milk and we drank it. As for bread, they had none. Then they put some hay in the attic of the stable for us to sleep on. It was understood that the next morning the man or his son would escort us through the forest and two villages into Kaminke, because when we were on the main road we had problems.

I immediately lay down like a stone. I could not touch any part of my body, or even turn over. As I lay on my back, my wounds hurt as if someone were stabbing me. Some of my wounds were bleeding. Before long, I managed to fall asleep. I do not know how long I slept. It seemed like no time had passed before the owner of the place woke us up, and told us it was time to be on our way. It is possible that we had slept two or three hours; it was still dark outside.

When the man saw my physical condition, he offered to hitch a horse to a wagon and drive us to Kaminke. I was unable to open my eyes or my mouth. But we asked the man to get the wagon ready and take only Baila. In the meantime, the two of us would stay in his house. Baila agreed to arrange everything in Kaminke, and said she would write to tell us whether it was possible to come into Kaminke or not. When Warszawski heard that he would be taking only one passenger and should set out as soon as he could, his wife gave Baila a kerchief to cover her head, so that she would not be recognized.

He left, taking Baila with him. Once again I fell asleep, and was soon awakened by the householder's son, but because of the unbearable pain, I could not fall asleep again. Since we were very anxious to hear what was happening in Kaminke, every waiting moment turned into days.

Finally, thank God, at four o'clock on Thursday afternoon [July 3], the Christian returned. First he asked his son to close the gate. Then, slowly, he took an object out of the wagon and spread it on the ground. In the object were about 20-30 caps and hats covered with blood. Baila's husband and I watched him through the cracks. He had come back alone, without Baila. The wagon was full of blood. Can you imagine, my dearest, what we experienced at that moment? We knew that under every government, people were killed. Here we were seeing lots of hats, while the heads were already buried in the ground.

Warszawski was in no hurry to come to us. He went into his house to eat. When he had filled himself with food, he came up to the attic and told us the news about what had been happening since Tuesday night in Kaminke. They caught him in town with his small wagon and one horse and forced him to take thirteen murdered Jews to the field in three trips. He was also given more than thirty bloodied hats. Baila wrote a note to her husband.

I got no information from home, though Baila wrote that in my home everything was fine. Father had run away and Mother did not have the patience or strength to write to me. I did not know what to do next. I still could not move my arms and legs. We concluded that there was no reason to go back to Kaminke. It was obvious that if we were caught there, we would be murdered.

How bitter it is to live with the Germans! Three years have passed since then, and today I can say the same thing: if caught, I will be shot right away. Oh, how sad it is! Not a pleasant end for me, though there are no more Jews walking freely on German streets. My dearest, can you imagine my situation? I was physically and morally broken. At present I am strong only physically. All my experiences, which you will learn about later, strengthened me.

Oh God, if only I can live to see the time when I will be able to talk about all this with my friends, and avenge, avenge my two beloved souls, my father and mother! They suffered considerably at the hands of our local Christians, who were well known to us. They did not let my parents alone, even though my parents never gave anyone any trouble and never belonged to any organization. They were tortured for the simple reason that they were Jews.

I will write to you about this later. If God spares the life of my dear and only brother, and if this notebook reaches his hands, let him avenge the innocent holy blood of our parents. Vengeance, and again, vengeance! You can believe me when I tell you that tens of thousands of young people, who have lost everything, want to live only for the sake of vengeance.

No, I cannot let them catch me.

And so I had to believe Baila's note, even though there was no sign of life. Though I was completely broken, I had enough sense left to ask Mr. Warszawski to send his wife to us. I realized that she was the kind of person who would help us for money or its equivalent. I arranged for her to make a special trip the next day, Friday [July 4], and bring me a sign of life from my parents. At dawn on Friday she went to Kaminke.

I was lying on a pile of burning problems. Thinking about them was worse than the pain from the wounds. Late in the afternoon the woman returned, and brought me a letter from my mother who wrote: "Motenyu, save yourself! Here is not a place for you." Father was hiding in Jaroni, and my mother [later] told me about what happened in town. [After the occupation, mother made three trips to Lemberg.]

My grandfather, my dear grandfather, earned his living with his ten fingers as a shoemaker and suffered all his life. He was the one whose candles were rejected in Dovid Postel's synagogue, because the elders looked askance at a shoemaker lighting candles there, even though all he wanted was to say

Kaddish on the *yahrzeit* [memorial day] of his father or mother.[4] (This incident was not in my memory, but it was part of the class struggle in our community.)

Grandfather did not know about any worldly matters. Apart from work and the *Beis Medrash* [House of Study], nothing existed for him. He never cheated anyone in his life. He was always the one who was cheated. Grandfather worked for us. Every few days he ran to the cemetery, to my grandmother's grave, to pray that no harm, God forbid, should come to me. This righteous Jew was murdered in a terrible way. (By July 4, when Mrs. Warszawski made her trip into Kaminke, he was no longer among the living.)

Mrs. Warszawski brought me a pair of pants, a shirt, and a scrap of a jacket. She was given a fine present by my dear mother. Despite her husband's misgivings, she proposed, especially to me, that I should stay with them a few days. I said that I would only stay on condition that my friend stayed with me and she agreed

I will tell you why I asked my family to send me some money. When they did send me fifty or a hundred rubles, Mrs. Warszawski did not bother to give me any of it, and I did not even bother to ask her about the money, though my mother had mentioned in her letter that she was sending me some.

Because of this, we decided that on Sunday [July 6], when the woman went to church, she should come see us in the attic [before she left]. On [Friday] night my friend washed himself a bit. The next day, I took my clothes off and my friend removed some gravel fragments from my back, while I removed the gravel embedded in my knees. I asked Mr. Warszawski if he could spare some vodka, so that I could forget the pain. His wife had gotten the vodka from my mother.

When the husband saw the state I was in, he hoped to get more supplies from my mother, so he gave me the bottle of vodka. In normal times I would probably have needed two specialists to care for me, but I had to care for myself. The vodka cleaned out my wounds and prevented infection. I attended to my head wounds by pouring vodka on a rag to make a compress. From day to day I was getting better — so much so, that after Shabbos, in the evening, I was

---

4   It is customary in Judaism to light a memorial candle on the anniversary of a loved one's death — *yahrzeit* in Yiddish — and to say the prayer in honor of the dead — kaddish.

able to climb down from the attic and went outside to enjoy some fresh air on a beautiful summer night.

On Sunday, Mrs. Warszawki [came to us]. I was lying down when she came in. I particularly wanted to ask her to bring me a written note from my dear father. Though my mother gave her bread for us, the woman never delivered it. She did give us milk, but I had no appetite for any kind of food. I was satiated with difficulties and suffering.

She went back to Kaminke and brought more supplies from my dear mother. They also gave her half a liter of rum for want of something else to give her. The Christian woman was surely afraid that I would ask her for some rum, so she told me that while she walked home through the forest, the bottle fell and broke.

On Monday [July 7], two Ukrainian policemen showed up and ordered Mr. Warszawski to return the wooden planks he took from the Doniebindik sawmill. Under Polish rule the mill belonged to Yankel Oksen, and under the Soviets it became a government enterprise. If Warszawski didn't return the wood, they would come back and conduct a search. Warszawski was afraid that when they returned they might find us, but I managed to persuade him that the two men would not come back, and that there was no reason for him to worry.

On Tuesday [July 8] Warszawski went to town with his wife. When he returned, he brought regards from home, but not from Father. Binshe Gever [Shaya's wife], the daughter of Meyer Leibush, came back with them. She had been told by my dear mother and by Baila that I was hiding with the Warszawskis in the forest, so she came to see me. At that time, Jews were not yet required to wear armbands [The edict was issued on July 21, 1941]. She had her sister Shaindel's two children from Lemberg with her, a red-haired boy and a girl.

During the Russian occupation, the children had come to visit Binshe, and they were trapped in Kaminke by the outbreak of the war. Binshe wanted to take the children back to their parents in Lemberg, and also wanted to find her husband. I could not provide her with any specific information, apart from what I already described in the previous chapter.

It was less than ten days since the Germans had invaded, and so Warszawski took Binshe and the children to stay with a Jewish family in the nearby village — though I knew that in Remenow all the Jews had already been murdered — and what would happen later. Binshe made a deal with Mr. Warszawski to take her and the children to Lemberg for items he was supposed to get from Shaindel's husband, and I wanted to send a message to Zlateh and her family.

At sunrise on Wednesday [July 9], the younger Warszawski took them to Lemberg. He returned home late at night and was unhappy about having gone there. I tried to persuade him to take me the next day and he was angry at me for that. I did not want to go to Lemberg alone, and Warszawski did not want to take me by wagon because the horse had just come back [and was tired].

All day Thursday I begged him to take me. After what my dear mother had given them for delivering a letter from Kaminke, they could not be happy, particularly after what they received from Shaindel's husband in Lemberg. It is possible that this had something to do with their decision to ask us to leave.

I had been warned by my mother not to come to Kaminke and [I should] try to get through to Lemberg. Though the Warszawski family was ready to keep me because I did not look like a Jew, they did not on any account want to keep Baila's husband. I did not want to part with him — how could I let him go to Lemberg all alone? Zlateh wanted me to come to Lemberg, but she didn't tell me that the men were hiding in all kinds of holes, and that their former servants were looking to report the Jews and have them taken "to work" — a place from where many Jews have not returned to this day.

And I was still afraid to pass through Remenow.

My wounds were healing quickly, thanks to various traditional herbal remedies, vodka, and my body's own ability to heal itself. I slowly began to stand on my legs, but I could not touch any part of my body. I realized that I needed two more weeks of rest, but I had no choice. I became afraid, and for fear there is no remedy. I was afraid of the people in Remenow, and for this fear, too, there was no remedy. It was enough that we agreed to leave on Friday [July 11], at dawn. I wanted to give Warszawski's son money to take the same road that we used to bypass Remenow, but he would not hear of it.

On Thursday evening [July 10] we climbed down from our nest in the attic, and slept on a pile of hay in the stable. The old man woke us up at midnight, but did not want to hear or think about going by wagon. The son was our escort and I made a deal with him to guide us to Lemberg for a hundred rubles.

I wanted to make sure that before it was fully light, we would pass Remenow. At first we walked on side paths and stayed off the main thoroughfares. We wanted to do this until we reached the main road to Lemberg. But it was getting lighter and the younger Warszawski worried that a military truck could come by.

It was too early to go, he said, and he was right. He completely persuaded me not to worry about Remenow, and by that point, I was ready to listen to anything he said. He brought us to Kapice, where we took a nap. It was already light when he woke me. "It's high time to leave," he said to me. "Let's go." He saw how hard it was for me to walk, but he kept assuring me that when we reached Remenow we would rest, and after that we could walk more slowly. This gave me courage. I wanted so much to get past Remenow, that I half-ran to get away from it as fast as possible and reproached myself for having taken a nap.

Remenow had been a terrible place during the period of Polish rule. To this very day, many Christians traveling with merchandise to Lemberg are killed and robbed on their way through Remenow. But as we approached the village, Warszawski reassured me. Imagine — I was entering the village where all the Jews had been murdered, although in other towns some Jews were still alive. I tiptoed through the place where they had beaten me almost to death, leaving no place on my body untouched. I did not look at the miserable house where I had suffered so much. I walked in the middle, with Warszawski in front of me and Baila's husband behind me. God helped us and we passed through the village safely.

Once we were in the forest, we sat down and rested. Various ex-Soviet military men passed us by on the road so I asked them about my beloved brother and learned that by that time he was stationed near Odessa. The three of us slowly made our way to Zidatyczsze, where the father-in-law of Melech Badner Lifa — brother of the "*Krimmer*" Badner [who limped] — lived.

We stopped at the Badners [July 11] and in Lemberg I was no longer afraid. Then Warszawski met a Christian from his hometown and joined him. We agreed to meet later near Zlateh's place. Warszawski already knew where Zlateh lived because he'd taken Binshe there earlier in the week.

At Badner's father-in-law's house, I discovered that Gever had been handed over to the Ukrainian police not far from there. The soldiers who brought him in said that after the incident in Remenow, Christians had pulled

Gever out of a Russian tank — from which he was [supposedly] shooting at Germans. He was handed over to the German Army, but the troops were heading to Kiev, so they handed Gever over to the Ukrainian police, who were still not properly organized.

The lying thieves in Remenow had turned Gever into an anti-German Russian soldier. If he'd had just one small identifying document they would have left him alone. Today there is no need for tanks from which to murder people. One word is enough — *zhid* [Jew]. The Jews told me how he implored the Ukrainian murderers for mercy, how he wept for the Jews: "I am a father of small children. Save me!" He surely thought that they were going to execute him on account of the false slander about him. The poor fellow was not aware of what had happened in Kaminke. They took him to Lemberg.

The first slaughter of Jews occurred in Lemberg on a Thursday to remember. Jews were taken out onto the sands. [Gora Piaskowa, a sandy hill in the city, is where the Jews were taken to dig their own mass graves and then were shot by Einsatzgruppe C.] No one was saved by any kind of pleading. That was the last news I had of Shaya Gever. He ended his life there, like the other Jews; but unlike some others, he did not have to suffer for years on end.

However much you may talk about suffering — when you want to live, the greater the suffering, the will to live becomes stronger. I am not telling you any old wives' tales. I felt it all in my own body.

I very much want to live, to live to see you who remain alive, and to speak with you. Oh, how long it is since I heard a Yiddish word!

It began raining hard so I asked Badner to give me or lend me a bit of something to put over my head because I did not want to be recognized near the city gates. I walked on until I reached the cannery, stopping there for a moment because further on, near the gates, they were catching people for a work detail.

Then I entered Zlateh's home. Warszawski met me there and was paid. Zlateh also gave him a shirt, a pair of socks and a good breakfast. When I arrived at Zlateh's, I began to understand the true meaning of fear. Mechel [her husband] was hidden behind the white closet in the corner of the pantry, where it was possible to hide someone. Everything that could be done to hide him was done and the room was kept locked.

They worried constantly. Maybe someone is coming, maybe someone is here. The fear was terrible. I hoped I might be able to get a good rest in my dear sister's house, but I had to admit that under the Christian's roof it had been much more peaceful — though during the few days we were there, we also lived in fear.

Baila's husband had family in Lemberg, but Zlateh did not let him leave the house because Jews were being caught in the streets and were instantly liquidated. He was so upset he was ready to go back to the Warszawskis, stay with them in the village and then continue on to Kaminke. That same day, I gave him fifty rubles.

I washed myself and I was helped all the time. When I finally went to bed, Zlateh locked the door and stood guard. People almost fainted when they saw my wounds. I kept telling them not to mention the beating, stabbing or burning to anyone in my parents' home. Zlateh didn't know what had happened to me, and my mother did not find out about it until months later. After the long ordeal, I was finally in Lemberg, the Lemberg where I had once enjoyed being with my sister and her two dear, never to be forgotten souls [Abish and Elish, her sons].

My dearest, believe me, I am talking about it, and it sets my heart on fire. I cannot believe that it was and is no more.

CHAPTER 4

Kaminke

I want to give you a brief overview of events in Kaminke from the time I left home. That same Wednesday, July 2, 1941, the first pogrom in Kaminke took place. I cannot provide you with a completely accurate account of the pogrom, because I was not at home. I can only write about events that I saw with my own eyes and experienced personally. However, I hope that some Jews will be able to escape this horror and go abroad, or go over to the side of the Bolsheviks; and they know what happened in Kaminke. I was interested only in my parents, who were at home the whole time, and that is what I will tell you about.

On that Wednesday, some Jews were caught in the street and others were dragged out of their houses and brought to an area near the public baths. Nearby, there was an egg cannery, with concrete huts where the eggs were canned. Our beloved grandfather was taken there. [Earlier] a German soldier caught Grandfather, but Mother had managed to talk the German into letting Grandfather go.

Mother told me that Jodek Jadenecki, known as Yoshki Kornik, came to our house. In the past, I had had a legal run-in with Kornik's brother, Karolki, over the cleaning of a rug, but he'd moved to Lemberg before the war. Kornik dragged Grandfather to the slaughter room at the egg cannery and proceeded to beat him until he murdered him. Dozens of other people were present in the room, and it is possible that more than one killer took part in beating and murdering Grandfather. My Uncle Chaim-Hersh was in that room, too, and was

53

murdered that same day. Uncle Meyer-Leibush — who was also there — was able to prolong his life for a while.

So there you have it: the terrible way in which our beloved grandfather lost his life — a life in which he had gone through so much. All his life he had worked extremely hard, and when the time came at last for him to enjoy some of the fruits of his labor, he was robbed of them in this dreadful manner.

On Thursday [July 3, 1941], Meyer-Leibush came out of the place half-dead from the beatings and told of the terrible suffering his brother and brother-in-law had gone through. He had been forced to urinate into my uncle's mouth to revive him — and he was not the only one who was forced to do this to others. Because of the people who were already dead, the killers dismissed those who were still alive, as fresh victims kept coming in. There were plenty of bandits, not all of them Kaminke Christians. Various murderers came from the surrounding region as well.

Grandfather and Uncle Chaim-Hersh suffered terribly until dawn on Thursday, when they both died. Uncle Meyer-Leibush was alive because when they brought him into the room there was a mass of other people coming in, and he was not so murderously beaten.

That same day, the townspeople buried Ukrainians who were shot by the Soviets for openly sympathizing with the Germans. The Ukrainian priests made a most imposing demonstration in the streets. And after their verbal agitation, the bloody pogrom began. I do not know how many Jews were murdered. I heard that the screaming of the burning Jews was horrifying. They were begging for a drop of water, but instead of water they got stones. Each one that was brought forward was beaten by all those who stood there, to the point of being battered to pieces, and then they threw the victims into a storefront. The heat in the store was unbearable because the iron shutters and door were closed. People were piled on top of one another and suffocated.

That same day, someone cut off Mechel Tohen's leg, right in front of his house and after suffering, he died at the door of his home. A rumor circulated that Broder, the pig butcher, was responsible for that act. People said that Broder was already angry with Mechel before the war began because Mechel had a house that was better than the butcher's. Then, when the opportunity presented itself, the butcher killed Mechel. Dolek-Avrom Kahl's son-in-law, Dr. Birger, had his head cut off. I do not want to go into details, because I did not see this.

Father hid in a stable at Anton Sztofel's [a Christian we trusted] in Jagonia for about six to eight days, and that saved him for the moment. First he went to Heranka Olnicki, who refused to hide him, and on Wednesday evening he went to Jagonia. During Soviet rule, I provided Heranka Olnicki with his entire livelihood. I got him into the regiment where Meyer and I worked, and he was given a job. He made salami and other kinds of meat products from government supplies and never had to buy any kind of fat or meat. Now, when it was a question of helping me, he refused to give shelter to my father. I will return to him later in my account.

All the murdered Jews were taken to the cemetery. The situation was very dangerous. Mother asked Wierczorik to let her into his home, but he and the two gentile women with him refused to let her in. They put pictures of saints in their windows and lit candles to let everyone know that Christians lived there.

The Jews of Kaminke were robbed, beaten and murdered, and their windowpanes were broken. Sef Jakobszej, a *Volksdeutsche* and pig slaughterer, came to our house, broke all our windowpanes and beat Mother to a pulp. In the course of eight days, they searched our house fourteen times. They dug in the ground, stabbed the furniture and searched the chimneys. A few months later Jakobszej came back, broke all the windowpanes again, and while Father hid under the bed, struck Mother in the face, hard, and kicked her a few times. Mother's suffering was indescribable and she became unrecognizable, a shadow of what she had been — during Russian rule Mother had looked like a bride.

We had a short-statured mailman, who during Soviet rule sometimes brought me mail from America. Whenever he delivered the mail, we gave him a drink of vodka — Polish vodka at that. After the pogrom he showed up at my parents' house with Roman, the shoemaker from the warehouse. They tortured and beat Mother, while demanding to know where the Polish vodka was hidden. They even dug up the floors in their search for it.

Blind Kashke also tormented us. She left Bari [a neighbor] alone in her house. [Blind Kashke was Bari's very near-sighted servant and robbed the family blind.]

Michal Krawiec, the hunchback, was our saloonkeeper during Pesach. One day, while drunk, Wladek Wotowicz, the electrician, grabbed Mother by the arm and dragged her to the local government office. He wanted her to transfer ownership of the saloon to Krawiec. Mother, for her part, wanted to transfer the place to Sztofel, so Wladek beat her up to make her change her mind. Mother wrote about this and said: "Child, if I survive, I want you to do the worst to him."

You can imagine that if our mother — who always looked the other way if she was wronged and never lost her temper at the person who wronged her — said such a thing, it was because that Ukrainian bandit had caused her unbearable suffering.

May God help me to survive all this!

Krawiec was always sucking blood from our parents. He became the business owner of our saloon with two partners: Ridnik Dmitro, and his brother-in-law, Romke Kosarowicz. Both partners married Kaczmari's daughters. Father was their servant. He would rush to order beer for them, swept the rooms, and performed any necessary chores. Our parents were glad to do all this, as long as they were left alone. But Krawiec, the hunchback, made their lives miserable. He did not let them lift their heads.

Szweneczycki, who had been an overseer in the slaughterhouse during Polish rule, became the town's mayor under the Germans. He also tormented our parents. Kornik, who murdered Grandfather, now put all his heart into robbery. He took most of the property from the Soviet officer who lived in our house and left everything in the bedroom. Blind Kashke also took a good dip into his belongings. I could go on and mention hundreds of particulars like these, but it would be pointless. The few incidents I have mentioned are not the most important, neither are they the least.

When our dear parents saw that the robbery was constant, they split up their belongings among their Christian friends. Anton Sztofel, the man who had hidden father for a few days, was given most of our property. It was understood that if the world would survive, he would return those things. Sztofel transferred all the spirits, wine, hard liquor, cognac and rum to his house — there were only seventy liters in all. There were liter, half-liter and quarter-liter bottles, a few boxes of liquor, and a variety of other objects from the saloon.

In addition, Anton took bedclothes and garments: a total of seven hundred items, including Father's and Mother's fur coats. Not one item was ever returned. Not one bottle of liquor ever found its way back — he kept everything. I saw his youngest daughter wearing our clothes. Everyone in

Jagonia knows he used our clothing. He let the police, the best-known murderers and bandits — and some famous SS men — get drunk on our liquor.

One of the bandits, Lachman, slept with Anton's middle daughter and supplied her with all kinds of clothes and shoes. This bandit terrorized all the Jews who were still alive, and even the Christians were afraid of him. He lived in the lap of luxury, while our parents did not have enough to eat. By that time, the bandits drank up all our liquor.

The second person who hid our property was Krach Foimes's brother-in-law, the former town hall worker. He kept a whole chest full of men's suits, fabrics and fur coats that had never been worn, mine and my father's — all of our clothes. The third person who took our property was Johan Jakacze, the secretary of the Jagonia community. He kept quite a few things, including some of our furniture. One closet and the beds were taken by Józef Streker. Semer took things too. You should know that our parents gave our property for safekeeping to people from Jagonia, people who were *Volksdeutsche* and who played important roles in the town.

And yet, how trivial this issue of property seems in the light of what we lost! It all amounts to nothing. My beloved mother would always write: "I want to live with just a shirt on my back, but let me survive." On many occasions Zlateh told me: "I want only a piece of dry bread with water, as long as I can stay alive with my husband and children." How often she would point to her two innocent, blooming souls and say: "And this is what they want to destroy!"

But my dears, they *were* destroyed, destroyed in a terrible way — the best, the most beautiful ones. Do you realize what kind of children Zlateh had? Two healthy, beautiful boys, one of them more intelligent and handsomer than the other. [Abish was the older one; Elish was a toddler.]

Everything turned into a dark, black dream. They are no longer among the living. They are not people any more. They were torn up by the roots. But they wanted to live so much! In spite of the dreadful times, the love of life was and is stronger than ever. They went to their deaths with their heads held high. Yes, I know everything about Zlateh's torment until the last moment of her life. I cannot control myself when the images appear before my mind's eye. I must end this chapter.

I am not writing in a room, at a table. I am lying in an attic with a bit of straw spread under me, and I write by a small light that shines through a crack in the little thatched roof. I am listening to the explosions of artillery shells. There was bombing tonight. The whole district was lit up by fire from exploding shells, but I did not see the light because I am always in the attic, where it is always dark. Every time I stop writing, I stop up the hole in the roof with hay.

CHAPTER 5

Pogodna Street, Number 19

[July 12] I washed and shaved. We realized that I could not stay with Zlateh very long. All the Christians on her street knew me from when the Soviets ruled, when I would visit her, driving there in all kinds of vehicles, in cars and in trucks.

We decided that I should get to Pepe's place. (We were engaged but not yet officially married according to Jewish law. We had expected to marry when the summer vacation started.) When I would visit Pepe, I would stop the car at her parents' house because her father [Yosl Haberkorn] was always in the synagogue in the morning. Zlateh went to Pepe's and asked if I could stay there. It began to pour again, and under cover of the rain, I took the opportunity to run the short distance from Prachtmana Street to Pogodna Street.

Everyone was home. They were afraid to show their faces on the street, where Jews were rounded up and taken to work. We quickly set a closet against the door leading to Shloime Barits's room. The closet was skillfully placed in front of the door so that it was impossible to imagine there was another room behind it. Among those hiding in the apartment were Yosl Haberkorn's brother-in-law and sister-in-law [Messing was Sheyve's brother] from Zamoarstinowska Street, and Messing.

During the first terrible days, Messing escaped from his apartment because his landlady was a fanatical Ukrainian patriot. When the Soviets took her husband away with them, the landlady decided to exact revenge on her

Jewish tenants. Messing stayed in Pepe's apartment only for a few days; then he went home.

For several months, many people lived in Pepe's apartment without reporting to the authorities, collecting their bread rations or going to work. But Yosl Haberkorn and Shloime Barits went to work on the sewage network, because the job was near their homes, near the train tracks where bombs had damaged the network of pipes. Before the war, Lonek [Pepe's brother] worked in the Podmet metal factory. Under the Germans, he went back to work in the factory.

The most important thing was to find work, so that it could be reported that you were employed, and therefore you could not be caught for other jobs. Every day, German "catchers" were in the streets looking for Jews. Everyone employed had a work card and I was the only man in our group who was not legally working.

I also remember how silly Shloime was. Although he owned a tremendous amount of merchandise, he did not sell anything because, he said: "When the war ends, I'll be the biggest and most experienced merchant in Lemberg." He was the type who envied the employee who earned 25 *złoty* more than he did for a 14-day work period — even though both of them were digging ditches by hand.

Because I wanted to remain hidden from my acquaintances, I spent all my time in Shloime Barits's room and Pepe provided me with books to read. I must say that this was the most pleasant period I experienced during the German occupation. The door was always locked because at any moment different characters could appear. Fear was a constant companion. But after four o'clock in the afternoon, when the three other men came back from work, we all felt more relaxed. We cheered each other up, and hoped that help would come tomorrow or the day after. But all we heard were rumors.

Late in June, when the Germans were only a few dozen miles from Lemberg, the Jewish community had been asked to make its first "contribution." Barrels of kerosene were placed next to all the Jewish holy places, synagogues and houses of study. If the community didn't come up with the "contribution," the religious sites would all be burned to the ground. The town was in a terrible uproar. The Jews gave the authorities the money they asked for and then the holy places were torched anyway. I do not need to go into much detail when writing about this, as I am sure that historians will describe the incident of the "contributions" thoroughly.[5]

At that time, Zlateh had 10,000 rubles in cash. Of course, it was not hers: Father had given it to her. The Germans were exchanging rubles for marks at a rate of ten to one, so Zlateh was left with a thousand marks. At that time, a bunch of parsley cost one mark, and a kilo of potatoes cost three marks. Mechel gave a contribution of 3,000 rubles, and Zlateh gave only 2,000. Sheyve Haberkorn, because her family was penniless, gave the only 1,000 rubles she had.

By the end of the *Aktion*,[6] Zlateh, Sheyve and Leytshe Barits had no more cash on hand. Shloime was a penny-pincher even when times were good, but after the contribution, he had only merchandise, no cash. A large part of his merchandise was at Leytshe's parents' house in Złoczów. It was certain that by then it was already spoiled. And he had no access to the merchandise he had at home, because he had no one he could trust with the goods.

Jews did not walk in the streets, except to go to work and back. Everyone stayed hidden. In short, we had no money and no food. Around that time, Zlateh sold the first gift she had ever received from Mechel: a small gold bracelet. She got about 700 *złoty* for it and used the money to buy one cubic meter of potatoes.

We received packages of foodstuffs from home, but the person who brought the packages would take the bigger and better part of it for himself. Our parents were always under the impression that their food packages arrived in one piece. What they did not know was that the hunger was so great that people acted toward one another without mercy. The Christians refused any kind of monetary payment to carry packages for Jews. They even feared entering a Jewish home. I had to ask my dear mother not to send us any more pack-

---

5 Hostages were also taken. The Nazis appointed a Jewish committee in late July 1941 that became the Judenrat (Jewish Council). In August 1941 they were ordered to pay a twenty-million ruble "contribution." The money was paid, but the Germans burned down the Great Synagogue (the Hekhal), the Sykstuski Synagogue, and the Tur Zahav Synagogue — one of the most beautiful neo-Gothic structures in Lemberg.

6 The Nazi term *Aktion,* literally translated as action, was used in such contexts to mean an operation against the Jews. The term was also used for roundups for deportation to death camps.

ages. I realized that it was extremely hard to find someone from Lemberg who was ready to deliver a package. And when someone was found, he wanted to be paid for the delivery with a variety of food products.

Once, our parents sent two loaves of bread baked by Christians that weighed about four kilograms each. The person delivering the loaves substituted other loaves distributed by the Germans for the ones that were intended for us. I immediately realized that there was no bread like that in Kaminke, but what could I do? On another occasion, a man delivering the packages kept them for himself, and claimed they had been stolen en route. So as you can see, we did not live in luxury.

The situation deteriorated so much that we started getting up later, just to postpone eating. We fasted two days a week, hoping that God would help us. I ate at Pepe's parents' home. (Zlateh brought me food at Pepe's, but did not want to be seen in the streets while bringing it to me.) However, I did not eat much of what Zlateh brought, as I told Lonek and Yosl to eat because they were working. When she looked at me, Pepe did not want to eat, either. She ate only with great effort. In any case, I was fasting to some extent.

Mother came to see us three times. It was very dangerous then to travel on the roads. And yet every time Mother came to us I was overjoyed. We could not get our fill of talking. My dear mother was constantly worried: "They must not see you or hear you talking. And you have to take care of yourself so that nothing, God forbid, will happen to you."

Such were the cares of my beloved parents. And when I said to my mother, "Go, Mother, Zlateh is waiting. Go to sleep. Tomorrow you have to return home," she at once replied, "I go to sleep — and where is my child sleeping? My dear Meyerinyu, does he have anything to cover himself with? He is still so [young]. Will he be able to fend for himself in the world?"

My father sent me a message saying that my mother cried day and night, wanting to know if her children had what to eat. Father tried to comfort her by telling her that my friends, the ones who had stayed at home, had all been murdered; but that did not help my dear mother. She went on weeping, night and day. She also had terrible dreams. She would wake up in the middle of the night, crying out: "Where are my children? Who is left to me? Where is my dear son Meyerinyu? He was always singing to me, and it made all of us happy. He was always hungry for life." Oh my beloved mother, how I understand you! Who but a mother could feel this way — a mother who had been robbed of her children?

Oh, how different the situation had been just a few months ago! How happy and joyful we were then, all of us together! And now? Yes, my dearest mother, you were right. Now we no longer had our dearest, our most beloved family. We were torn apart and scattered. But dear mother, until this very day I have been drinking from this cup of bitterness, and it is clear that I have not yet drained it dry.

As I write these words, tears flow from my eyes and my heart bleeds. Oh, how I wish I could meet my brother, my one and only, my dear brother, my Meyerinyu, and at least tell him all of this and hug him to my heart! Because of all this, I do not care about life or the things I have been through. You will understand this when you read the following chapters.

Whenever Zlateh and Abish came to see me I would hide. I was afraid that he might talk about me to strangers, as children do. They were looking for me and very much wanted to murder me. Zlateh was repeatedly visited by various messengers searching for me. Money was what they were after. You, my dear brother, knew particularly well the bandit from Lemberg, the notorious Mishke, who had married Koideieh's daughter from the Lanes family. Wasil Demczine, in particular, made me out to have been a leader under the Soviets. In addition, he told the Lanes all kinds of stories about me, with the result that Mishke, accompanied by several other bandits, came looking for me. Because of these searches, even Zlateh refrained from visiting me too often.

As I mentioned earlier, every time Abish came, I hid. Every time someone went to open the door, Zlateh would tell me whether she was with her elder or her younger son. When it was the older boy, I immediately hid in the attic, in the closet, or in the bed, covering myself up. My heart ached every time I had to hide from Abish, the boy for whom I would give anything just to make him happy.

In this situation, I had no choice. I hid from Abish, and for weeks watched him from a distance, admiring his beaming face. Zlateh's second son [Elish] was small, but he was as clever as the day is long. When he was only two years old, he already watched over his mother. He understood what we were going through because of the Germans.

Right before, *Yom ha-Kodesh* [literally, the holy day; Yom Kippur, October 1, 1941), Mechel began work as a mason at the municipal slaughterhouse. Until then he hadn't worked for a long time. When he worked for the army, loading wood and stones, thirty of the people working with him were killed in one day — and the next day, too, there were victims. Though nothing happened to Mechel, he stopped working for the army because he didn't want to die. The job in the slaughterhouse was different: it was close to home, and he worked with many Christians he knew personally. From time to time they gave him a piece of liver, lung or regular meat.

On *Yom ha-Kodesh*, Mechel did not work. He had a *minyan* [prayer quorum] in his home and led the prayers. As usual, I did not leave the house. But that same day, a regular army soldier from the front, who happened to be a jewelry expert, went from one Jewish home to another demanding gold watches, chains and rings.

The winter frost started much earlier that year and we lived at Pepe's until November. During that time [November 8-December 15, 1941], plans for a ghetto were drawn up many times. People moved from the streets in the city center to the ghetto quarter, but as soon as Jews moved, so did the location of the ghetto. The only purpose in changing the location was to force the Jews to lug their possessions from place to place. By then, all Jews were required to wear armbands. The horror of that patch can be known only by someone who has worn it.

Bands of robbers stood on all the bridges and various street crossings along Krajcigon Street and did nothing but steal from Jews. At times, even ordinary citizens robbed the Jews. Nobody paid any attention to the robberies, because the victims were wearing armbands. Shloime Barits' stepmother gradually carried bundles of household items from Kościelna Street to Shloime's house on Pogodna Street. During one of her journeys, the Christians took a bundle of linens from her and gave her [just] three *zloty* in return.

Goods, no matter what they were, were being requisitioned for the army. In short, the authorities were taking everything. In an attempt to do something about it, we on Pogodna Street decided to hide some of our household goods. We built a double room in Yosl Haberkorn's attic and hid Zlateh's, Sheyve's and Leytshe's best things in it, hoping that the next day there would be an end to the slaughter.

We did not know then that this was just the beginning. The three apartment owners [Yosl, Shloime and Mechel] agreed to conceal items they would not sell for any amount of money. It was decided that if it became necessary to abandon the house, the items would be left behind, and that is what was done. The items were packed with mothballs, into boxes, sacks and milk churns. I did the technical work, and eventually everything was stowed away.

While we were still living there, we opened the small attic room only once, when Pepe took out a piece of fabric that would make a good summer coat and traded it for potatoes and wheat flour; and Uncle Kver [his maternal uncle] put his fur coat into the hideout. Shloime Barits's possessions made up seventy percent of everything in the hideout. While the door was still open, he shoved the whole of his eiderdown into the space with great difficulty. It barely fit in. His Leytshe begged him to leave it out, but Shloime did not want to hear it. It was just one eiderdown…oh, how he needed it later on! But by then it was too late.

Zlateh, too, hid no small quantity of things. She even slipped her two wedding rings into the pocket of Mechel's town coat. I cannot list everything for you, but that closet hid the best and most beautiful items. Later we found no trace of those things. Before we left, Mechel said we should take some items out, but Shloime Barits did not want to hear of it. He said that he would rather beg than open the hiding place, and he won the argument. Everything was left there to this very day. If we could have known the problems caused by leaving everything behind, we would certainly have taken some of the items with us.

On the day we were supposed to move to the Jewish quarter, SS men and Ukrainian police stood along the streets we had to walk, and it had a terrible effect on us. Trucks drove up to the house on Samojele Street, and everything was carted away. Then a rumor spread that those found in their apartments after the next half an hour would be shot. Later another rumor spread, saying that those who missed the deadline would be allowed to take along only fifty kilograms [of belongings] and no more. But who cared about possessions? Everyone wanted to escape with his life.

Shloime Barits had sold his beds and closets. The rooms were empty, but I did not go to Zlateh. Just imagine: the janitor was supposed to take over the apartment after we left, but Zlateh was being robbed by everyone. Hania, her former servant, picked things out for herself. A Ukrainian policeman took all her furniture and better items. Other people just walked in and helped themselves to whatever they wanted. Mechel drove off to the new apartment with two wagons of wood and coal, but when the wagons returned, Mechel and Shloime Barits had to hide from the work roundups. Many people never came back from that kind of labor.

As Zlateh stood there in the abandoned apartment, alone with her two children, a policeman demanded that she give him her two down quilts, which had to be delivered to his home by four o'clock that afternoon. If not, he would not release the Christian who was delivering the furniture to him. The Christian had five cubic meters of potatoes in his wagon, which he was supposed to deliver to our new apartment. Zlateh had asked him to do that; he took the best wagon for Mechel's sake and then gave them the five cubic meters of potatoes. Then my dear sister brought her younger son [Elish] to me, and ran, with [Abish] her elder son, to the Messings on Damarstinowska Street, where she was able to secure a few quilts to give to the bandit. Later we met this bandit again, and he robbed us again.

Our apartment was left unprotected. Anybody who liked anything in our apartment could simply take it. But we didn't care about that. To us it was a question of saving the best wood and coal and the foodstuffs that were left. Zlateh was trading everything for food, for it looked like it was going to be a severe winter, and the deadline for leaving the quarter had come.

It was, I think, November 10 or 11 and it was difficult to get to the apartment. Zlateh had to renovate the [new] apartment — for we needed to have room there for thirteen people: Shloime Barits's father and stepmother, Shloime and Leytshe, Yosl, [Sheyve], Pepe, Lonek Haberkorn, Mechel and Zlateh, Abish and Elish Eisen, and me. Zlateh gave up one of her rooms and the kitchen. All of our firewood and coal, and there wasn't much of it, was stored in the kitchen for lack of space. There was a lot of water in the basement: it was a meter deep.

Yosl Haberkorn leased an apartment near Kaszczarna Street, where we all had lived together [before the ghetto was formed], and moved a man named Piotrowski into it. His brother lived in Zlateh's house.

We were glad to have a place where we could live and keep some of our belongings. There were many people who had no place to live. Officially the Christians were forced to leave their quarters as the Jews were leaving theirs, but the Christians were not threatened with any sanctions. Basically, the Christians and Jews traded their apartments, and most of the people making exchanges knew each other. When it came to renting or exchanging apartments, the Christians only wanted to know if the Jewish apartments had gas, electricity, running water and bathrooms. They wanted comfort. None of the "new" Jewish apartments had these luxuries, and so it was hard to get a decent apartment. There would not be enough space in the whole of this notebook to list all the people from Pogodna Street [who were forced to move].

Zlateh's former servant Hania had a one-room apartment on the other side of Znieszenie, beyond the gate. She and Zlateh were trading apartments, but she did not want Zlateh's whole apartment with the kitchen and the other room filled with furnishings and decorations. She took the down payment for her apartment but did not let us move in. Why? Because she and her husband were Ukrainians, and her mother-in-law used the money to immediately send her sons to work in Germany. Instead, Zlateh's landlady was paid 800 *złoty* for everything that remained in the apartment and it was all taken away.

The entire Eisen family — Shaindel [Mechel's mother], Esther [Mechel's sister] Chaim Katz [Mechel's brother-in-law], Hersh-Leib Strassler [another of Mechel's brother-in-laws, married to his sister, Rochel] and Yosl Eisen [Mechel's brother], all lived on this side of Znieszenie, beyond the gate, far from edge of the ghetto.

At this point I want to give you an overview of the situation. I will do the same thing in future chapters, if I can succeed in writing it all down.

We had already lived through a variety of troubles. Here I want to mention one in particular. [The summer before the ghetto was formed,] on one Shabbos day, we were told that the following day, Sunday — I believe it was on the Ninth of Av [August 2, 1941] — that it was Petlura's memorial, and the Jews would be slaughtered to commemorate him — and they were. [Symon

Petlura was a Ukraine Nationalist who was assassinated by a Jew in Paris in 1926.[7] The pogrom began on July 25.]

Yosl [Haberkorn], Shloime, Lonek, their neighbor Eisenberg, his son Mendl, and I, hid in a small wooden room in the home of a Christian who lived near Yosl. We went into hiding at three o'clock at night. All the people living in that apartment block were Christians. We had to keep quiet during a whole scorching day, until nine in the evening. Under pressure, the proprietor gave us the key, and Sheyve locked us in from the outside. At the time, it seemed to me like torture, but today things like that look like a game. I would be able to stay lying down like that for weeks, and it would have no effect on me. Though by then I was no longer free, I was still in a house and among people. I could cough and groan. Still, that first day was very hard.

Later, the householder who hid us refused to hide Jews again, for any amount of money. The family is Zaba from Bataticze. They have a son who is a university professor. During Russian rule, the son was in Moscow. The war caught up with him when he was traveling in Davist [unclear reference]. His mother told herself that she would live to see the day when she would see her only son again, and invited us to stay, but later on, we couldn't convince her to help us again.

Yes, Pogodna Street! In spite of all the hardships I experienced under the Germans, it was there, on Pogodna Street, that I had the best time — though I have to add that it was very hard for a free man to adjust to such conditions.

7　Tisha B'Av — the Ninth Day of the Hebrew month of Av — is a solemn fast day commemorating the destruction of the ancient Temple in Jerusalem. According to Jewish tradition, many other catastrophic events took place on this day throughout history.

　　Semyon Petlura was a Ukrainian nationalist leader and hero who was the last leader of independent Ukraine and was murdered in Paris on May 25, 1926. Ukrainian nationalist leaders transformed the anniversary of Petliura's death to July 25 and conducted massacres of Jews in Lwow that came to be called the Petliura Days. Villagers from the nearby villages participated, as did Ukrainian policemen. More than 2,000 Jews were murdered in the three-day massacre.

But it was still the sweetest time. We were still all alive then. You know what it means to be alive. By that time, thousands of Jews were no longer among the living. I still had parents, a sister, a brother-in-law, two small beloved diamonds [nephews], and what a Pepe! Everyone was entitled to breathe, to look at one another, to laugh at times, and of course, to cry at any time. We cursed the moment when we had come under German rule, but it was too late. If we had known then what we knew later, we would have escaped to Romania or Hungary. We were told that for money it was possible to escape to those places. And yet, how tragic it was for the Jews in Hungary!

It is certainly no better for them than for the Jews in Poland, Ukraine, Czechoslovakia, Austria, Germany, etc. As I write these words, the Germans are marching into Hungary, and the government is changing. Soon the German bandits will show the Hungarians what kind of suffering they can inflict. The Jews who fled to there from Poland already know what kind of suffering the Germans impose.

It is April 24, 1944. We have been under German occupation for [three] years. We do not get much news, but I can find out a lot from an old newspaper. Oh my dearest, living family, it is near and yet it is far away. I am still hoping to survive, although nothing in my situation has changed. If I am caught, I will be shot at once. The same regime of bandits is still in power.

CHAPTER 6

13 Bilinkiewicka Street — or The Jewish Quarter

The rooms in Yosl Haberkorn's old apartment were already empty, and I was the last to leave Pogodna Street. That last day was a bit warmer — there was snow, but it was melting, and there was plenty of mud. In the evening Pepe came to tell me it was time to move to the new apartment. Zlateh, the children and Mechel were already there.

Pepe and I waited until it became dark outside. Then we began walking. At that time I did not have an armband, and Pepe pulled hers off. And so we walked. For the first time in five whole months, I was on the street. I never would cross Pogodna Street; I did not even step over the threshold. And for the first time in my life I was now on the other side of Znieszenie, beyond the railroad tracks. The tracks led from the train station at Podzamcze to the oil refinery and the municipal slaughterhouse, as well as to the "Raiker" canning factor. That meant Jews could not reside on this side of the railroad tracks, and the area on the other side of the tracks became the Jewish quarter.

Living in the new place were Shloime, his wife and parents, and Yosl Haberkorn with his children and wife. Hersh-Leib Strassler, who had a house of his own on the wrong side of the railroad tracks and had exchanged it with someone who lived on the ghetto side of the tracks. When we arrived that night, I did not immediately enter the apartment, because if there were strangers in there I did not want them to see me. As it happened, the landlady [Maria Ignatowicz] was there, so I waited outside until she left.

The first thing I did when I got into that apartment, was hug Abish to my heart.

Later, on more than one occasion, I hid in the closet so that [the land-lady] wouldn't see me. Mother insisted I not show myself to anyone; if it was not possible to be completely hidden, then only a few people should know about me. I followed my mother's advice very closely and to this day, thank God, everything worked out as my mother would have wished.

Zlateh brought the kitchen cupboard with her from the old apartment and also the white linen closet, the one I used for hiding. I also would hide with the Teppers, our next door neighbors.

The new apartment had a room and a kitchen on one side, and a room and a kitchen on the other side. There was a small hallway with three doors between them. Two doors led to the two apartments, which were on the right and left sides, and a third door led to another room with a tiny kitchen. From this little kitchen one could use a ladder to climb up to an attic, or take the stairs down to the basement.

The Tepper family — a mother with two young daughters, lived in that middle apartment, [which had another entrance]. The elder daughter was about eight or nine, the younger about six or seven. Their apartment also had a door to our apartment. Although the door was always closed, it was not locked. We removed the door handle, and kept it on our side. Whenever I needed to hide in the Tepper's apartment, I kept the knob handy, next to the door, and I would go in.

Zlateh and the children slept in the bed nearest the door, and Mechel and I slept in the other bed [on that same wall]. There were two more beds on the other wall. Shloime slept in one with his father, and Pepe and her mother slept in the other. At night, they would put pillow cases on the couch pillows, for the couches in the middle of the room, where Leytshe Barits and her moth-er-in-law slept. Lonek and Yosl slept on a bunk bed in the kitchen.

(I describe the apartment in such detail because more than one memory is connected with it. In the winter, snow blew into the apartment and stuck to the walls. There was always a layer of snow, two to three centimeters thick on the outside walls. Zlateh slept where it was dry. In one kitchen there was a middle wall black [with mold]. Water ran down the walls into half of the kitchen, where the wood and coal were kept. It was always cold, whether we heated the place or not. It was the epitome of the "cold, and miserably dark" apartment — and it was slippery! It was pretty dark there, because although there was a small lamp, the apartment had no electric lighting, we lived by the light of eleven candles — still, we somehow managed.)

The landlady was our constant guest, and helped herself to our things — she could not get her fill of them — and she would gossip. When she came around, I hid in the closet for hours on end, or I would sit in the attic, or on the stairs that led down to the basement. The basement was full of water, so we kept the door to it closed. When I knew the landlady's visits were going to take some time, I would go to Mrs. Tepper's, where there was plenty of room to move around. When the landlady would end her visit with us, [and if I was in the Tepper's apartment when] she would knock on the Tepper's door, I would seize the opportunity, before she could open it, to climb over the beds into our apartment. I always kept the door handle with me, just in case.

Mechel still worked in the slaughterhouse. Shloime was working at his trade, in the fur cooperative. Yosl Haberkorn was working for Benbenko, a Christian from Pogodna Street who had a horse and a small wagon. Yosl had worked for him for ten weeks, but the man could not provide proper certification. Luckily, when they traveled together, they were not stopped by the Germans or checked for identification. They were able to make money, and as you know, money was in short supply. Yosl made money by going to the marketplace and getting hired to move people from the Christian streets. Lonek worked in his metal factory. [I continued to heed my mother's advice,] and stayed indoors so that no one would see me.

The day after we moved to the new apartment, all four men went to work. [There was a man in a large apartment next door who didn't work and we stayed together.] [His name was Stengl, and his sister-in-law and niece would join us later.] Both of us were in a very bad situation. When we first met, we didn't know that both of us, together, would be saved from the murderous hands of the Germans. During the course of a conversation we had [later] while in hiding, we realized that he was one of six people who had emerged alive, along with me [from a mass murder].

I ate Zlateh's food because Zlateh absolutely did not want me to eat the Haberkorn's food. Zlateh had stored a considerable amount of food for us, with plenty of flour, potatoes, beans and onions. She stocked enough of everything, because everyone was saying that no Christian would be allowed to enter the Jewish quarter. She had over 20 liters of oil and chicken fat, butter and all the other things needed in a household. Ironically, we secured food supplies, but we could not secure our lives, not for all the money in the world.

At that time, I derived the greatest satisfaction from Zlateh's two lovely, sweet children. I did not need anything else. They were substitutes for everything. In their company I found the world I had lost. I never wearied of them. Zlateh's children sat with me for days on end, and so did the Tepper children.

The fur *Aktion* soon began.[8] The Jewish police ran from apartment to apartment, searching for furs. Then an announcement declared that Jews were forbidden to own anything made of fur. Anyone found with furs or clothing trimmed with fur, after the *Aktion,* would be executed.

My sister did not have her good furs with her — they were stowed in the hideout; but there were two short fur coats, one Mechel's and the other mine. Abish had one too. I had it made for him during the Soviet period, by Uncle Chaim-Hersh — a complete, child's-size, fur coat. [Elish], the younger boy, did not have a finished fur coat: the little sleeves hadn't yet been sewn on. Zlateh surrendered an old hat of Mechel's and an old pair of fur gloves. Shloime handed over a fox fur, but Sheyve handed over nothing. We quickly took some pieces of clothing to our Christian neighbors, Rzadkowa and Bobe. Mechel gave one of them his fur coat. Some Christians were still living in the neighborhood even after the Jewish quarter was established, so I immediately thought of bartering the furs.

Jews were now also not permitted to own sweaters, pullovers, scarves or gloves made of wool. It pained our hearts to barter the children's furs, Mechel's sweater and my short fur coat. We waited until after the *Aktion*, because then the value went up. Later, when we wanted to sell items, we had to show them to the buyer, but our Christian [customers] did not want to go back and forth to Jewish apartments.

We built a hideout [for our valuables] in the basement by dividing it into compartments. We dropped several boxes and some coal-weighing bins Mechel owned into one of the compartments, and built a scaffolding of planks

8 In late December 1941, all across the so-called Generalgouvernement (General Government), which included the Lwow/Lemberg area, the German authorities ordered the Jews to hand over all furs and winter coats. The clothing was to be remade into warm clothing for the German soldiers who were freezing on the Eastern front in the Soviet Union.

on top of them. We laid some straw down on top of that, with another row of planks to create a crawl space, and we crawled along a plank from the stairs to the scaffolding. The last person to crawl across to the compartments would pull the first and second planks into the scaffolding, making it impossible to reach — since in the winter months the basement was filled with more than a meter of water.

The items [we hid] were what I bartered for wheat flour and rye flour. I [also] traded Zlateh's and her children's fur coats, and Mechel's wool sweater — hand-knitted by Zlateh — for flour.

All my bartering was done with only one person, Kozar, a Polish Christian who came from Prose, a village near Lemberg. I would give him items and money and he would come back with flour. Relatively speaking I did good deals with him because we had enough flour for the winter. I did the bartering because Mechel was always at work and also because Kozar did not know me from before. I also understood the nature of my "customers," and not just from the period in question. When I bartered the sweater, I asked Kozar to hold on to it. I was planning, if we survived this ordeal, to buy it back. I believe he did as I asked — he wore that sweater all through the winter and did not sell it.

Soon there was dissention. [Yosl's wife] Sheyve would shout: "If I had my things from the attic, I would have something to barter. As it is, I have nothing." Shloime traded a splendid little fur coat of Leytshe's and other things, but Sheyve had nothing to exchange. The only thing we could have done was go back to the attic [in Pogodna Street] and reopen the hideout.

Because of the fur *Aktion* we were glad we did not have our important furs with us and that they were hidden in the attic. But from then on, Sheyve cried and said she would die of hunger because she had little or nothing to eat. She cried until the last moments of her life. She constantly complained to her husband and children. And yet she was a very devoted wife. She was used to a life where she made sure that Yosl did not, God forbid, have to do without anything. That was what caused her to act in this way. Meanwhile: Her eyes! It is not for nothing that, after death, shards are placed upon the eyes.

Every time it snowed, the Jewish police rounded up Jews for snow removal — that included women, except for women with young children — who were released by the chief of police. During roundups I would climb into my hideout in the basement, which I called "Robinson Crusoe's Island," once I pulled in the two wooden planks.

All the men who worked had their certificates posted on the doors of their residences, indicating that the Jews within were employed. On two separate occasions I was caught off guard when the Jewish police came to round up Jews for forced labor. Once it happened in the evening, when they were not expected, and I had no place to hide. The policemen who found me never saw me before in their lives, so I spoke to them in Polish. I pulled the bedspread off Zlateh's bed, and tried to give them the impression I was buying it from the Jews. The policemen didn't ask if I was a Jew. Later, I met one of them in the streets of the ghetto, and we both had a good laugh.

I could write several chapters about the problems caused by the Jewish police in the ghetto, but I will leave that to others. The second time I was caught, the Jewish policeman arrived while I was visiting my next door neighbor. We both jumped out the window and ran. During that winter of 1941 to 1942, the Jewish police caused me to suffer a great deal.

A policeman once walked into the apartment while I was sorting potatoes. Zlateh threw the bedspread over me and began making the bed. It was quite early and the men had just left for work. Yosl Haberkorn wasn't working for his Christian employer, because moving season came to an end, and the Christian did not want to keep the horses over the winter. The police arrested Yosl and took him to the Jewish police station, but he was released since, for the moment, no men were needed.

In those years, people were sent to a labor camp in Winike, near Lemberg. Those who entered there never came out. Soon after he was arrested, through a connection, Yosl began working in the Lemberg shoe factory. It was lucky he got that job so quickly, because otherwise Sheyve would never have let us, or her own children, hear the end of it. Once he was working, she calmed down. Yosl also began to work with horses, earning extra income. The Germans were constantly stealing goods and Yosl delivered those goods to their homes. They always paid him on delivery.

Then the season for potato deliveries began. Everybody was issued a potato card, and Yosl brought some potatoes home. We were overjoyed when Yosl brought home money, because when he came home empty-handed, Sheyve would be out of sorts and we would hear nothing except, "If I had my things from the little attic, I would be able to do business."

Sheyve was not intimidated by the events happening around us. One man sold a fox fur coat. Later on, the man who bought the coat informed on the Jewish seller, who was arrested. Yitzchok Krats, a Jewish policeman from Lemberg, sold a fur coat in Kaminke to the Kaminke commander, an SS man, a bandit, who wore civilian clothes; (he is at his post in Kaminke to this day). He was then arrested on the order of the SS man who bought the coat, and was taken to Kaminke. Other Jews were also arrested in connection with the sale of that coat. Among them were: Moishe-Meyer Lindvorm, the tailor who made the lining; Berl Lafayavke, who made the fur coat; Meyer Kleyner, the president of the Judenrat, who used Jewish community funds to buy the coat; Matyas Baran, who sold the fur coat to Yitzchok Krats in Lemberg and Krats himself. The same SS commander issued Matyas the permit to travel legally to Lemberg!

The men were taken to Sokal by the SS and were never seen again. I could tell hundreds of stories like this one — they are endless. However, Sheyve stuck to her own point of view. These kinds of stories did not bother her. What did restrain her and have a great influence on her was the fact that we were together.

We all cooked in one kitchen. Only a housewife knows what it is like to share a kitchen with two other women. That was the greatest curse. If Sheyve had been alone to use the kitchen she would have considered herself rich, but because she had to share it with other women, she considered herself poor. I cannot describe how much we suffered because we had hidden those items in our old apartment attic. There were times when we asked God to burn down the whole small house and everything in it, just so that there would be no more talk about it.

The Germans passed another law: one could once again live in one's own apartment. Jews who had not entirely moved out of their previous apartments stayed put. For example, Mrs. Tepper's [family]. Her husband was caught by the Jewish police and was in a forced labor camp in Korowice near Zloczów. She had parents and two sisters who always lived on Tokarzewskiego Street and she had rented an apartment above them. When Mrs. Tepper moved to the ghetto, they stayed in their old apartment. Some of their things were hidden behind the closet in the ghetto apartment, and some were in the old apartment.

There were quite a few Jews in this predicament. The Christian who had Yosl Haberkorn's apartment moved back to his own. The Jew who lived there had to move out, so now Yosl's apartment [on Pogodna] was empty. Yosl moved Pietrowski, his Christian friend and a wagon driver from the shoe factory, into it. After a while, Pietrowski, moved out.

That's when we could have removed the things hidden in the apartment because nobody was living there. But just then a terrible German *Aktion* was carried out against our people. We thought the younger people were being taken to Germany to work, while the older ones were being murdered either in Lemberg or in Belzec, so we abandoned everything.

I was still not working, and I had no documents so I always had to hide. Hiding from the Germans was not the same as hiding from the Jewish police. With the Jewish police, I always figured that if I was caught, I would use all means not to fall into German hands. I thought I could escape the Jewish police because they carried no weapons. Now it was no laughing matter. The SS men were walking around with Ukrainian and Jewish police.

Our small Robinson Crusoe's island no longer existed because the water in the basement had dried up. Now one could walk into the basement and the worst that would happen is that you would get mud on your shoes. Ukrainian bandits did not worry about their boots, because their boots were robbed from Jews.

A few illegals were now hiding in our house: Shloime's parents and Mechel's mother, as well as one of our neighbors, Mrs. Rab and her daughter. The man [Stengl] who hid with me all winter began working when Mr. Rab took him to a job on Liczakower Street, where they had always lived before the war. There was also a widow named Gold and her sister. Together with Pepe and me, there were nine people who had to remain hidden.

Mechel, Shloime and I built a second hideout. To provide a route to the hiding space, we nailed planks under the stairs, and next to the lowest step we removed one small plank from the step above the lowest one. We made a small door in the wainscoting that closed from the inside, and we inserted planks there. We made seats along the sidewalls. All the women hid there with Shloime's father. The wooden planks that we nailed underneath the benches were old, black and warped by water because we took them from the wainscoting in the basement. The small door was cut out from two fairly long planks, so that it was like one piece and it fit like a wooden square on a chessboard. It was very well made.

I had my own special hideout, where no one else could hide with me. I would push myself into a baking oven, right next to the floor. I would slide into the oven feet first, so that my head would always be next to the small door. Then, with a big effort, I would pull my arms into the oven and place them on my chest. After that, I would disguise my head with rags, and there I lay. Before I did that, though, I would make sure that all the others were in their hiding places and that the door was closed.

I gave everyone in the basement candles and matches and told them they could move around freely, but that if they heard anyone knocking in the apartment above, they should not cough or talk. Those who remained in the apartment kept very quiet, so as not to alarm the people hiding under the stairs. Little Abish, Esther's son, and two other boys roamed the streets. It was unknown whether they were Jews since they did not wear armbands. If they saw something, they immediately informed us: "They are already in the streets. They are already on our street."

We lived right on the edge of a field — a big potato field faced our window.

A Jewish policeman lived two apartments down from us. He never took part in the *Aktions*, because he belonged to the crime squad. The Jewish police had a special crime squad because night after night, particularly in our neighborhood, there were robberies and muggings.

We got on well with a few [Christian] families on our street, and for that reason we always kept two bottles of vodka and some food available. Believe me we did not eat the food ourselves. We used it for entertainment — we had to entertain the murderers. One of our neighbors was a certain Senie Naihaus. His wife was from the Friedhoffer family, and before the war, Senie got the bakery near the railroad tracks from his father-in-law. Arnold, a Hungarian and former journeyman for Naihaus, lived there with his wife and children.

At that time, foreign nationals did not have to wear armbands, so the Hungarian and his family could constantly wander through the streets. Every time the bandits showed up in the potato field near our apartment, Mr. Arnold told us about it. The bandits were drawn to Naihaus's apartment [to drink] and when they left, they no longer searched as hard. More than once, their drinking went on for more than two hours, while we, hiding in mouse holes, were in deadly fear.

I would always cough to alert the people in the basement. Hiding in the kitchen oven, I would listen to Zlateh and Leytshe talking, and I would become aware of what was happening in the street. On more than one occasion, a second party of bandits would appear, and we would bring out another bottle of liquor, just to put out the fire.

The thieves would arrange to stop at our apartment to drink after work, so we had to have some liquor ready and some food to go with it. I still remember how the people in the basement always asked me to let them know what was happening on the street. More than once I crawled out of the oven to go down to the basement to calm them down, because I was the only person who could and I would try to give them courage. If not I, then who? I, who was in the same situation. The people in the basement would bless me. Mechel's mother always said: "Nothing will ever happen to you. You will be protected from all bad things. No ill wind will ever blow on you."

This pious Jewish woman always kept her *Korban Minchah* prayer book[9] with her and did not let go of it until her very last moment. Other people blessed me in their own ways.

Mrs. Rab, an old kerosene seller from Liczkow, did not know Yiddish well. Her young daughter was like a good Christian — we heard nothing from her lips but "Jesus, Maria," and she knew no Yiddish at all. Mrs. Gold liked to chant Jewish prayers and blessings, and to say *Krishmah* [*Shema Yisrael*, the Hear O Israel prayer]. The people kept blessing me. Thanks to that, maybe I am alive today. At any rate, if all these blessings are heard, I may, with the help of God, live to see my dearest brother.

The *Aktion* lasted almost four weeks. I think it ended before Pesach. It was quite hard to get through it. I had a particularly difficult time of it with Mechel's mother. Poor thing, she was always a suffering woman. I believe she had asthma. In any case she was always coughing. The other women rebelled: "She will be the death of us. Because of this one Jewish woman we'll all go."

I always would tell the people in the basement to move about as freely as was possible in that hole. Pepe would say that thanks to that old Jewish woman [Mrs. Eisen], we would be saved. But go talk to Charlottke [Rab's daughter]. She did not understand a word you said to her.

The *Aktion* went on day and night. We no longer slept. I would stand, all night long, watching the flashlights as they moved along the street. The

9   A special Yiddish prayer book specifically written for women with Yiddish translations and commentaries.

people in hiding sat with their clothes on. I did not let them go to the basement. Above, in the small kitchen, they would lie on the floor, where it was airier than in the basement. I did not sleep or eat.

Then it became possible to get work with very good documents for $100-$200. But I didn't want to go to a job while Pepe stayed at home. Even if I was prepared to go to work, it was possible that the others would not have let me. Old Mrs. Eisen said: "Protect us, and God will protect you." In fact, by that time, I was so bound to the home and the children that it seemed to me that I would not be able to survive on my own.

Meanwhile, events ran their course. One Monday, Miss Charlottke and Mrs. Gold's sister went out in the direction of Leczawka Street. People were saying that there would be no *Aktion* that day, but they were caught and never came back. Mrs. Gold was caught, too. Early in the morning she had joined the men on their way to work. Mrs. Gold's brother-in-law was Stengl, the fellow who hid with me in the basement in December. He was able to save his sister-in-law only when he shouted to his work supervisor that she was his wife and had forgotten her papers at home. The other two women could not be helped by any means. They were taken away and were the first two victims from our house.

Chaneleh Eisen [married to Shayeh Pardes] was very sick, so her old mother, [Shaindel] wanted nothing more than to visit her daughter and help her a bit. We implored her: "Don't go because the small Christian children will see you, and then they will send the guys in to search the house. In this house there are old people who do not work."

One afternoon Mechel came home from work with the news that an *Aktion* had started beyond the railroad tracks. A few trucks had arrived, along with their thugs. "Where is my mother?" Mechel asked. "At Chaneleh's," we said. It was not possible to restrain the mother's heart: she had gone to visit her daughter.

Mechel quickly went to Chaneleh's place on our same street. Old Mrs. Eisen was hiding in Chaneleh's closet because they'd heard about the *Aktion*, but Mechel swiftly brought her to his place. We only just managed to hide ourselves when the gang showed up. They stopped at Chaneleh's place first, then jumped the fence because they did not know how to open the small door. They came in and looked in the [linen] closet, but there was no one there. Then they entered our apartment, but did not find us. It was not the first time. They searched the rooms, the beds, under the beds, and in the attic. We had covered the basement entrance with an old blanket, so that you would not know there was a basement below.

That is how we suffered day after day, night after night.

We also helped plant potatoes, and Yosl, who went to the field with a horse and wagon every day would bring home about 40 to 50 kilograms of potatoes. At that time a potato was, as they say, "a hand in the fire" [a popular item to sell]. Sheyve or Pepe would go to the field to bring Yosl his lunch in a basket, and on their way home, would manage to bring back a few potatoes. The Christians would haul potatoes from the field by the cubic foot and immediately sell them on the road, so they paid no attention to the few kilos taken by Yosl. While this was going on, Sheyve was in an excellent mood, because she knew one kilo of potatoes was worth 10 or more *złoty*. I make a point of this because at other times Sheyve gave her husband, their two children, and the rest of us a terrible time.

In winter, before Christmas, the bandits attacked us for the first time. If I am not mistaken, our landlady had a hand in the attack. Yosl went to the toilet at seven or eight o'clock in the evening and heard someone trying to break down the little door to our courtyard. He quickly came into the house and told us.

Zlateh and I were standing in the chicken-plucking hut, doing the laundry. We happened to be taking a large pot of laundry from the kitchen stove and we were transferring it to a tub in the hut, so that it could soak overnight. At that time, Zlateh was still using the pre-war washing system: first the clothes had to be boiled, then starched, then rinsed. Later this was no longer possible — flour and also other quite important substances, such as starch, were unobtainable. But we did have a pot of hot lye in the kitchen, and logs for the fire.

Yosl, Shloime and I went outside but could not return to the apartment because the bandits hurled themselves at us. I was the last out and I never made it down the steps. Yosl and Shloime were beaten with a variety of metal bars. Yosl took refuge in our neighbor's apartment, but Shloime could not. Meanwhile the tub and the large pot full of laundry left little room to maneuver in the hut.

There were four bandits. In the course of the beating, one broke Shloime's arm with an iron bar. Then formal war broke out. They came into the hut as we came out of the apartment with pots full of hot lye. They realized that they could not rob us, so they wanted to beat us up and broke all the windows in the apartment. The children and Mechel woke up. We started throwing bottles and lumps of coal through the broken windows. The screaming was terrible. I also remember how the two darling children [Abish and Elish] stood there in their nightclothes, shaking with fear.

There were two Ukranian families in apartment number 15, but they did not come out. What did they care if people wanted to murder a Jewish family? The attackers would not have quit us if neighbors hadn't come to help us: the Jew Naihaus, the Hungarian [Arnold] who was a boxer and soccer player, a real sportsman, and several Jews from the street came to our aid. Arnold threw himself on one of the guys. One of them was about to stab Arnold with a horribly big knife, when Arnold tripped him and he fell to the ground. The bandit dropped an iron bar, the knife, his cap, and ran away. The others had run away even earlier.

When the neighbors came into the apartment, we saw what happened. The entire wash, the staircase and the path leading to the street were full of blood. The bandits had learned their lesson. We were almost sure that one of the bottles hit one of the bandits, because the broken bottle was full of blood. The apartment and courtyard were littered with various trays, plates, kettles, pieces of wood and lumps of coal. The bandits had even thrown things from the street back into the house.

The next day we took Shloime to a Jewish doctor. (There were still some Jewish doctors left.) Shloime's arm was put into a plaster cast, and as a result, he did not go to work for several weeks. On the same day that Shloime, Leytshe and Zlateh went to the doctor, we made shutters for all the windows. We had two windows in the main room and one in the kitchen. In the main room, we boarded up one window completely and only half of another. We had to leave half a window uncovered in order to let some light into the room.

In the kitchen we made one shutter out of boards, and every evening we fastened it to the window. Lonek brought home pieces of iron, and we made these into bars to protect the light fixture. We secured all the windows in the attic and the entrance hall with iron bars, and in the same manner, the chicken-plucking shack, so that the windows could not be pulled out or pushed in.

We had a premonition that those guys would be back to take their revenge. We also secured the basement door, the attic door, the windows in the Tepper's apartment, and the three windows in our neighbor's [Stengl's] apartment on the other side. The door of the building and the door of our apartment were secured with iron bars. We were, so to speak, inside a fortress. Two days went by, and then the second attack came, but this time there were only two beatings.

At nightfall, we carried water into the house, and when the men came back from work in the winter at four or five p.m., we closed all the doors and did not go out. More than once people came to visit us at night, but we did not open the doors. However, in cases when we had to open the door, all the men in the house came to the door with axes. Don't think that was a joke. There were Jewish families who had been robbed of everything because they did not close their doors.

Uncle Yehuda's eldest daughter [Dina Stromer Apfel] lived not far from us on another small street. She had never been a wealthy woman. Once, when she was not home, she was robbed of everything she had. All their linens were stolen and the family slept in the ragged clothes that they walked around in all day. She had two beautiful daughters, who from a young age, wanted to be movie stars and were splendid dancers. I did not know them personally, but they would come and visit when we lived on Bilinkiewicza Street. Zlateh always fed them, and from time to time sent their mother a piece of meat, some flour, and things of that sort for Shabbos.

One night two bandits who had been there before returned. They tied up the parents and raped the two daughters. The day after this terrible ordeal, the family moved into Uncle Yehuda's empty apartment. It was empty because the Christians only wanted to move into places that had conveniences [gas, electricity and running water]. I could write much more about incidents of this kind. They ended in the murder of whole Jewish families.

Those guys would visit us almost every night. Who cared about Jews? We even considered taking a stand and putting a stop to the attacks, but it made no sense because our Ukrainian neighbor in apartment 15 was their partner and informed them of everything we did. He was home all the time and observed everything. I would stay awake at night and sleep during the day because we were always afraid of another *Aktion*.

But the bandits would not leave us alone until we moved out. We figured out that the landlady was the ringleader because after each attack, she would show up early in the morning. [She] wanted us to move out so that she could rent the apartment again. We were not permitted to speak. What we did tell her was that we would move out only when the house burned down.

Three or four days later we found a bundle of straw soaked in gasoline under the wooden stairs, but they did not set fire to the straw, even though we did not hear them when they entered the courtyard. They also never threw anything into the well in the courtyard because the Ukranian in number 15 drew water from it. When the weather warmed up, we set up a watch. There was an *Aktion* going on at the time, so the bandits were afraid to walk around because the police were prowling the neighborhood.

Once the bandits crawled through the basement and reached the attic with ladders, but nothing happened to us. The landlady promised me that we would not be evicted. We made it clear to her that if her gang attacked us we would burn the house down. That had some effect. They gradually began to let up on us.

Our landlady's name was Maria Ignatowicz. Her husband was a trolley car conductor and quite an activist. The Soviets sent him to Siberia. They had one son and one daughter. We will write more about them later.

It was our first Pesach under the Germans. One morning before the holiday we baked matzos in the kitchen. We ground the wheat in a coffee grinder and I did the sifting. Zlateh and Leytshe rolled out the dough, and Sheyve, who was in a good mood, did the actual baking. When we baked the matzos, we still did not believe that this was the end of the Jews. If I am not mistaken we had to hide on that day, and maybe also on Pesach. I do not remember clearly.

We kept the house clean even on the worst days of winter, when snow was settling on the walls, and I do remember that on that [eve of the holiday] we cleaned the house a little bit. The Teppers contributed a little wine for *kiddush* [the blessing over wine that begins the Sabbath or festival meal]. That night, Mechel led the Pesach Seder. His mother joined us. Abish asked the four questions and our whole family and the Teppers shared the few matzos. We shed more tears than the wine we drank. Everyone cleansed his or her heart with the flow of tears, and we hoped… maybe, maybe…

By then all of Zlateh's oil was used up, so she had no cooking fat. All the same, the food was very good. I do not remember whether she had four or five eggs for Pesach. This was the first Pesach under the Germans; what was important is that we were all still alive.

One day, around that time, we sold Elish's brightly colored stroller. I remember how little Elish cried "*Jozefa, mama, ja niechce sprzedac wozek. Ja chcem sam jechac na nim.*" ["Jozefa, mother, I don't want to sell the [stroller]. I want to ride in it myself."] when a Christian bought the cart for his child on March 19, and we got 500 *złoty* for it, an excellent price. Elish was promised that when the world changed, Uncle Meyer would buy him another, more beautiful [stroller].

But the boy said: "I don't want it. There will not be another world." He felt that he would never ride in that or any other carriage. The child actually fought us when the Christian took the carriage away. "*Mama, ja niechcem, ja niechcem,*" he cried. ["Mother, I don't want to, I don't want to."] Meanwhile Abish was trying to persuade Elish that it was necessary to sell the carriage so that we could buy bread.

Finally, when the carriage was actually taken from the apartment, Elish had tears in his eyes, as I do now, as I write these words. My beloved ones, whatever I write about the children cannot compare to the reality. My dear sister, imagine kind Zlateh's feelings, when she had to sell the carriage while the child was screaming: "*Mama, ja niechcem.*" ["Mama, I don't want to."] The Christian grabbed the carriage, threw down the 500 *złoty* and ran out. He himself could not bear to watch the child cry and had tears in his own eyes. Do you think the child had ever ridden in the carriage? No. It sat on top of the closet, as shiny and new as when it came from the store.

I tell you, I bartered and sold many items, but selling that carriage made my heart ache. The little boy was so bright and intelligent that he could read a newspaper. He would have grown up to be a prodigy. You should know that daily a private teacher came to tutor Abish at home in exchange for a bowl of soup. Sometimes he taught little Elish the *Aleph-Bayz*. In a just a few weeks the boy learned to *daven* [pray] and eventually caught up with his older brother. The teacher never grew weary of observing that child.

When the carriage was being taken away, the boy said to me, for the first time, something that I will not forget as long as I live: "*Wiedz sobie do babci do Kamionki. Co wujcie chce odemnie?*" ("You should go to Grandma, in Kaminke. What do you want from me, uncle?")

My head is exploding! I cannot read my own writing, I must take a break.

Dear sister, when I write these words I turn hot and cold. Do not think that we had to sell the carriage because we did not have bread. No, there were worse times when we really had no bread. However, I never thought that buyer would give me the asking price for the carriage. I asked for 500 *złoty*, though I knew that a similar carriage was sold, by Mr. Messing's son-in law to his nanny, for 300 *złoty*. And yet the offer was made. The Christian was very anxious to have it. He liked the color, and the carriage was in perfect condition. The Christian accused me of exploiting the situation, and that he was overpaying for the cart by about 150 *złoty*. But I said I wanted 500 and got it.

On one occasion, Zlateh was walking with Elish from Esther's place when they met the Christian with his wife and the carriage. The little fellow ran up to the carriage and shouted in Polish: "Please give me back the carriage." The Christian woman, who was carrying bread from the store, gave Elish a whole loaf of bread. At that time a kilo of bread cost about 20 *złoty*, or even more.

The carriage came with detachable storage bag that could hold food or a bottle of milk and had not been attached to the carriage when I sold it. Zlateh looked for the bag, found it and gave it to the Christian woman, who gave her another loaf of store-bought bread.

My beloved ones do not be surprised that I spend so much time writing about the carriage. When you take our situation into consideration, you will understand that the whole Jewish tragedy was reflected in the child's words: our whole bitter situation, our panic, our experiences, had only just begun. Only the person who saw and experienced all this can understand it.

If, after I have described all these events, you could ask me all kinds of questions and I could answer them, I could be satisfied after experiencing all this. Yes, I could be happy if I could still see you, my only, dear, sweet brother. Maybe!

As spring began with its bright sunny days, Jewish hearts grew darker and darker. Jewish property and holdings were divided. Entire Jewish families were uprooted. Inflation steadily increased. Christians grew nervous about entering Jewish homes.

The most disturbing thing was that there were some unemployed Christians walking the streets all day looking for those willing to enter Jewish homes to sell something or barter. When they found a Christian who did this, they took away his goods and then blackmailed the Jew who sold it to him. If the Jew did not buy his way out, he [the Christian] immediately brought in the police. By then, many Christians had Ukrainian policemen as partners, and, in more important deals, they brought in the SS. They'd make a deal with the Jew, take the money, and then the [Ukrainian] police or the Schupo [Schutzpolizei/German urban police] would burst in and seize the merchandise. The Christian was ostensibly victimized along with the Jew because his money was lost.

It cost more if the Jew had no spare goods for the robber to take, because if he wouldn't allow himself to be robbed, the thugs had plenty of companions on Felczinska Street or Lonckiego Street, or in the two jails, who would leave more than one Jewish life bleeding. They did not nourish these people with bread [did not spoil them]. Those who were victims of the bandits settled on the spot. It was always cheaper that way. Who wanted to oppose the gangs?

A loaf of bread cost about 30 to 40 *złoty*. We had a little wheat, so every day I ground two kilograms of wheat in a coffee grinder. A kilogram of wheat cost between 20 and 25 *złoty*. During the winter months, our supplies dwindled and we began to ration our food. Father sent us $400. A single dollar was worth between 25 and 40 *złoty* and could buy about two kilos of wheat.

The food situation grew worse when Christians stopped wagons on the roads and confiscated the contents. When some of the smuggled goods were allowed through, a high price had to be paid for the privilege. As a result, ten thousand Jews walked around swollen from hunger and cold and died of starvation in the streets. At the bread stores, where bread was distributed for ration cards, dozens of poor people begged the people who were leaving the store "Give me a little piece to revive me!" The bread was distributed by weight and pieces of it went to dozens of recipients.

Zlateh had regular guests all through the winter, even when there was not too much to eat. But Zlateh always managed to make summer soup from young beets, their leaves and some buckwheat. She would provide soup for her sons' teacher every day, and to Eliakim and his son Boruch, who were both swollen from hunger. Eliakim was a *shames* [sexton] in a *shtiebel* [a one-room synagogue] on a small street next to ours. She [Zlateh] fed Zia Supartke, once a week on the Shabbos, and provided for Fach, a cantor, and his two sons. He was once a well-off person. Our permanent guest was Uncle Yehuda's eldest daughter [Dina]. There were Raden's two sons. Raden had once owned a candy store very near the tracks and was handicapped. I could go on and on. The crazy Mintshe's daughters were also constant guests of my dear sister, who never let anyone leave empty handed. Hunger began to take a look around, every time — into yet another Jewish apartment. Some Jews who yesterday had been givers of food became recipients of food the next day.

Examples are Avrom Wasserstein Sapir, a partner of Shloime Barits during the good times; Esther, Mechel's sister; Hersh-Leib and his six small children. I am mentioning only a few acquaintances and family members. That is enough. Leytshe Wasserstein came to us, and we would make her feel better with a little bit of soup. Mechel's mother fed Mechel and Yosl. Esther would do anything she could to get a bit of cooked food to her two small children. (Abeleh was a child who already understood a lot.) Esther would deliver kerosene to people, just to be able to provide her children with a slice of bread or a spoonful of cooked food.

[We would grind wheat in a coffee mill] and I would bake small, round, flat cookies from the ground wheat. Then I would divide the cookies among the children. Oh dear God, please forgive me for refusing to give cookies to the small children on more than one occasion. You can imagine how big the cookies were — I was able to make between 104–112 cookies from two kilograms of wheat flour.

The golden souls [my nephews] would ask, "*Wujcio, niech wujcio da nam jeszcze jeden placek.*" ["Uncle, give us one more cookie"]. Can you imagine? I would give anything in the world, for these two children, and there I was, rationing a cookie that weighed just three decagrams.

Abele would remind me about those times when his grandmother from Kaminke would run after him with a buttered ruggaleh [a pastry], and he did not want it. He didn't like it when his mother fed him bananas, oranges and chocolate.

Twice, when Elish became angry, he would order me to go to Kaminke to get him a cookie, as he did when I sold the carriage. I couldn't, can't, and will never forgive myself for it. The boy was like an adult. When he was told something once, he never forgot it. He remembered all the street names where members of our family lived. Street names like Kardinal Tromba, Szochczinskiego, Wniebowstanie, names even his own the parents could not pronounce. Whenever he got his hands on a Polish newspaper, he immediately pointed to the letters of the alphabet, A, B, and so on. Later, he read entire sentences in Polish.

Whatever I write about the children would not exaggerate the truth. Many times my dear sister would point to the two children sitting at the table playing dominos. The older boy was serious, full of devotion to his parents. Oh, how many times did he give his piece of bread to Abeleh, Esther's son, or to Eti Gitaleh, the smallest child? She [eventually] died of starvation. They were all dying of hunger. Later on, when the girl was given a chance to live, she was already dead. I will write about her later on.

Zlata's youngest [Elish] was very grown up for his age. He looked at everybody with his two smart eyes, and Shloime Barits was crazy about the boy. Both boys, the older and younger, always said good morning. When the father came home, they always ran to meet him before he could get through the door. When their father brought some wood home from work, they would take it from him and carry it into the house.

Oh, how happy we were during those fleeting moments, in spite of all the problems we faced.

From day to day, Mechel's sister Chaneleh grew weaker, and she passed away on a nice summer day. On Thursday, she was taken to the Jewish hospital and died the following Tuesday. Shaye, her husband, killed her with his stinginess. He refused to sell anything from the house and gave her nothing to eat. When her brothers eventually forced him to do something, it was too late.

Chaneleh [finally] gave Mechel and Yosl her diamond ring, and they sold it for 8000 *złoty*. She could have been saved but by the time the ring was sold, it was too late. When she was still strong, she was afraid to give them her ring to sell because she was afraid of what her husband would do when he found out. I believe Chaneleh is the only one of our family members who was buried in the cemetery. Her only [surviving] brother, Levi Eisen from Eretz Yisrael, should be told about it. Let their children know how the Eisens finished their lives.

Everyone else died in Hitler's system. I will write about them in a separate section.

I want to live to see the day when I can take the remaining members of our family and show them the places where our brothers and sisters, nieces [and nephews] suffered immeasurably and lived through the hell inflicted by the German government. They suffered until their last breaths. If there is justice in this world, not a single German would remain alive. But even this would not be enough to pay for the innocent old people and small children the Germans barbarically murdered.

Today the Germans are screaming because they are being bombed. Let them look at the mass graves of innocent Jews in every small shtetl, and they will see that [in comparison] what is happening to them is nothing. Even if they would be completely uprooted, it would not be enough of a punishment — because what we have lost cannot be brought back.

CHAPTER 7

Registration – Identity Card or Mr. Krajewski[10]

As the price of work cards slowly began dropping, everyone tried to persuade me to go to work. It did not make sense to stay home. Besides, the Jewish employment agency began registering people again, and every worker was given an armband and a number. People were saying that we would not be able to stay on our side of the tracks; a real ghetto would be established, just as in the other large cities, and Jews without armbands would not be allowed into the ghetto. Women who worked and were assigned a number would be able to enter. Those who were not working would be killed.

How much truth was there in what was being said? Jews were murdered, workers and non-workers alike. But I also began to think seriously about the problem. Moreover, every day another one of our men came home with a new number. The first was Hersh-Leib [Strassler], then Yosl Eisen, Shloime, Mechel, Lonek, and our two neighbors, Rab and Stengl. All the men who lived on our street were registered. I stuck to my opinion that there would always be time to go to work. However, we are only human. Zlateh would yell at me: "If you don't register and get an I.D. card and an armband, I won't be able to endure it." She reminded me of the problems she had on my account during the last *Aktion*.

10 Although this chapter appears here in the order of the manuscript, these events may have occurred before the events described in previous chapters. The chronology is unclear.

I struggled to make up my mind. To go or not to go? There was no position for me — one could not get a job without paying for it. The Germans did not understand how to deal with bribes for jobs, but Jewish brokers taught them how. Meanwhile, just imagine — I would be going into the street! Since the German occupation, I hadn't set foot on the streets, except to run from Zlateh's to Pepe's, and from there to Bielenkiewicza Street.

At first, there were only a few forged documents available, but later they were widely used on the Jewish streets. I bought a forged "Christian" passport for myself and thought of using it to escape to the outside world. It was a Soviet passport, most likely taken away from a fellow named Penczerski, a Pole born in Lemberg. The forger inserted my photo and the necessary stamps.

During the Soviet period, I could not resolve to leave my parents. Now, I could not decide whether or not to leave Pepe and Zlateh with the children. So I held on to the passport and hid it in a good place so that no one, God forbid, would find it. The passport was so useful, that I twice showed it to the Jewish police.

The first time was when the policeman were searching for men to put to work.

I asked one of them in Polish, if he would prefer to be a Pole or a Jew wearing his police cap. Another time, I casually showed a Jewish policeman my passport and asked if I could trade with my Jewish friends. On both occasions, [when the police encountered me] I did not have time to hide. It never crossed their minds that I could be anything but Polish.

Meanwhile, the ideal job for me became available. Pepe's uncle, Mr. Messing, lived in an apartment house where [a fellow named] Krajewski had his carpentry shop. He made products for Fontes, the German firm doing work on the main railroad station. Messing and his son, Mondik, worked for him. Messing's daughter's husband, Czaf, who was from Radziechów; Perlmutter, a former mercer [a dealer in fine textiles] from Belsk, and a few other Jews also worked there. Krajewski sold me a blank registration card for 1,300 *złoty*.

Today is April 26 [1944]. Just now a Soviet airman dropped a few bombs.

People hid in the basement. I had to stay in my place in the attic. What do you think of that? This is a fine place to hide from airplanes!

I did not have to actually work for Krajewski. I bought the I.D. card and could stay home. It was perfect for me. Other Jews also did not have to work. Every month we gave Krajewski a few *złoty* to add a new stamp [to the card], and we could stay home. Pepe and I went to the employment office and registered me as a carpenter. I had to tell them from whom I learned the trade, where I took the examination and where I practiced. I answered all the questions and received my I.D. card. My registration number was 35107. Mechel's number was 425.

A lot could be said about Vayber, the head of the employment office, but it is enough to note that the young ruffian frequently came out of his office with a whip in hand and hit people over the head. Yet, he was not the worst of the lot.

As soon as I received the I.D. card I put my efforts into getting Pepe an I.D. card. Since she took care of my household, I tried to get her a registration card for housekeepers. That card could only be issued with Judenrat approval. [Housekeepers' numbers matched the numbers on the armbands and cards of their husbands, brothers and fathers.]

One day, I think it was a Wednesday, June 24, 1942 at two o'clock p.m., an *Aktion* suddenly began.[11] Anyone without a registration card was caught. At the time, Pepe was visiting her aunt Messing at Damarstinowska Street 41. Yosl Haberkorn's sister was also visiting the Messing family. That same day, Pepe's aunt, who traded in fabric coupons, took Pepe with her when she went to barter something. She accidentally took along her daughter's registration card, while Pepe had only a little bit of white paper [her temporary I.D.]. When the street filled with smoke, Pepe's aunt Messing sent her back to Damarstinowska Street to switch registration cards. Instead of sending the

---

11 There was no major *Aktion* that day. It is possible that Moty Stromer confused this with
    an *Aktion* of the sort that he describes that took place on July 8, 1942, when some 7,000
    Jews without work permits were rounded up and murdered in the Janówska forced-
    labor camp.

Christian woman she sent Pepe! In the meantime, Mrs. Messing stayed with the Christian woman who was trading with her.

Mrs. Messing was not someone to dismiss; she was a shrewd, wise woman, and yet she did not think — she sent Pepe. When Pepe reached Kinge Street, she was stopped [by the catchers] and taken to the assembly point on Podzamcze Street, from whence one was taken to the Podzamcze train station. The Polish cavalry barracks were located to the right of the station.

Pepe was caught at two p.m. We didn't find out a thing until Lonek came home at five p.m. He had stopped at the Messing's place and discovered what happened. By the time Lonek got to the Messing's, Mrs. Messing was already home.

Imagine what went on in our apartment! Terror spread through the house. Sheyve, Zlateh and Leytshe were stunned. Pepe was able to let Mrs. Messing know where she was — she had an old newspaper with her and wrote a few words on it. A young man, who was released after someone brought him his I.D. card, took the newspaper [Pepe's message] and delivered it to the Messings.

I quickly grabbed a saw — after all, I was a carpenter — and put on a pair of glasses. Then I ran to the assembly point. The situation in the street was horrifying. Jews were being dragged into the streets from all directions. Older people, children, and parents with parents of their own were being beaten. Everyone was bleeding.

Yosl, Mechel, Shloime and Lonek ran with me. We heard continual screaming: "Oh, my mother! Oh, my father! Oh, my sister!" People were shot where they were caught. We quickly ran to the assembly point. Hundreds of people were crowded there, but no one was allowed into the barracks. People were being held in the stables. Hundreds more had been caught and there were other assembly points. Every few minutes, trucks full of people left for the Janowo station, which was always the last stop [before mass] murder.

There we met the younger [Mondik] Messing and his brother-in-law, Czaf. Jews were being brought in from everywhere. They were beaten and half naked. Blood flowed everywhere. I quickly pushed myself toward the entrance [to the stables], and forced my way in with a group of those who had been caught.

Pepe — or I — had luck. I showed my registration card and told the SS man: "I've just come from work. I work on the Ost [eastern] railroad, and my housekeeper was taken away." He actually heard me out, even though just before I approached him, I had seen him beating a young man who held two small children in both arms — twins, I think. Blood flowed from the father and the children. I went over to that same murderer, and he heard me out; then he went into the stable among the people and called out "Pepe Haberkorn!" An older person reported first, but he took Pepe by the hand, led her out, and brought her to me.

Here I break off. The [Soviet] airman is still dropping his loads. Today is April 27. Last night I stopped writing. I had a splitting headache. The Poles continue to move out of here, because the Ukrainian gangs keep setting fire to Polish villages and murdering the Poles. Near Kaminke they burned down the Polish [villages of] Jazienice-Berbekes, Taurkes and Ptasznifes. The Poles are fleeing to the other side of the San [River].

A few times, my landlords planned to move out, but so far, they have stayed put. It is a very lucky thing for me that they are not moving. Thank God for that. Yesterday they had a community meeting about that, but so far, nothing happens. Meanwhile our [the Soviet] front is not moving even one centimeter closer.

I visited Jodel Streker from Jagonia.

When Pepe was in the stable, she knew it would be difficult for her to get out of there alive. But she had hope, and pushed herself closer to the walls when she noticed that people standing around the entrance were constantly being taken away in trucks. As one of the first to be brought in, she quickly found her bearings, and when she realized [what was happening, she stayed in the shadows. Because of that] I was able to find her even after she spent five hours there.

The people who accompanied me to search for Pepe did not know what to think. They thought that maybe I, too, had been caught in the "warehouse" — because that's what would happen to others. [A person would present his documents], then the documents would be torn up and the Jew would be shoved into the "cage."

You can imagine our companions' joy when they saw Pepe and me on the street, free. They all wept for happiness. German officers were walking around the stable and intervening and preventing Jews from leaving, and here I was — a person who had not exchanged two words with those guys, or ever seen them in my life before that day — and [we were] allowed to go free. We ran toward home like lunatics, along Bielenkiewicza Street.

New victims were constantly being led away. The cries of the tortured were terrible. Every few minutes we were forced to hide, because we ran into Ukrainian police and Germans everywhere. The police on patrol made many mistakes when they checked people's documents, and we were afraid that, God forbid, Pepe would be caught a second time.

On the way home, we encountered two people from Kaminke — but how different their situation was from ours! I saw dear old Taube-Shifre, our former neighbor, being led away. She could barely stand, and in one arm she held a small child, while a second child, perhaps four years old, held on to her dress. She wore no kerchief on her head. Poor woman, she had been beaten and she was bleeding. The children were screaming and it was horrible to hear.

I saw a Jew being led into the [the stables]. He had a long beard as white as milk, his head was held high, and he turned his sweet eyes upon his murderers. It seemed to me that he was laughing at all of it. He was not afraid of death.

There was a second man from Kaminke, named Sliwka, whose name means prune and who was also a neighbor, who lived near the slaughterhouse. He worked in the tax office. This bandit went from our house to the Zolkwia road. He was full of glee, and his mug expressed huge satisfaction at these events. It is possible that when he drove out of Kaminke he did not expect to find such festivities going on in Lemberg. It would have been very different if I was the one in power at that moment.... In another, more tragic case I met his brother, traveling into town by car; but I will write about that later.

With great difficulty we made our way home. No one in our apartment believed in [the success of] our race toward home. They thought one of us would be caught. We had to convince each of them that it was a fact that Pepe had been released.

Then something spoiled our brief happiness. Mrs. Tepper was detained. She would often go to town, to the community [Judenrat], to send packages to her husband, who was in a camp. She also visited her parents every day, for she was an affectionate daughter and an even better wife. We knew that if she was not in the house, something must have happened to her. We sent Lonek to her parents to find out.

Lonek wore very dark overalls, the kind usually worn by metal workers. He also took various keys with him, so that dressed in work overalls and carrying tools in his hand, he would appear to be coming home from work. He hurried to Tokarzewskiego Street, because Jews were still allowed to walk in the street until eight p.m., but he was home by nine p.m. and did not bring good news. Her [Mrs. Tepper's] father did not know her whereabouts, and her mother and sister had been taken away. We assumed Mrs. Tepper was caught, because she would have done everything possible to return to her children.

Imagine the Jewish tragedies that occurred at every step: here a mother and sister, there a mother of two small children. Mrs. Tepper had a document similar to Pepe's. Lonek had given it to her, based on his registration card.

We took the Tepper children in for the night. They cried and asked, "Where is our mother?" They spoke German for they had been raised in Danzig. You can imagine our happiness when their mother returned at daybreak. She had seen her mother and sister. In very good German, she'd told the authorities about her husband, who was in a camp for more than a year, and so they let her go.

Of the thousands who were detained, about forty people were released. Mrs. Tepper was one of the lucky ones and told us what was going on in the detention place. The detainees were brutally beaten and shot. Men and women were stripped and ordered to dance and sing, while the naked bodies of young Jewish girls were lashed with whips. Old women were ordered to lie with their faces to the ground and crawl around.

The area was surrounded by machine guns. The searchlights were so powerful that you could find a pin in the sand. Later, when I was in a labor camp, or was, as the Germans called it, a *Zwangsarbeitslagerarbeiter*, a prisoner of the SS or the police, I often saw dreadful scenes like that.

Pepe and Mrs. Tepper both told me that at that moment [the moment they were released] they were born a second time. Mrs. Tepper was separated from her mother and sister and returned to her two small children. She had people to live for. However, those souls did not have much time to enjoy their lives. They were pulled up short, like cattle not yet ready to be slaughtered, and were led back to the cattle shed. In the cattle shed they had no place to run, and whenever the SS wanted to, they could be taken from the shed [to the slaughter].

But it was even worse for the Jews. Cattle are fed by their owners until they are slaughtered, and they do not know that a knife awaits them; but the Jews, poor creatures, had to fend for their own food, and they knew that Bełżec was waiting for them.

CHAPTER 8

The Shameful Aktion

In the Jewish world there is always a month of troubles, suffering and tragedies; nothing can compare to the month of Av of the year 1942 [August 10–31], not even in the times of Spanish or Roman rule. Nothing can compare to the suffering inflicted on the Jews in the twentieth century, in the presence of all the Christians, in the age of electricity-radio-air warfare.

Only Hitler, the greatest murderer of human beings in the twentieth century — and his helpers — could have invented such a scheme. I cannot call them his devoted helpers, because every one of those horrible bandits thought only of filling his own pockets. However, for the benefit of others they always had on their lips the familiar *"Heil, Hitler!"*

After Pepe's [terrible] experience, we began looking for a job for her, but it was hard to find something suitable. We were afraid because people were being taken from workplaces to the camps. We felt a dreadful period beginning for the Jews — though it had already been terrible when the Germans first came in. Now we felt something ghastly was hanging in the air.

We knew the German Minister of Justice, the biggest leader of the gangsters in the General Government, Dr. [Hans] Frank,[12] was [in Lemberg]

---

12 Moty Stromer was mistaken. Whereas Frank was the General Governor in Poland, he was not minister of justice of Nazi Germany. Rather, he was president of the Academy for German Law.

on an official visit. He definitely brought along a gift for the Jews, and we did not have to wait long for it.

The factories began sifting through the workers. The SS came to the larger factories, where a considerable number of Jews were employed, and every worker was inspected. Anyone who did not please them had his registration card taken away, whereas those who passed the inspection received a red stamp [on their cards] from the SS and the police.

About 400 Jews worked in the factory where Yosl Haberkorn was assigned. Right at the start of the [*Aktion*], fifty men were removed by the authorities, and camp-guards took them to the Janówska camp.[13]

A distressing event took place where Shloime and Mechel worked. This time, it was not a question of victims, but money. Because only Jews worked in Lonek's place of employment, no Jews were touched. Mechel's workplaces, in the slaughterhouse and on the construction site, employed about one hundred Jews, but no one was taken, as a large sum of money was paid to protect them.

Butchers earned money because they could smuggle out a little meat [to barter], so it was not a problem for them to pay a bribe of tens of thousands of *złoty*. At that time, Mechel contributed 100 *złoty*. There were others who gave a few thousand *złoty* each. Their supervisor was a German named Schmaltz, a big meat merchant. He employed Jewish workers in particular — only Jews — and had his office at the distribution site, where he also kept the meat in refrigerators. Because he gave meat on credit to many customers, he had opportunities to meet the "right" people. Schmaltz and his Jews made a deal that for 60,000 *złoty* he would arrange it so that none of his Jews [at the warehouse], and none of the [Jews] working in the slaughterhouse, would be taken.

The Jews working in the municipal slaughterhouse did well, but those working for Schmaltz did much better financially. Stamps were added to the I.D. cards. Then the women's cards were taken. Each card stated that the owner of the card had a red stamp from the SS, and that the woman was taking care of [the card holder's] household. This kind of stamp was called a second-

---

13   The Janówska Road camp was a brutal forced labor and concentration camp in Lemberg. It also served as a transit station for Jews being deported to the Bełżec extermination camp. It is estimated that tens of thousand of Jews were murdered there.

ary stamp, and prevented its owner from being taken in an *Aktion*. Jews were receiving stamps for the World to Come.

Pepe was still without a job. We were afraid to send her to work, because every day there were cases where newcomers were sent directly to the transports. At that time, the *Aktion* had not yet started in Lemberg, though Jews were being taken to Bełżec from all the cities in Poland. Transports were arriving from Kolomei [Kołomyja], Kuty, Kosów, Kraków, Berzan Podhajce, Przemyślany and Przemyśl. I could list many more cities and towns from all over Galicia.

In addition to Bełżec, there was another execution site in Poland called Sobibor. It was in the Chełm area. Jews from Galicia were taken to Bełżec. The people going to the transports were first brought to an assembly point. Can you imagine [what it was like]? Fresh, healthy people were thrown together with those who were in transports for eight days — people who were half-dead, crazed, half-suffocated by the cramped quarters, swollen from hunger; there were small children whose parents were already dead or still at home — all of these people were undergoing the *Aktion*, or [being held] in the railroad wagons.

Those who thought that young girls and boys, or very young adults, were being sent to work were now convinced that they were all going to their deaths. The Christians were smiling and saying: "*Zydki, idziesz na mydlo.*" ["Jews, you are going for soap."] "The Germans don't have any soap."

My dearest, if you read these words, do not think that I did not see these things with my own eyes. I did see them. Later on, when I was in the camp, I saw far worse things; yes, far worse things. At first, people had garments on their backs, but later on, people were led [around] naked. I saw a few railroad cars that were specially used for small children. Those small Jewish souls lay in [freight] cars once used for hauling pigs.

Oh God, if a single German is still alive today, there is no justice. How many precious hours did those tiny souls bestow on their parents? How much effort, blood and sweat did it cost their mothers to raise them? It would have been better, if the mothers had not lived to see this.

GOD PUNISH GERMANY.

At this very moment, as I write these words, planes are flying overhead. I hear machine-gun fire. I do not know whether it is an air battle with Russian fighter planes attacking German bombers, or the opposite. I cannot see the sky. I have only a small ray of light falling on the spot where I write: I move the light higher or lower, left or right, in order to see better. But I am laughing at this. How happy the Jews would have been, had they lived to see this!

[This must have happened before August.]

All the men had their registration cards stamped, except me. One day Pepe came to tell me to bring my registration card to Damarstinowska Street as soon as possible because my boss [Krajewski] was sending the cards to be stamped. The boss collected all the cards and sent them to the German firm [Fontes]. We did not have to go there for inspection. They looked at the pictures on the cards. Because most of the workers lived near the workplace, they were able to bring their cards to [Krajewski] very early in the morning. But by the time I was informed, it took some time for me [to get there] because it was quite a distance from where we lived on Bielenkiewicza Street.

I was home when Pepe came to tell me about it, so I quickly dressed and ran to Damarstinowska Square. This was not a good time of day for Jews to be on the streets because Jews were out only when they walked to or from work, but were never to be seen in between times — except for those who worked for *Altes Eisen Flescher*. Those Jews wore tin badges with numbers on the lapels of their coats or jackets.

When I arrived at the workshop, Krajewski had already taken the registration cards to the main railroad station, where the German firm Fontes was located. When Krajewski saw me he began cursing me. He was a common, ugly drunk, a lowlife and had a mean expression on his face. I will write about him later — his name will have to be mentioned again. Confronted by this man's curses and abuse, I stood before him, taken aback. I did not know the gangster all that well. My blood boiled me within me. Krajewski would have to take my registration card by trolley car to the firm, a small thing, but he refused to do it.

I personally took my registration card to the German firm at the main train station, where its office was located in a barracks. I went on foot. And though Lemberg is a big city, and I saw acquaintances, they did not recognize me. I still did not want people to know about me. I always had my eyeglasses with me and I grew a mustache, which I still have to this day.

I left my document at the office. They told me to go back to work and said they would return my document to the workshop, so I walked back from the main train station without the document. I was stopped by the Schupo from the so-called Extermination Brigade on Kazimierzowski Street. They asked me what I was doing in the street during working hours. I told the Schupo that I had taken my registration card to the office. He laughed, because he found it funny that I was working for the railroad, for a German firm. I did not want to mention Krajewski. I thought that if I said: "I work for Fontes," it would make a better impression. It looked as if he had more than one Jewish family on his conscience.

He said to me, "I'm sure the firm has Christians who could be sent to take care of such things. It isn't necessary to send out a Jew during work hours. Besides, if you are working for the German firm, why are you walking toward town?"

I realized that nothing I could say would do me any good. I merely wondered why he was arguing with me. Usually these men wasted little time on encounters like this. Soon two of his friends arrived, leading several Jews. He had been waiting for them, so in the meantime he talked to me. Later he kicked me several times. He took me to the Ukrainian police station, together with the others.

About fifty Jews were already there. I tried to persuade them to telephone the firm and ask whether I worked there. In response, I received two stinging blows. I already knew their tactics. It became clear to me that words would not help, so I said no more.

People were being brutally beaten in the station. I knew the best thing to do was to stay in a corner near the wall. Others pleaded and screamed. We were all ordered to sit on the ground, feet folded underneath us. I grabbed a corner spot. I had already seen this kind of thing in Remenow. I did not utter a peep — and I did not receive any blows.

I was glad about just one thing — that I had told Zlateh I might sleep over at the Messing's or maybe at Klara's house, because only Klara, her child

[son] Manye, and Klara's husband still lived on Gazowa [Street]. The rest of the family had already fallen victim [to the murderers]. [Klara was Moty's first cousin by his maternal aunt.]

I'd told her that I might sleep over so they wouldn't worry about me all day and would also be able to sleep peacefully through the night. I was afraid only that there might be someone at the Messing's who would ask about me, but no one was there that day.

There were various kinds of beatings and they never stopped administering them. Finally, we were ordered to leave the room, and lie on the ground outside, face down in the mud. They counted us. There were eight rows and nine people in each row. Most of the people were middle-aged. I think that the first group of people, of about fifty, were from some kind of institution, while the rest, like myself, had been caught by chance. Stengl was also there, but we did not see each other. I only found out about him later, [when we had that conversation on the basement stairs.] They lined us up, five in a row, and led us to the burned-out jail on Kazimierzowski Street.

That morning I had had nothing to eat for breakfast. Now it was three o'clock in the afternoon. We were lined up in a single row. Once again, I made the effort to be the person at the left end of the row. Ten Ukrainians and four Schupo with machine guns started beating us. It does not make sense to describe the beatings in the light of what was about to happen.

Soon a murderer appeared: a tall, strong bandit and sadist. He was a German wearing a coat made of oilcloth, with gloves on his hands and a black helmet on his head. This character did not play around too much. Shortly afterward, another man approached carrying a blacksmith's hammer, the kind that weighs ten kilograms. Later on, I worked with a hammer like that on a construction site.

[The German sadist] walked over to the first man at the right end of the row, and told him: "Say to me the following words, which I will say to you." And then he said, in German, "'*I must die because I am a Jew.*'" He then hit the first man over the head with the heavy hammer, smashing his head to bits. The brains ran out as the man fell down. And so he went on to the second and third man. Each time, the Jew had to say the words before being hit with the hammer. When he had murdered eighteen or twenty men, a few men fainted and fell to the ground. In fact, I think that when the German murdered the first Jew, the third or fourth man in the row fell on the ground, unconscious. After he murdered about a quarter of the people, a few fell to the ground, causing a disturbance.

I seized the opportunity to fall among the murdered. I pushed myself under five or six dead bodies whose warm blood was still flowing. None of the bodies had heads. I took care to hide my head beneath the dead. I felt very ill. I was completely drenched in blood, and it stuck to me. But I could still hear the murderer screaming, in German: "You dog, you're going to get it, you vile Jew-Bolshevik," and other expressions of that sort.

The hammer continued to strike. Then the sound was drowned out by a few dozen shots from automatic weapons. People ran over me. One man was killed with the hammer, and fell down right on my back. I heard his last cry: "My wife, my little children, my God!" — followed by a heavy thump on my back. My back became wet and warm with blood. It was the murdered person's blood, flowing over me. I felt even weaker than before. At one point I actually fainted. I did not faint in Remenow.

When I came to, it was pitch dark and I could not orient myself. I didn't know where I was; but I was not wounded, I was not a prisoner, and I was not being beaten. I was terribly cold. I struggled forwards and upwards, but quite a few murdered bodies were piled on top of me. For a moment, a dreadful shudder went through my whole body.

Then, in one second, I was on my feet. I was covered in blood from top to toe. The blood on my face had dried, but the blood on my back was still wet. I could not figure out how long I had been lying there, but it must have been a few hours at least. I was surrounded by a whole heap of murdered corpses.

I soon became very frightened, because in the dark I noticed a few shapes stirring near the high fence that led to Karna Street. I was about to drop back onto the ground, but then, as I watched, I saw them motioning with their hands as if beckoning to me. I did not understand right away, but when I saw that they were indeed gesturing to me to come to them, I very slowly crept out from the mountain of bodies and then swiftly ran over to them.

Five men were standing there, including a father and his son. I heard one man calling another "father." I was the sixth man. When I looked at them, I realized what I myself looked like. We did not talk. We were terribly afraid that someone might hear us. We all had the same idea: to escape from that place as soon as possible. There was no time to ask "Who and what are you?" We had just one thing on our minds: to run away, far away.

The fence was very high. We quickly gathered a few mortar [ammunition] boxes and created some scaffolding. We hurried about as quietly as little mice and assembled everything. Two of the men had strong belts that held up their pants. We tied these together and attached them to the wire. Barbed wire ran around the fence. The first to go over the fence was the father. The son suggested his father be the first and that he would go last. I was the fifth [over the fence]. One of the men with a gunshot wound in his leg was the second.

When I jumped over the fence I found only the father, who was waiting for his son. The others had vanished into the dark night. One of the men had taken some time to get over the fence, but no one else arose from the mass of bodies. I worried about the wounded young man, but he was a sport. He jumped like a cat. The three of us walked over to the corner of Szpitalna Street. Then they went on their separate way. Later I regretted not asking them their names. But at the time, who thought of things like that? We were unfortunate Jews, and the catastrophe made us all equal.

I tried to figure out where to go. It was a long way to Bielenkiewicza Street. I had to traverse the whole of Zin Street, then Zolkwia Street, and pass through Baczewski Street. Then I still had to get through all the small streets near the city limits. At one point I was sure that a patrol would catch me. The Messing family lived on Damarstinowska Street, but the main gate to the house was locked, and when one rang the bell, the Ukrainian landlady would open the door. During the first period [of pogroms] Messing was hiding from her, so that wasn't a good [idea] either…

Klara! But Stroizowa, her landlady, might get scared in the middle of the night [if I knocked] and cause a commotion and raise an alarm — meaning I would be caught again. Christians might emerge from their homes on Gazownia Street and punish me on the spot. I balanced this against my survival instinct, which was pretty strong at that time.

I sneaked across the street where the trolley turns from Sloneczna Street to Szpitalna Street and ran into the alley where the fish stores were. Ackerman, who had a son who was a furrier, ran a fish store there. From there, I walked to the shop stalls. Luckily I did not meet a living soul. It had to be close to daybreak — it was surely about three o'clock at night.

I approached the shop stalls where, in the past, Jews used to sell meat, and pushed myself between the stalls and waited — I myself did not know for what. However, I knew that if anyone were to see me, he would run away in fear. I stayed there until four o'clock — the town clock struck the hour. I became really cold. It was [by now] Thursday morning.

At one point, a shade in a storefront window rolled up, and, in fear, an elderly, gray-haired Jew looked out. I waited until he finished slowly rolling up the shade with the stick, so as not to make any noise. It occurred to me that as long as he could pull down the shade, he would do so out of fear if he spotted me. So when I saw him putting down the stick and — begging your pardon — standing near the stall to urinate, I ran over to the shop door and prevented him from running inside and closing the door. I could see he was half dead from fright.

But when I told him, "Don't be afraid. I am a Jew who has survived a mass murder — I'll say no more," he let me into his house. Everyone there was still asleep, except for him. He had risen very early to pray. I washed up a little bit. Then he loaned me a jacket and a pair of pants. I wanted to leave him my own jacket and pants until I could bring his clothing back to him, but he declined to take my bloodstained garments. He gave me some paper and I wrapped everything in it.

It was now five-thirty in the morning. At six, I went to Klara's, and the gate to the house was open. Gas had been installed during Soviet rule, so I was able to wash myself with hot water and was also able to wash my things. Manye gave me some of his father's clothes: a shirt, underpants and pants. I managed to hang on to my hat when I was among the murdered people. I asked Manye, who was on his way to work, to give the borrowed clothes back to the Jewish man. I also asked the people in the house not to say a word to anyone about what had happened to me. I wanted it to appear as if I had slept in their home, but I was actually there for the first time. Krajerson's sister and her son lived in their house.

I took an armband and ran home to Bielenkiewicza Street. Zlateh was surprised when I returned in different clothes. I told her that I had taken my registration card to the German firm, and therefore had decided to change my clothes at Klara's house. [In the meantime] my registration card had been stamped with the SS seal.

A few days later, Stengl and Rab moved, and the landlady took their apartment. They moved closer to the synagogue, into a neighborhood that had been designated as the future ghetto. The Jewish apartment association had assigned the newly vacant apartment to the landlady. The Christian woman, as well as handing the Jews an official notice and full rights, took a few hundred *zloty* from them because she said that the apartment was in such a bad state that she could not move into it. She painted the apartment and put in window-panes, paying for it with money from Jews.

She took Zlateh's tables and chairs, and Levin's desk, for herself, and when she was done, she moved in. She left Zlateh's apartment, but took all the windowpanes, window frames, and the grates from the doors and windows, along with anything else of value. We had to put on carefree, laughing faces so that she would not, God forbid, develop a grudge against us.

Firewood was an important issue at that time, so I went to work every day (wearing my own glasses), running to work quite early and walking home together with everyone else. Everyday, I brought home a bagful of wooden shavings. The package I carried served two purposes: it gave me something I could use to start a fire, and — taking care not to be seen by my Christian acquaintances — I was able to sneak a few fairly thick pieces of wood into the bag. Because of that, we did not have to worry about firewood.

Krajewski, the Christian, was in a good mood only when he received a bribe from the Jews. This consisted of a liter of liquor or two hundred ciga-rettes. For a few days after he got the bribe, Krajewski would keep quiet. That meant that he did not say anything to the workers who bribed him. Young Messing was the one who would deliver the payment.

Perlmutter and Koyen, an innkeeper's son-in-law from Damarstinowska Street, always played cards at the Messing's and did not go to work. They did not care if there was a search. They were living in the same building as the carpentry shop, and through the window they could see if a stranger ap-proached.

A few Jewish families lived Krajewski's carpentry shop, as well as the landlord's [place], and it so happened that everything was on the ground floor. The apartments at the front of the building had been destroyed by a bomb dur-ing the Polish-German War. The courtyard had a small door. There was also a large gate, but it was opened only for deliveries to Krajewski's workshop. This situation allowed the card players at the Messing's to go on playing without worrying about intruders.

The Messings' place was visited by various kinds of Jewish dealers who exchanged currency; gold and diamond merchants, and good-for-nothings of all sorts. The Messings were the only ones in the group who were very wealthy and owned hard and soft currency. The elder Messing was not happy with his job in Jan Krajewski's workshop, so he switched to another job at the airport in Skulow that cost him several thousand *złoty*. In a way, he was right. All husbands and wives had to have work registration cards from the same firm and from the same residence.

A few days after our landlady moved into the apartment [next door], the most dreadful *Aktion* began — the most horrible of that time. It was the most shocking, because during that period people still thought that it was not right and not possible that everybody would be killed.

On a lovely summer day, the conflagration began. [Aug 10–31, 1942] I started for work as usual. Walking out on the street, I saw hundreds of patrols: SS, police, Ukrainian police, and a special group from the extermination brigade. I was stopped every few feet. Patrols were placed on every small street, on both sidewalks and in the middle of the gutters. No one at all was allowed through. Everyone carried his registration card in his hand. They did not handle the [cards], they only looked at the stamps. Those with a stamp were allowed to pass. Hundreds of those who were caught stood on all the street corners, holding their registration cards in their hands. There were young, old and middle-aged people. Some of the detainees had been caught during the night. Other people were lying on the ground, murdered.

On the way to work, I saw three women and eight men who had been shot to death. They had surely tried to escape or had defended themselves. Perlmutter told of the tragedies that took place in his apartment building on Panienska Street. Fourteen people were shot dead there, among them a woman and her three small children, two of them still small enough to be carried and the third standing at her side — they lay on the ground, murdered by the janitor of the house. The husband of the murdered woman was in the Russian Army.

Arriving at work, I found out that in the city the *Aktion* had been going on since midnight. All the streets were closed off. By daybreak, when I headed to work, the lorries were already taking Jews either to the Janów[ska] camp, or later on, directly to the railroad station. Imagine our feelings, our pain, our anxiety about what was happening at home. Was there anyone at home to go back to?

Yosl took Pepe with him to the shoe factory on Marcina Street. He smuggled her into the factory on a hay wagon so that no one would know, and hid her there in a hay loft. She was safe there, although every day, a few times a day, trucks arrived at the factories and bandits rushed inside. They locked all the doors and checked every man and woman's identity card to see if strangers were hiding there. The director of a factory of this kind always had to give his word that there were no strangers in his factory.

Yosl would spend the night in the factory, go home early in the morning, and then return again. Because he had a horse and wagon, he had a permit that allowed him to move freely in the streets during work hours.

The *Aktion* shifted from one neighborhood in the city to another. People were dragged out of every hole and there was no place at all to hide. Old people, young people, people who could barely stand on their legs, were all packed into assembly places. People from around the area of the city limits were brought to the assembly point. The Sobieski School of Lemberg and the [city's] bridge both have a special place in the Jewish tragedy. Thousands of victims died there during that *Aktion* and during the relocation of Jews from the surrounding areas to the Jewish quarter.

During the August *Aktion*, the school was once again an assembly point. Jews were brought there in lorries at night and at dawn. For days on end, the tram cars carried only Jews. Everything was guarded by the police and by the Ukrainians. When the people were brought to the camp on Janówska Street, they were counted as they entered the main gate. Apparently Frank had stated what kind of contingent of Jews was needed.

In the meantime, the Jews were being annihilated. On the walls of Lemberg announcements addressed to all Aryan residents appeared: "Anyone hiding or helping a Jew will be punished with the death penalty." The notice was signed by the well-known Lemberg general, police and SS commander, Katzmann.[14]

One day, those interested in our present tragedy will be able to write something about this mass murderer. There was also another murderer, a special expert on the Jewish question; and a known sadist, Webke [his speciality was hunting down young mothers and their babies]. I leave this matter for

14 *SS-Brigadeführer* Fritz Katzmann was the *Höhere SS und Polizeiführer* (HSSPF; Higher SS and Police Commander) of the Galicia District from summer 1941 to summer 1943 and commanded the murder of at least 434,000 Jews.

others to research all this. I mention only two or three of the big fish in the German destruction machine of the Jews.

We all worked in Krajewski's workshop, where we had gotten our registration cards. Across from our workplace we saw an SS man push a young man and small child off the roof of a three-story house onto the street. The unfortunate man and child had tried to hide on the roof. From the roof on Damarstinowska Street, where we worked, I could see someone shooting and killing two Jewish boys.

Every day we had problems and suffering. The whole *Kahal* [Jewish communal organization] was taken away, with all its officers — their registration cards had not been stamped. Later, all the housekeepers were taken away, with or without stamps. Nothing was respected anymore. Everyone was taken to the slaughterhouse. Gradually we realized that everything was headed toward death.

For me, it all became difficult when I saw them taking away the housekeepers. Blackness fell before my eyes. At work, every minute lasted a year. To make matters worse, I had to stay in the shop until four in the afternoon, in horrible anxiety, watching as children were taken away without their parents and parents were taken without their children. The lamentation and screaming of the abandoned was horrible to witness. People were shot to death in the streets. Wagons driving through the streets were commandeered to take the old and the sick to the assembly point.

It was not enough that the Christians did not want to help the Jews, but there were special groups of Christians who pointed out the Jewish hideouts. Small Christian children would run through the streets yelling "Jew, Jew!" In this way they helped to destroy the Jews.

More than once Sheyve took off her armband, took a milk can wrapped in a sheet on her back, wearing her shawl like a peasant woman in the countryside, and got away from the house. The old guy would hide Zlateh in my oven. Shloime's stepmother would hide out in the basement. Zlateh's boys and the two Tepper children were the only children in the house.

Very early in the morning, when only a few people were on their way to work, Shloime would take Leytshe to the factory with him and hide her in a crate of leather scraps. On a few occasions Leytshe slept in the crate overnight, so that the supervisor would not find out about it. Pepe had to leave her hiding place because very wealthy Jews brought in their wives, children and parents, so that the place was no longer safe.

She came by wagon to the Messings who lived in the same place as our workshop. Once, when Krajewski was away, I hid Pepe in a pile of wooden planks. She crawled into the middle of the pile, and I surrounded her with pieces of wood. She stayed hidden all night long, while outside it rained cats and dogs. At dawn she was taken out.

A certain Diamenstein, a neighbor of the Messings, spent the whole of the August *Aktion* in a basket of old rags. People sought out various hiding holes. Every day, new public announcements appeared, contradicting the announcements from the day before. "The *Aktion* is complete. The quota was met. We have more people than were required by the quota."

The next day it would start all over again — the same thing, but more horrible. The Ukrainian police bathed in Jewish blood. They searched every hiding hole; they crawled into every cranny where a human being could possibly hide, using pocket flashlights, poking around, and got help from the civilian population. All this affected me so much that I felt as if pieces were falling off my body. I could not find any peace of mind.

One day it was said an *Aktion* was to take place that very morning near the city limits. The *Aktion*s in that area always would take place in the afternoon and at night, rarely in the morning. On that day, Mechel took Abish to work with him, but when he drew near to the slaughterhouse he saw a lot of SS men. The registration card of every person, Jew or Christian, was being checked. The other bunch was inside the building, conducting a search. Someone had informed the Germans that Schmaltz was keeping Jews who were not working for him in his shop. It was a known fact that Schmaltz allowed the families of his Jewish workers to stay in his meat stores for money. As it happened, however, no one was found.

When Mechel saw what was happening he ran back, but the streets were already closed. He always used Pogodna Street to get to work. What should he do? He wanted to stop at the home of a Christian acquaintance, where he once lived, but she refused to let him in. A Christian woman, Bogockien, lived near Yosl Haberkorn's apartment. She shouted that on Monday she had barely escaped arrest. She did not want to help, though she liked doing favors for Jews. There was no way out. He wept in front of her, begging her to take the child to its mother. He was ready to give her anything she wanted.

In the meantime, he had to run back to the factory gate because it was getting late.

He left Abish with her, but the woman did not take him to his mother. She let him go home by himself. Little Abish walked on his own from Pogodna Street all the way to Bielenkiewicza Street, making his way through the SS men and policemen. Nothing happened to him, but he returned home half the boy he was when he left. Imagine the feelings of the father, as he worked from seven in the morning until five in the afternoon. Imagine his mood! You can also imagine the mother's eyes when she saw the child entering the apartment alone, without the father, while the storm raged in the Jewish street.

Sheyve became very sick. She could not get out of bed. She was visited a few times by a Christian doctor, but it did not help at all. She simply could not stand up — her legs would not support her.

Then all the city's workshops directed by the Jewish communal organization were evacuated and shut down. The organization had carpenters, tailors, shoemakers, sweater and hat makers, all working for the city of Lemberg. Men, women and young girls with stamped registration cards, hundreds of workers, all with stamped cards — all of them were taken away. That was when we realized that the issue was not a need for workers, but the annihilation of all Jews.

CHAPTER 9

Zlateh and the Children in the Camp

A s I prepared to write this section, I recalled the moment when the terribly tragic events occurred, tearing our Jewish hearts to pieces, when the existence of Jewish families was shattered. We were as if blown up by dynamite and torn up by the roots.

I now want to give you a brief overview of what has happened to the Eisen family up to the present, and follow it with a detailed description of their personal experiences.

The day was Friday (as is today), the 28th. I do not remember what month — possibly August. Many people had already gone along the bitter road: Esther with her small child; Rochele with her two smallest children, twins [Rivkeleh and Adele]; Yosl's only daughter, Renye; Abeleh, Esther's older son (she was taken away with the smaller child in her arms); Yosl; his brother-in-law, Yosl Hochberg; his sister-in-law, a sister of Chaneleh; Chaneleh's father and mother from Dorosziew; Shaye Pardes's mother, sister and [the] child, Mondzi.

Now I want to move on to the issue at hand. I could go on listing and counting people, but so far I have not mentioned anyone from the Stromer family. By that time Herman [Stromer, Meyer-Leibish's son] had already been taken away.

On the morning (of the 28th) we went to work. At nine o'clock a driver came in who had just arrived from the slaughterhouse. Mechel sent him to me with the message that Zlateh and both children had been taken.

The carpentry shop had a special pass, which permitted me to walk in the street. After I survived the mass murder, I always kept this pass handy. I took the document, which had my armband identity number written on it, [with me]. By this time, we were no longer people, we were just numbers. But many people couldn't believe it. Unfortunately, when they were finally persuaded it was true, it was too late to do anything about it.

I did not know what to do. I took a droshky to the slaughterhouse because I thought Mechel was there, but he'd already gone. The landlord's daughter was the one who told him about the tragedy, so he ran to the assembly point on Podzamcze Street. He went with his neighbor, Mr. Blank, who was also a worker in the slaughterhouse. They had taken Blank's wife and his three-year old daughter.

I had the droshky take me to the assembly point. When I got there, Mechel was standing near the entrance, making a request while he showed his registration card. Blank and he had passes, though the assistant director [at the slaughterhouse] did not want to give [Mechel] a card. He'd gotten his pass card from Schmaltz, even though he didn't work for him. The assistant director was a Ukrainian named Stocki, who could not bear to look at a Jew. The director, Mr. Mekel was a piece of gold compared to his assistant.

But Mechel's talking did not help. It was of no use. I ran to the gate. The three of us [Mechel, Blank and I] wept in front of the bandits. They hit us several times with a cudgel and repeatedly told us to leave, and threatened to rip up our registration cards and pack us into the transport. We ran to various Germans. Then we went to Schmaltz.

He told us that the day before, the wife one of his workers had been taken away. He took a car and went to intervene on her behalf and met a tall SS man who warned him not to take an interest in Jews. Schmaltz replied that he was not interested in Jews but that the wife of one of his best meat workers had been taken. He was told that if he showed up one more time to intervene, the SS would immediately be notified by telephone.

The conversation took place in the presence of a barrack commander whom Schmaltz had indeed approached. After this, he said that he could not drive there again. We had 250 *zloty* to give him, but he refused to take it. We did not have a penny more. We ran around, but nothing came of it.

Christian onlookers moved among the masses of people. Every two minutes, lorries were leaving with victims. The Ukrainian policeman was there, the one who had taken all of Zlateh's furniture, the down quilts and many other items. I saw him then for the first time in my life, but Mechel knew him. He came over to Mechel. When he saw us crying he asked us what happened. He was elegantly dressed, in civilian clothes, and it is quite possible that he worked for the secret police. Mechel told him about our problems, and he said: "Give me 2,000 *złoty* and I'll bring her out of there." I told him that I would give him 5,000 *złoty* if he also brought out the children.

"Give me the money," he said. I did not have one Polish *złoty*, so I ran to the Messings on Marstinowska Street, to borrow 2,000 *gildn* [*złoty* and *gildn* both mean gold]. Whether they did not have the money, or did not want to give it to me, [I left with nothing.]

I worked with a young friend of mine named Gross. Before the war his mother was in the butter, eggs and cheese business and was a very wealthy woman. I ran to her. She, too, lived on Marstinowska Street, across from our workplace. Without knowing me personally, she gave me 800 *złoty*. She had 2,000 *złoty*, but was home alone during the *Aktion*, and was afraid that she'd be left penniless at a moment when she might buy her way out. I ran to Mechel with the money.

The bandit was ostensibly having a conversation with a Ukrainian policeman in uniform. I gave him the 800 *złoty*, and told him my sister had 10,000 *złoty*. He took the money and disappeared. We ran back to the gate to plead, but it didn't help. They began loading the lorries again. A teenage girl threw herself upon her old mother, crying out "Mother, dearest mother!" and ripped up her registration card. She was not one of the detainees. Zlateh and the children were put on a truck. I did not see her, but I did see Blank, our neighbor and Blank's wife with her child in her arms. Zlateh held Elish in her arms, and led Abish by his little hand to the slaughter.

I sprang toward the lorry, but the SS men began shooting at us with automatic weapons. The teenage girl was shot to death, as were two men. They had all come to see their parents, children and wives for the last time. It didn't take long, maybe ten minutes, for the lorry to be loaded, crammed full of people. Schutzpolizei stood around it to prevent the people from escaping.

My dear family, how do I know if you will ever have a chance to read this, or if I will ever be able to tell you about it in person? I am facing a situation that has never before occurred. I do not at present know what will happen to me an hour from now. However, I can tell you that anyone who has not seen all this will live longer. Let God repay them. *May God punish Germany!*

My heart is shattered. At the moment the lorry left, a few hundred Jewish, small, old and all innocent souls were erased from the register of the living. The cry from the open truck was: "God, don't forgive the murderers!"

We went home with our heads hanging down and with broken hearts. Oh God! When we came home, lo and behold, the apartment was a mess. The only person still there was Leytshe. Sheyve and Shloime's parents had been taken a few hours earlier; so had Mrs. Tepper and both children. Empty. There was no one there. A horror.

The pots which my dear sister used to prepare the Shabbos meal for us were there, but the owner of the pots was no longer. Mechel ran over to the coffee mill with which little Abish would grind a bit of wheat. He kissed the wheat and the flour and cried out: "My dearest child ground this wheat for his father, for Shabbos. This is his work."

Oh God, do not forgive the murderers for breaking us.

It was only then that we found out about the dreadful events. At seven a.m., a truck with Schupo and Ukrainian police drove into the narrow street. Christian children pointed out places where Jews lived. Sheyve was lying in bed, and the old man had not yet hidden himself. Zlateh happened to be in the street at the time, near the house.

When she realized what was happening she wanted to hide, but did not have time. Both of her children were in the backyard. Zlateh grabbed a hammer which the landlady was using for something in the garden and tore up the floor of the latrine! Lifting one son in her arms, while holding on to the other, she leaped into all that filth with both of them. Poor thing, she did not know the latrine was full, so much so, that one could see only their heads.

I write this with blood. The smaller boy was yelling: "*Mamo, ja tone, ratuj mnie!*" ["Mother, I'm drowning, save me!"] Being a mother, she wanted to save her children. If she would have been willing to abandon her children, she would probably still be alive today.

At that moment the bandits arrived. They found Zlateh standing in the open toilet pit holding onto the two children. Our landlady played a big role in this affair. She wanted her *Żydki* [Jews] to be taken away so that she would be free of them. Leytshe told me that the *shikse* [pejorative term for a Christian woman] had an argument with one of the bandits who spoke Polish.

When the landlady had seen that Leytshe was left behind, she tried to get them to take her. The [bandit] went into the apartment one more time, to check Leytshe's identification card. When he returned to the *shikse*, he told her that Leytshe's papers were all in order, and therefore he could not touch her. Leytshe heard what he said because he was talking very loudly. He did not understand that the landlady did not want the "little Jew" to know that she had informed on her. The SS man might never have looked for Zlateh in the latrine if someone hadn't told him where to look. I am sure of that.

They ordered Zlateh to come out. First she set her two sons down on the ground, and then she climbed out. All three of them were covered in filth from neck to foot. They ordered her to take tubs and fill them with water, and they ordered all three to strip completely and wash. Later, we gathered up the clothes and threw them out.

Zlateh washed herself and the children. We had a bottle of eau-de-cologne that Mechel used when he shaved. Zlateh now rubbed it on herself and the children. Then one of the men went to escort Mrs. Tepper and her children, Sheyve, and old Barits to the truck; the other man stayed with Zlateh. She pleaded with him, but he beat her cruelly. He also beat the children. They were all naked at the time. She, the mother, shielded the two souls with her naked body, and received most of the blows from the cudgel. I saw her cauterized back with my own eyes. The children had blue marks on their little bodies.

This man also shot his revolver into the apartment a few times. Then the second man returned. Zlateh and the children were now dressed. She dressed the children's in their best clothes, took the winter coat and put a shawl on her head. It was the month of Av [July/August].

She said to the second man, who was older: "Maybe you also have children and a wife. Let me live. I am only thirty years old. I have not lived yet. Here, take my diamond ring. Take it for your wife, and let me and my children go. Or leave my children with my little cousin (Leytshe), and take me."

He might have let her go, but just then the other murderer walked in and began to beat her afresh. This time, though, the three of them were dressed.

Zlateh told me later that she deliberately dressed herself and the children in many layers of clothing so that they would not feel the blows. Moreover, the extra clothing helped them in the camp. Oh, how useful the clothing was to them in the camp, with all those murderer-sadists around!

They were loaded into the truck and driven away. Oh, what kind of a Friday we had! I did not lie down, eat or sleep. Mechel walked around, distraught. It worried me. The *sheygets* [pejorative term for a non-Jew], the landlady's son, came home from work, took out his guitar and began playing various mazurkas and polkas — a kind of music that, at that moment, hardly matched our mood.

On that Friday, I swore to myself that if I survived all this, I would pay him back. He said "*Durna Żydowka. Ona skoczyla do ustępu.*" ("The stupid Jewish woman. She jumped into the latrine.") After hearing this mockery, I had a plan to take immediate revenge on the boy. I wanted to go away, and then come back and burn their little house down. The boy's mother could no longer endure his sarcastic comments. This Staszek was certainly a brat — but what was important was that he was an Aryan.

On Saturday we left the apartment. We made a hiding place for Leytshe to sit under a closet and told the landlady that Leytshe was leaving with us. We gave the landlady the keys to our apartment and to the Tepper's apartment. We knew that she would do everything possible to get into our apartment. She saw what was happening in the streets. Wherever Jews were removed from their apartments, landlords were dragging out linens, furniture, clothes and anything else they could find.

A special Schupo brigade of Jewish laborers in striped uniforms, from the camp, worked on this. They were called the *Raumungs Brigade* [cleaning brigade]. When all the people were removed from an apartment, the place was sealed off and the key was given to the cleaning brigade. But our landlady could not accept the fact that not all of us had been removed. The moment we left, she opened the door and started searching everywhere. She turned over the beds.

Leytshe was sitting under Zlateh's white closet in the corner. The landlady took all the best things from the Tepper apartment. We had a jar of fat drippings that she took away. She took the salt and even the wood I brought home from the carpentry workshop.

We had a feeling that if she moved into our apartment she would not give us any peace. At first, she ripped up everything. So we closed everything up. She tossed everything onto the floor and took the beds apart. When we got back, she told us the SS had been there and searched. [She said that] anything that was missing had surely been taken by [the SS] because they had not been able to find anyone.

Leytshe, sitting in the closet, heard their whole plan. Staszek was a good-for-nothing bandit and a Hitler sympathizer. He would say "I, myself, with my own hands, would stab all the Jews." We had to live under the same roof with that kind of person. And he was the one who had informed on Shloime's stepmother.

[This is how it happened.] Once, at five p.m., after work, an *Aktion* took place near the city limits. Two Ukrainian police were passing by just as that good-for-nothing Staszek was coming home. (He was employed by a German firm in town.) When he saw the police, he told them that two unemployed old people lived in number 13 and that they did not have registration papers. The old woman was lying hidden in a pile of maize-cobs, while I pushed Shloime's father into the oven, my former hideout. The two Ukrainians quickly came in, like murderers, saying: "Gdie je tu dwa stari Żydi? Żydowka o Żyd, skazy gdie wy. Wsie pudietie." ["Where are you, you two old Jews? Jewish woman or Jewish man, tell us where you are. You will all go."]

They found the woman because Stach [Staszek] climbed onto the roof of the latrine, saw her, and immediately reported her whereabouts to the Ukrainians. She was taken away. You can imagine how she screamed and wept. She was an intelligent Jewish woman and knew what lay in store for her.

While the two Ukrainians were searching the apartment, a drunken SS commander walked in. He was a tall, strong ruffian. *"Alles heraus!"* ["All out!"], he ordered — an expression the Germans used during every *Aktion* and arrest. We thought it was over for all of us. He lined us up in the small courtyard: Yosl, Sheyve, Leytshe, Zlateh, Mechel, Abish (the younger son was sleeping in the apartment and happened not to be at the Teppers) and me. He took everyone's registration card, and said: "If I find anyone in the apartment you will all be taken away, and I will immediately tear up your registration cards."

The SS man returned. They searched for old Barits but did not find him. One policeman held on to the old woman. We were still standing with our hats in our hands, and at this point, Sheyve had to get dressed. The policeman arrived when the SS man began asking who had registration cards. Those with cards were told to move to the side, and [the SS man] took everyone's registration card in his hand. The only person who remained standing in the middle of the courtyard was our dear Abish.

"Who does he belong to?" asked the SS man. Zlateh said: "Mr. Officer..."

"I'm not an officer," replied the murderer. "Well, let him go."

Only later did we learn that the German had stopped at our Hungarian neighbor, where he drank deep. He had not planned to search our small street — but the *sheygets* caused all the trouble. When he [the SS man] left, he took all the registration cards with him, thereby sentencing us to death.

Oh, if only I could live to see the day when the Soviets come!

At the time, we did not know why the German was looking at Abish. Later on we learned that on that day they had an *Aktion* to catch children. During that *Aktion,* the following were taken away: Renye and Esther's Abish (Abeleh). In an *Aktion* before Pesach, they took the great-grandson of Szprocer from Liczaków, a baker who lived with Yosl [Eisen]; a friend of Mechel's from the slaughterhouse, a certain Zinger, and his two children, boys, similar in age to Zlate's children, were taken away too.

I could not understand why my sister jumped into the latrine. At one point, indeed, we had discussed the possibility of making a hideout there. Mechel reproached me for not hiding my sister in the basement, though he knew very well that Ignatowicz [the landlady] and her children would not allow a Jew to remain alive. Later, my sister told me she wanted to save the children and had no other place to hide. She thought that this place was the best available spot. When she jumped in, of course, it was not so full. It was only later that the filth reached to their necks. That is how a mother saves her children.

My dear, beloved brother, if I will merit [living] to see you, you will see all of these places. I will show you where our loved ones spent their last, bitter weeks, days and hours. If I can share my experiences with you, dear brother, and relieve some of the burden of my poisoned heart, I may possibly feel better. Am I, then, able to cry? Experiences like these can be related only to a brother, a sister or a Jew.

Oh, dear brother, what a long time it has been since I last spoke Yiddish! If only I could tell this to my dear Meyerenyu while we give each other a hug! Dear brother, I think that there is just one country in the world that could recompense us for our catastrophe — the Soviet Union.

CHAPTER 10

An Impossible Event
(Or: Halfway to the Other World and then Saved)

To get out of the Janow[ska] camp — and with two children — was like returning from the other world, and from there one could only come back dead. At best, a man already assigned to a work detail might be allowed to flee by his foreman. However, in the August *Aktion* there were people in the camp who were loaded with money but still could not buy themselves out. In the camp, gold, gold dollar-coins and diamonds were like trash.

The well-known SS men in the camp ran around searching for people. They carried baskets full of paper currency, dollars and *złotys*. They kept yelling: "Anyone who won't give up the money will be shot immediately! There will be a strict inspection, and anyone found with gold or valuables will be shot." Jews were discarding all the valuables they had on them. Some buried valuables in the sand, in order to at least avoid giving it up to *them*. Everyone sat on the ground. The sun was blazing. Some people had nothing to eat or drink for a few days. When they asked for a drink, they [the guards] screamed that there was no water for Jews: "For you, there is poison." Because of hunger, small children bit their own fingers so hard the blood flowed. One small child even licked the blood of his mother, who had been struck and killed, and whose body was lying on the sand.

A few months later, on several occasions, I walked across the sands [the sandy hill in Lemberg],[15] where people had been beaten and killed. Everyone going to Bełżec had to pass through this central location. To reach that fate, people went through a terrible fire, or were exterminated in Bełżec, and then their corpses were burned. I am not making up fairy tales. Later you will find out that everything I am describing here is [tinted] in grey and sad colors. I cannot write about these things because there is a dreadful pounding in my brain.

It is Friday evening. I am putting my writing away. I wish it was already Sunday so that, God willing, I could live to continue my writing. I do not write on the Shabbos.

It is Sunday, the last day of April. All the things I write here are mere fragments of the suffering we experienced, because there is not enough paper to tell the whole story of what we went through everyday. Moreover, a human being does not remember—and does not want to remember — everything that happens to him.

Zlateh met her mother-in-law, Mechel's mother, [Shaindel] in the camp. Until that time of the August *Aktion* Esther lived with her mother in a house near the city limits with Hersh-Leib Strassler, on Kardinala Traube Street, a street beyond the railroad. They had to leave the apartment because the landlord evicted them. So Hersh-Leib moved to Żołkiewska Street 65, and Esther and her mother moved to Marczina Street 41. Esther and her youngest child were taken from there about fourteen days before her mother was taken away.

At the time they lived together, old Mrs. Eisen and a few other Jews from the house hid in the attic. When they were all in the attic they would pull up the ladder.

Every day, Zlateh would cook for her mother-in-law, and every day at

15 The Piaski sand hills in the city were the site of many mass murders of Jews — many thousands in all.

sunrise, on my way to work I would take the food to the attic where she was hiding. I would take my filled basket and send it up at the end of a long stick to those in hiding. At four in the afternoon, on the way home, I always brought her mother-in-law cherries or sour cherries as a refreshing snack and I would gather the empty vessels so that I could bring food again on the following day. Whenever it was quiet, Mechel would run over to them from the slaughter-house and bring his mother something.

It was a very difficult to get the food up to the attic. There was a black-smith living in the building that was visited by strangers. Because of that, we had to be careful, so that no one, God forbid, would see the hiding place. That last Friday, I brought them food in the morning. Old Mrs. Eisen took all the pots and the bread out of the basket. I can still see her standing at the edge of the trapdoor in the attic, wearing glasses, holding her prayer book in her hand.

That was the last time I saw her. None of us ever saw her again. I left the pots where they were, because when we went to inquire about Zlateh, we found out that Mechel's mother and the other people who were hiding in the attic had been taken away.

Besides her mother-in-law, Zlateh also met Uncle Yehuda's wife Shain-del, Uncle Meyer-Leibush and Mrs. Tepper in the camp. She was with Zlateh during that entire time. One of Hersh Lindvorem's daughters had a husband near the city limits, a man named Grinberg. She and her only child, a five-year-old girl, were also transported.

Later, the children told me that they saw small children and elderly people being shot. They [Abish and Elish] had given their food to those who had been without any food in the selection area for two to three days. The constant selections determined who would be shot on the spot and who would be sent to Bełżec.

Suddenly, in the great crowd of people, Zlateh saw Feyge, the daugh-ter of her mother-in-law's daughter Rochel. When Feyge saw Zlateh and her grandmother (Zlateh stayed together with her mother-in-law), she cried out in surprise: "*Ciotka!*" [aunt in Polish]. She was less surprised to see her grand-mother. [Feyge] was afraid, because since her mother was taken, her sister Chaneleh was hiding in our apartment with her two small children and her younger sister, Sima. Another person hiding there was Hersh-Leib's only son, Motek. She was certain that all of them were taken away at the same time.

But in fact, very early that morning they all went into the basement and stayed there. Our landlady did not know that we were keeping them in our apartment, because if she had, she would have gone looking for them.

Because of all this, on that particular Friday, Hersh-Leib's three children were saved. Feyge, who had a stamped registration card, would visit our apartment when she ran around looking for her mother. [Feyge] worked for one of the biggest German clothing firms, Schwarz and Company.

Rochele was reported walking around streets designated for Christians without her armband, and her daughter was running around looking for her. [Feyge] was caught during working hours and taken to the Janow[ska] camp. There she met Zlateh. At four p.m., she saw Hersh-Leib, her father. He was caught during the *Aktion*, but was allowed to work in the camp as a glazier and was not sent with the transport.

When he saw his Feyge, he let out such a terrible scream that all the thousands of people present heard him. She was his only hope, because his older daughter had no documents. She worked for the Jewish community, where the registration cards were not stamped. And now his last hope, Feyge, was lost too. All this was made even worse when he saw his mother-in-law and Zlateh. Yosl Eisen was allowed to work in the camp.

That was when Hersh-Leib realized that, if they were still alive, his three children on the outside had no means of making a living and no chance of survival, because the rest of the family was in the camp. Feyge's cry was not meek, either, but their cries were swallowed up in the screams of thousands of people. Hersh-Leib was, at that time, on the other side of the fence; the people being loaded onto the transport trains were behind wire fences — cut off — in [that] ghastly, sandy place.

Zlateh had $400 on her, wrapped in a handkerchief. She threw the money over the wire fence, and Hersh-Leib grabbed it. At that moment the guards in the observation booth, who could see everything, opened fire. Hersh-Leib went back to his group and Zlateh mingled with the people around her. A few SS men came out immediately to search for the person who threw something over the fence. Because there were thousands of people, they [the SS] could not find [the culprit].

At seven p.m., a certain Glück, the director of the Schwarz firm and a member of the [Nazi] Party arrived. The Schwarz firm — the largest firm to employ mostly Jews, employed about 3,000 workers. The director came to intervene on behalf of the people who worked for him and had registration cards. The Germans fired a few rounds from their automatic weapons, and the mass of people fell silent. Then the camp commander, the well-known *SS-Untersturmführer* Wilhäus, called out: "Anyone who works for the firm Schwarz and Co., come forward! — but those only. Anyone else will be shot on the spot."

My dear sister understood that this was an opportunity for Feyge to escape from the fire. Feyge saw her director, who was in the company of another German employee from the Schwarz firm, a certain Klopotek. The head of the Jewish workers' organization, Weber, and another group of SS men stood right next to him. They began checking the Schwarz firm's registration cards. Zlateh asked Feyge to rescue her two souls, as she [herself] had no choice but to stay. She knew that she would not pass the inspection. She told Feyge to tell the Germans that the two boys were her [Feyge's] two little brothers and that she was supporting them. Maybe, just maybe they would let them go.

Feyge took the children. Imagine my dear sister's feelings! She parted from her children and handed them over to Feyge. But the two children did not want to go without their mother. At last, Zlateh talked them into it. Feyge quickly ran with both children to her director, and showed him her registration card. Just at that moment a Jewish woman standing next to the inspectors who was not being allowed through, took poison. [Distracted], part of the gang looked at the woman, who was still in convulsions, while Feyge and the children ran over to the group of the luckiest people.

Zlateh, without the children, did not know what to do. Then she made up her mind, said goodbye to her mother-in-law, and walked over to the gang. Because she did not have any documents in her hands, the gang began beating her across the face and legs with whips. During the beating, Zlateh screamed that she worked for Schwarz and that her registration card had been torn up. They questioned her. It happened that Feyge, when she visited us, always talked about her job. As a result, Zlateh knew which section Feyge worked in and the name of Feyge's foreman. And when Zlateh sent Feyge out with the children, she gave her coat to her and took Feyge's trench coat — and it had the armband with an identity number on it.

The director knew the numbers of his Jews because each factory usually received consecutively numbered armbands and registration cards for its workers. This proved decisive. [Zlateh] was allowed to pass to the other side of the fence. Imagine the joy of the children, who all the time had been shouting: *"Ja chcem do mamy."* ["I want to go to Mommy"), when they saw their mother coming toward them.

That Friday, at nine p.m., Zlateh was brought back from halfway to the other world. She was driven to the city in a lorry, one which, only a short time earlier, had taken a group of unfortunate people to the camp.

Zlateh and both of her children were rescued that time; it was an unusual case. It appeared they were destined to suffer at the hands of the Germans for a few more months. During that time they would go through hell — hiding and gasping for air in basements. They struggled for a sliver of hope [and had faith] that things would somehow improve. For another ten months we had the joy of their being alive. For our loved ones' sake, we accepted whatever happened to us. More than once my sister said: "I would settle for a plain potato, if they would leave me alone to live with my children and my husband — just to live!"

Indeed, it was this, the dearest thing — life — which was stolen from the Jews; and until the last Jew was eliminated, the Germans carried on the work of extermination. There was no way to escape, even for those people who had large fortunes to pay for it. The Jews wanted to save themselves, but the bandits thought up various ways to exterminate them.

Until the August *Aktion*, many Jews with armbands would walk around the Christian quarter. Later, every suspicious-looking man in the street was checked. In the case of Jewish men, it was easy to check. It is possible that some women traveled clandestinely to Germany and worked there, and it is even possible that they are still alive, but a mother who had two sons could not have saved herself and also her children.

I hope that after the war, no German will be allowed to be in a position of authority. They must be wiped off the map, or we will never have rest, never. They must be eliminated like a venomous snake, without leaving a trace.

CHAPTER 11

In Schwarz's Factory
(Or: Supplies and Money)

On Friday night, Zlateh and her children were brought to the Schwarz factory on Marcina Street, where there was a whole complex of buildings that belonged to the [company]. The main building was across from the Podzamcze railroad station, and the buildings continued all the way down to the place where you turn off into Panienska Street.

The people [from the camp] were brought to the factory at night. Some food was prepared for them right away. Like all factories, Schwarz's had a canteen for its workers, and once a day they were served a bit of hot soup. During those days [the days of the *Aktion*], many workers did not go home.

Mechel and I went to work on Saturday. On the way, I sat down on a stone and from [sheer] weariness I fell asleep where I sat. Mechel soon woke me up and told me the good news: that Zlateh and the children had been rescued and that they were here in Schwarz's factory. Mechel was holding a shovel in his hand, so it would look as if he was on his way to work. I got up, and without taking the street pass, began running with him.

Hersh Baumwald's daughter [Lusia], who also worked in the factory, was the one who told Mechel about Zlateh. We got to the factory, where a janitor named Garfinkel stood at the gate. For about fifty *złoty* he immediately opened the gate, and we entered the factory. Inside, it was like a fair, full of thousands of workers. The workers spent more time wandering around than working.

I spotted Zlateh right away. Imagine our joy! "Where are the children?" I asked, because I could not believe that both Zlateh and the children had escaped the killing-grounds. Then I saw little Elish and Abish. They jumped into our arms and cried out *"Tato-wujcio!"* ["Daddy-Uncle!"]. People were looking at us. They must have thought we were the most fortunate of Jews. Very often we heard quite another exclamation: "Where is the director? They have taken away my mother, my father!" The *Aktion* was still going on.

Soon we were told that anyone who did not work in the factory must leave the premises, because those who had been saved would now be registered and would receive confirmation that they had been taken out of the camp. The SS would approve their registration cards with an official stamp. However, those who had used the name of the firm to smuggle themselves out of the camp, but had never actually worked there, must leave the factory by 12 midnight.[16] After that time, the director himself would summon the SS and hand all of those people back to the camp.

Imagine our situation! What were we to do? Where could we hide them? We were the most fortunate of people, to be able to bring three souls back from the other world; but what could we do with them now? We ran to the Christian woman Esther was living with and asked her if she could hide them. It was a waste of words.

We ran to every possible place. Mechel ran together with me to the slaughterhouse, to Mr. Schmaltz, who, as it turned out, was about to leave on a journey. Many leading personalities left during the August *Aktion* so they would not have to intervene on behalf of their workers, and it is possible that [these vacations] were initiated by the authorities. What could we do? We had no choice but to return with the children to Bielenkiewicza Street. Maybe the landlady and her children would not be home. Then we would be able to smuggle the children into the basement without their knowing about it. There was no other way. But how could we take them through the streets while the *Aktion* was in full swing?

We found a covered military truck, used for transporting ice, in the slaughterhouse. I talked to [the driver] and told him what our problem was and

16 A few lines later, Stromer refers to "12 noon" as the deadline. It seems the latter time is correct.

that we were prepared to pay him well. He said that at a time like this he was afraid to put a woman and two children in his truck.

We asked Mr. Schmaltz to lend us his luxury car. He said yes, but we could use it only after two p.m. In the factory they said that Zlateh and the children had to leave the factory by noon, and it was getting late. There was nothing we could do. We went back to our souls [Zlateh and the children].

When we returned, we talked to a man named Schwarz, a Jew with lots of influence at the factory. As it happened, he had the same name as the firm and Zlateh had already spoken to him. He wanted a diamond ring, but a Ukrainian policeman had already taken Zlateh's ring when she sat in the truck on Bielenkiewicza Street. In return, the Ukrainian had promised to let Zlateh and her children leave the truck. But after driving them to Podzamcze, he gave her several blows with his rifle-butt, and she no longer had her ring.

I will not write too much. We had $247 that we gave Mr. Schwarz so he would take care of our three souls and not toss them out onto the street. He took us into a timber storeroom, where he took the money from me, and putting his left hand on his head — he was not wearing a hat — and giving Mechel and me his right hand — he asked us to give him our word that we would not tell anyone how, and for how much, we had taken care of this problem. He registered Zlateh on the spot and she would have to remain in the factory until such time as she would receive the red stamp of approval from the SS.

However, he told us to take the children home. We begged him to hide the children for the time being, so he hid Zlateh and the children in an attic. We also gave the janitor a piece of meat and a handsome amount of *złoty* for taking care of Zlateh. We [Mechel and I] could not stay in the factory. We also asked Mr. Garfinkel to make sure to provide [Zlateh and the children] with water so that they could take a bath, after [being covered with] all the dirt and sand.

We went home, and I prepared food that Mechel carried over to the factory in the afternoon. We also took Feyge's registration card with us, and gave it to her sister Chaneleh. We somehow managed to sneak her and the small meal into the factory. And because Feyge obtained a new card, claiming that her old one had been destroyed, Chaneleh remained to work in the factory. Then Feyge submitted Chaneleh's picture for her new registration card, and had to wait, like Zlateh, for official approval. Schwarz knew about this, but he also knew that they were Mechel's sister's children, so he helped in this matter.

Secondly, the $247 was an argument in itself. In this way Zlateh, Feyge, Chaneleh and Sima were safe in the factory. Although Sima and the two children were illegal visitors in the factory, they stayed there on Shabbos, Sunday, Monday and Tuesday, until they had to leave.

Bitter troubles now began for me. I was the sole provider. I had to go to work every day, and cook for the six people in the factory, and for Mechel, Motek and myself. Meanwhile I did not have a single decagram of flour; I had no sugar and no fat.

Two things had been missing for a long time: meat and buckwheat. In a word, I had nothing. I did have 20 kilograms of unground wheat. Every day after work, I went to a neighboring Christian woman to grind two kilograms of wheat in a hand mill. While Leytshe kneaded for me, I baked flat bread on the stove.

For such items as two kilograms of rye flour, a bunch of carrots, a head of cabbage and some green beans, I would barter various old clothes with my Christian neighbors. Everyday I managed to put together a good pot of soup, and took it, together with the flat bread, to the factory. Sometimes Mechel would bring home a piece of liver or meat. All I could bring home was wood shavings. I no longer put pieces of wood among them, firstly, because they were too heavy to carry home, and secondly, the landlady would take them away. We always would leave the key, and Leytshe would hide behind the closet. A few times, Mechel brought home an unborn calf [from the carcass of a slaughtered pregnant cow].

That called for a celebration. The meat did not need to be cooked long. I cut it into pieces, broiled it with an onion, and added a little water. The meat made a first class meal. I would add borsht made from young beets and their green leaves. I would often bake flat bread and cook until midnight or one o'clock at night.

Sometimes, when I made the flat bread from rye flour, the [dough] stuck to my palms and fingers and to the baking pan. Then, at two o'clock, I would go to bed. I would throw myself into bed still wearing my clothes, because I was so tired and because I had only three or four hours to sleep. I had to run over to Zlateh and bring everything to her. When the food was ready, I would carry it down to the basement to cool off. The people hiding in the basement had a gas stove they could use to heat up the food.

It is hard to believe what was going on in factories of this kind. People were swollen from hunger and people were cooking in the factory. Those who had two potatoes cooked them, and so did those who had just one. A person who had 10 decagrams of buckwheat flour was considered a lord. Many workers lived off the one daily portion of soup they were served in the factory [canteen]. They fasted the rest of the time. Every time I brought my pots to Zlateh, she gave some of the food to her co-workers in the same work group, people who were dying of hunger.

Yet there were those, like Schwarz, who ate bread and butter. He took money, supposedly for the director, for favors rendered; but he kept it in his pocket. He ate white rolls with butter and ham. There were plenty like him.

However, both the starving people and the important people died at Bełżec, because they were all Jews.

After the August *Aktion,* there were fewer hunger-swollen people in the streets because most of the people caught in the *Aktion* were swollen from hunger. Luckily for those who remained, Jews now gave each other, and received, more support than before — even from those who, up to that point, thought they would need their money for after the end of the war.

On Wednesday morning, at about ten o'clock, Sima and both of the small children came to me. They were told that an *Aktion* would take place in the factory. Zlateh was not afraid, nor was Chaneleh, because they were registered there. But Sima and the two small children had to be hidden. What should I do with the three people in my courtyard? As it turned out, nobody noticed them. I took them and went to Bielenkiewicza Street. The street that we walked on happened to be quiet. I knew that this was the best time, because the little bandit [the landlady's son] was at work, the *shikse* [the landlady's daughter] was visiting a girlfriend, and the old lady would visit a neighbor every day and work in the garden.

As it happened, I met no one. As we walked along the street, I covered Abish's face with a handkerchief, and Sima held [Elish] close to her skirt, so that nobody would notice us. The door of the house was open, and I had spare keys to all the other doors. I stowed all three people in the basement — that was the safest place. I wanted to bring Pepe to our basement, but it was impossible to take her through the streets.

That Wednesday there was a terrible massacre in the factory. Children, wherever they were found, were taken away, including the family of the janitor who lived in the factory: they took his wife and his only child. The Jewish workers hid children under their worktables, where they had thrown army coats waiting for repair. The children were wrapped in several coats and carried from one courtyard to another that had already been searched by the SS.

A whole lorry full of people was removed from the factory. Our small children, as it happened, left the factory where they had been for five days, so they were saved for the time being. I ran quickly back to the factory and ran over to a street level window, near where Zlateh worked at a sewing machine. I gave her the good news: I succeeded in smuggling all three people through the streets. Imagine what my sister went through, not knowing if I succeeded while she witnessed what was going on in the factory. She could not have known that the quarter that I walked through was quiet. I told Zlateh that when I went back, I ran into the *shikse* on her way home.

Zlateh calmed down considerably. She knew that if the young woman was home without knowing someone was hiding there, then no one would search the house for Jews. Then she told me that she could say that she was sure that no one would find us — we were safe.

We had no alternative. We always gave something to the Christian woman for watching the house. Later, whenever the SS set fire to apartments with Jews inside them, we told the Christian woman that if they found an apartment with no Christians in it, they would just burn it down. As a result of that, the Christian woman stayed home all the time.

My dearest family and friends, what we suffered from the small Stach [the landlady's son] is indescribable. We did not tell the Christian woman about Zlateh's release. On Saturday, the little bandit began to rub salt into our wounds by saying: *"Już nie ma Abosza i Elisza. Już napewno znich toaletowe mydło na dwa tygodni będzie."* ["Abish and Elish are not here anymore. They will certainly be made into toilet soap in the next two weeks."] We had to keep our peace because, so far, we had no other apartment. We simply could not argue with the Christians. We had often asked the *shikse* to let Abish stay in her apartment, as if he were a brother of hers, but she would not hear of it.

My sister was full of Jewish pride. She would say: "I won't give my child to just anybody. Don't trust them [these Christian neighbors]. I want either to live with them [the children] or to die together with them."

Yes, dear sister, you accompanied them on their last journey. Dear parents, if only I knew that my suffering during the last nine months would lead to a goal. It looks as if it has become quiet on the fronts. Everyday, I hope that maybe the Russians will break through. I stayed hopeful about the front at Brody. We heard shooting from far away and bombs being dropped. But because I have not seen even a scrap of a newspaper for the past eight days, I do not know what is happening.

Around Friday, [Aug. 28. 1942?] Zlateh and Chaneleh received their registration documents and went home. The landlady opened her eyes *this wide!* We did not tell anyone about the children, because we were not sure of their safety. When we showed Stach the stamped documents, we did not tell him when and what arrangements had been made, because we did not want to give him a reason to inform on us. Zlateh went back to work in our kitchen.

I would be willing to suffer for my entire life, not to eat and not to sleep, if only I could take care of my dearest parents, my sister and her children, and all the rest of my dearest family. Unfortunately, it seemed that this was fate, and I had to experience and go through the entire German hell, and be a witness to it all. Everyday I lived through something different and [through] various degrees of fear. Up to the present, it has gotten worse daily.

Part of the Polish population is moving out of Jagonia and across the San River. They are afraid of the Ukrainians who burn down their houses and kill some of them. If the Christians in our area move out, I will be stranded. I cannot step into the street because every small child knows me and would turn me in to the same murderers who killed the other Jews. The same mass murderers are also here in Kaminke.

That is why I say once again that [freedom] is so close and yet so far away. My situation has not changed, though just the other day the Germans were near

Moscow or Stalingrad, and now the Russians are near Brody, Tarnopol, Kowel or Lutsk. But God can help. *"Der Mensch trakht, und Gott lakht"* ["Man plans and God laughs"] is how the saying goes.

CHAPTER 12

The Loss of Pepe

Pepe hid inside an actual factory chimney with her aunt Mrs. Messing. The chimney was in the same courtyard where they lived and I worked. Her aunt had a registration card, but because her daughter lived with her and also had a housekeeper's card, she did not want to have two housekeepers in the same apartment [so she decided to hide]. [At that point,] the situation was so bad that even workers [wage earners working outside the home] were disrespected, so she decided to hide with Pepe . A Ukrainian worker who worked for the landlady — she owned a small factory that manufactured brass doorknobs — took a few hundred *złoty* from Mondik Messing and let them into the chimney. I was sure nobody knew.

On Saturday I spoke to Mondik and asked if Wasilka knew that they were in the chimney. He assured me that no one knew about it. I said to him, "Mondik, maybe the *sheygets* knows. In that case they ought to leave the hideout this very night and hide in your attic, in a small room." He gave me his hand and assured me that no one knew about it. Satisfied with this answer, I went home with a quiet heart. In the meantime this Wasilka knew, and I was sure that no one else did.

On Sunday morning I went to see Pepe. [She was gone.] She had been in the hideout that same Saturday afternoon, when Wasilka got drunk on Mondik's money, went to the Ukrainian police and informed on them. A Schupo man and two policemen came to the place and fired [their weapons] right into [the chimney]. Two Jewish souls [Pepe and her aunt, Mrs. Messing] were taken out of there and put into the waiting automobile.

Can you imagine? The Messings were willing to give any amount of money requested. Mondik was not shy; he pushed a few thousand *złoty* into the hand of the Schupo man and promised him an English jacket and a suit. The man had already allowed the two souls out of the auto again, when someone from the building began yelling, "You are letting them go for money?!"

Mrs. Messing was very smart. Realizing the situation, she grabbed the son of the woman who was yelling from the window and was about to enter the building. But the Schupo was annoyed and pushed her back into the truck. The Schupo knew only about the two women, not about the child who was also in the hideout.

It was in this way that Pepe met her fate. Nothing helped, though many ways were sought. One of Messing's brothers-in-law, and his wife, worked for the SS in the camp on Czwartaki Street. On that same Sunday, the Messings sought a favor from him.

On Monday, the camp commander personally ordered Mrs. Streit to leave the camp on the next transport. All was in vain.

[Later, Streit moved in with Messing, his brother-in-law. Yosl Haberkorn and Lonek moved in, too, when the Germans ordered that three people were to occupy one square meter of space — under the circumstances, families tried to stay together.]

My dearest Pepe, who knows better than I do how much you had suffered, how many problems you had endured because of me from your own mother. We understood each other. Your mother wanted my parents to transfer their property to her. I would rather go hungry than write to my dearest parents about money. I knew what they were suffering and what kind of problems they were living through each day. We were always content with the fate that was delivering ever harsher blows.

Dearest Pepe, how much you suffered on account of me because you had a rich fiancé. At this hour, not knowing what tomorrow will bring, I ask you, dear Pepe, for forgiveness. I believe that I did not, God forbid, do you any harm. You know what I suffered because of your mother, who recognized only money, but we both had to remain silent — after all, it was your mother. You, dearest Pepe, the one who bore the name of my deceased grandmother Perl — you were as pure as a pearl. You fell like thousands of other Jewish daughters, a kosher sacrifice to Hitlerism.

God, allow me to see Hitlerism's downfall!

CHAPTER 13

In the First Ghetto
(Or: On Ordonia Street 23)

Every day, Zlateh went to work with Feyge and Chaneleh. Little Sima hid with [Chaneleh's] two other small children and Leytshe at her place. But before the *Aktion* ended, we had a bit of an incident with Motke, Hersh-Leib's son, who [never wanted] to stay in the basement until we came back from work. He would go down in the morning and leave after a few hours, or, if he stayed, would pester the others.

Sometimes he didn't go into the basement at all. He would eat breakfast and then go hide in the garden, which wasn't such a bad idea, but you had to stay down all the time [and keep out of sight]. In his case, he would lie on the ground for a little while and then get up and take a walk without his armband. [One day] he went through the fields towards Kaminke and was caught by a Ukrainian policeman in a roadblock during the *Aktion*. He was detained and ordered to sit on the grass.

[Motke] had been sitting there for a few hours because the policeman was waiting for his replacement. It happened that a Christian woman who lived on Hersh-Leib's street passed by and recognized the boy. He asked her to tell Mechel where he was. (Luckily, Mechel's apartment was on the woman's way home and she stopped by and told us about the boy, just as Mechel, Mr. Blank and I were returning from work.)

We did not have a penny on us, except for Blank. We went to the policeman and begged him to release the boy for a few hundred [*złoty*]. He let the boy go because [he knew that] Mechel and Blank had lived in an apartment on Bielenkiewicza Street. Later that day the policeman came to the apartment, and we gave him 300 *złoty* and a jacket. He told us that he wasn't wearing a uniform because he could not bear to watch what was going on. We were lucky to get the boy out of their hands so easily. By the time Zlateh, Feyge and Chaneleh came home from work, Motek had already been returned to us.

Every day, Zlateh, whose legs ached, would walk into the neighborhood designated to become the ghetto in search of a place to live — [even then] Jews were paying thousands of *złoty* for apartments, My dearest sister found an apartment in a building made of clay, but my sister did not care. After every-thing that had happened, she did not want any other apartment. Its landlady lived in the city, so Zlateh went to see her. She said Zlateh could move into the little house at once. It consisted of four apartments, with a dark corridor [down] the middle, and a small porch. A man named Pasternak lived in the first apartment on the right. The next apartment had a tiny kitchen with a grill in one corner. The room had a framed window. When I went to see the apart-ment, I was taken aback. Mechel cried out, "Oh my God, a living grave!"

However, Zlateh did not want to listen; she just thought that she wanted to be there, and alone, without any partners. Mechel's search was useless; he wasn't able to find anything. A good apartment cost up to 5,000 *złotys*. You can imagine how we felt when the landlady took 100 *złoty* from us. When she came around and saw how we had fixed up the broken-down apartment, she was very happy.

Mechel was a builder and I was a carpenter. We hauled in bricks and sand. We quickly repaired the wall with bricks. We also found a little bit of lime in a ditch. I bought a small window and a frame from Krajewski. The window and frame measured 70 by 70 cm [approximately 28 inches] [and] we inserted the window and patched up the wall around it.

We soon constructed a hideout. I bought a few wooden planks and two large plywood boards from Krajewski. We built a double wall, which was also very narrow because the whole apartment was a mere nothing. The hiding place was 60 cm. (23.6") wide. We dug a foundation ditch along the whole width of the wall, below floor level. We'd learned from the previous *Aktion* that the bandits would run into apartments and often shoot into the walls [this trench would offer some protection].

Our hideout was directly opposite the door. [It was connected to] the only available wall in the apartment because in one wall there was a window, in the second [there was] a door, and on the third [wall, there was] the stove. We figured out that it was better to sit in [the wall] than to stand. Once the [false] plywood wall was in position, we covered it with clay, spreading it with our hands. The clay dried very quickly and was hard to detect. We also used some clay on the ceiling. Then we whitewashed the whole apartment twice.

In the corner, near the double [false] wall, there was a bed, so we built a small trap door [behind it]. The bed was always made. In order to enter the hideout, you crawled under the bed on your stomach, then slid feet first through the trap door. That way, you landed inside, standing up. The last person to enter closed the trap door from the inside.

At that time we had no wood, coal, flour or potatoes. We took the white closet [with us from the old apartment], along with the lower part of the credenza. The upper part had been burned as firewood.

Chana Eisen gave us a bed, and we had our own small table. We also had a couch, which only just fit into the apartment. The closet could not even be squeezed through the door, but we lifted it in through the broken window before it was fixed. Later, when we moved out of the apartment, we had to leave the closet behind — we could not get it out. We put the credenza next to the stove, the bed next to the double wall, the closet in one corner near the window, and the couch under the window — where it fit perfectly between the bed and the closet. Now the whole apartment was furnished. We moved the table next to the closet. When the floor was washed, our apartment had a very pleasant smell.

Oh, how my sister prayed to God that she would be able to survive in this little apartment! The Schwarz firm had enough work for several shifts, day and night, but Zlateh stopped going to work. She realized that she was not helping herself at all by working. Both boys would go around hungry and dirty — and she was right.

I [finally] went to work, and the workplace was nearby. Every day I brought home wood and wood shavings. Mechel brought home meat he bought from the Christian or Jewish workers. He wrapped it around his body and in that way was able to smuggle it out of the slaughterhouse, so we always had meat to sell. As a result, the meat our family ate did not cost us anything; in fact, we made a profit of a few *zloty*.

I began dealing in flour. I had a Christian acquaintance, Szwiferski, who worked in a mill and I bought small quantities of flour from him. I smuggled it myself because the most important thing was getting it home. Here's how we did it: we took a strong bag and put eight to ten kilos of flour in it; then we patted the bags until they were flat, and wrapped them around our waists, securing them with a belt, and covering up everything with a trench coat. Zlateh also did this a few times.

I bought a bottle of liquor for my boss every week and [that way] I did not [have to] go to work. By now, I had merchants who bought flour and meat from me. Sometimes I came across some butter. At times, the Christian also had venison, buckwheat [and] barley. I became his regular customer.

Zlateh arranged the purchase of four [cubic] meters of potatoes from the area near the town limits. At that time, you could still walk in the streets alone. We stored the potatoes in the trench between the [false wall and the real wall]. Mechel also went to the train station to get potatoes, so that we would have [enough] food. What I did not have was money. However, I made money: over 2,000 *zloty*. It would have been possible to live — but we were not allowed to. At that time, my father sent us an additional $160.

[Father] had hidden the rest of our belongings underground, where we used to hide the liquor. Dear brother, you surely know where that place is. You remember the time we lowered a milk can, with all our property in it, to mark the spot. This time, our dear father put everything in the same place, but not on top. If someone searches the place, he will find it; but only you know the place. Maybe Henia remembers where we used to hide liquor against a rainy day. I would use the ladder to get down there.

Things are getting worse daily. My landlady was washing clothes today to prepare for a move. I do not know what I will do, but God will help. The peasants keep leaving for the train station with wagons full of household goods, cattle and horses. The worst is that I can no longer show my face in the street; otherwise I would be looking for another place to live. I have no money. All I own is ten single dollars and 150 *złoty*. That is not money! However, as I said before, God will help.

We would walk up and down Ordona Street. There was not, God forbid, any shortage of food or *groszen* [pennies]. Sima and Motek were living with us and we would send food daily to Hersh-Leib to eat in camp.

At first, Chaneleh and Feyge did not know what to do, but Zlateh took them with her a few times and they soon learned how to make money. They would sell their goods in Schwarz's factory and would also walk up and down the street. They always made a profit: two loaves of bread and a few decagrams of butter — enough to send their father a loaf of bread.

That's when I remembered the times I was stingy about giving the children flatbread; but now I had various kinds of flour. I asked people to bake bread and rolls, since we had a first-class oven, which made Zlateh open her eyes wide in surprise. We wanted to make all our acquaintances happy, so we let them bake and cook with us.

On Friday evenings, Zlateh would light Shabbos candles. Beforehand, she would bathe the children and change their clothes. When Mechel came home from work he washed up, prayed and said *Kiddush*. We had challah for Shabbos and meat almost every day, and he [Mechel] often had 20 kilos of meat, or more. We also had rendered beef fat, so we were never short of fat. The profit from selling meat was very good.

Mechel used to take me to his Christians' homes, where I was able to get meat from them more than once. We wore special pants and jackets for smuggling the meat, with a coat to cover everything so that we would not become bloodstained. I always carried a carpenter's saw and wore my eyeglasses. Mostly I walked along the street at dawn — twice — back and forth, looking for trade before people went to work. Things went well until we received news from Kaminke: a terrible *Aktion* was taking place there.

We stopped running around looking for business. I cannot describe to you what we lived through during this period. Every day we sent a few telegrams to Kaminke, but received no reply until God helped us and a telegram came on Yom Kippur eve [Sept 20, 1942]. The telegram contained one word, in Polish: "We live!" We began to breathe freely again.

But did we enjoy the good news for long?

Tuesday, May 2 [1944]. I cannot collect my thoughts. My heart is suffering terrible stress. People keep leaving. It seems that my landlords will also have to leave their home.

Wednesday. [May 3] I cannot write at all. On Monday, on Zkliniec Street, a Jewish family named Ekonumiu was shot in the Zkliniec courtyard. The Jew had definitely been hiding the whole time in the house of a Pole; but because the Poles had to leave their homes, the Jew was compelled to leave his hiding place. He was with his wife and two children. Someone saw him in the forest, and the Ukrainians came and killed all four of them. Just think: [The father] had hidden them all for nearly three years, and now, in this critical period, he and his lambs were slaughtered.

I have no plans. I do not know what to do with myself. I cannot show my face because everyone knows me. If they did not know me, I could have slipped away to another place. And if I had a plan, I would cover my face with a kerchief so that I would not be recognized.

What should I do? My heart feels light, but I cannot sit or lie still in my den. Today again, early in the morning, someone came to my landlady and told her that they [the Nazis and their collaborators] would visit her here in Jagonia to search for weapons. My landlady became very frightened. She was afraid that someone might find out about me living there and that they would come around looking. She was right.

Some time earlier, I'd dug a trench [in their cellar]. For a time, they [the landlady and her family] used it to hide a trunk full of clothing; but recently, [when] they took the trunk out of the hole I did not let her fill it in. We covered it with planks and then covered [the planks] with dirt. There was a way to get from my attic to the place where the opening was. I asked them today if I could hide in the ditch, and whether they could cover me, but they did not want to. They insisted that I stay up in the attic. If I was caught, I was to say that I sneaked into the attic on my own.

Then Józef Streker, the landlord, went to the village to find out if the gendarme was coming. He went in the morning, at about seven o'clock. Now it's just about five p.m. and he has not returned. No doubt he seized the opportunity to get drunk and is sitting there drinking.

I cannot write any more. May God help me!

Thursday. I am fasting today. For the past ten months I have been fasting every Thursday. The [first] meal I eat after Wednesday is on Thursday evening and often not until Friday at nine or ten o'clock in the morning — but it is foolish. My brain is drying up from thinking. I do not know what tomorrow will bring.

Yesterday a Christian woman moved into the Streker's house. She is to stay in there after the rightful owners move out. I know this Christian woman. She does not have a husband. Her husband was Szczor, a Ukrainian from Malechiw near Lemberg. The Germans arrested him because he was an activist during Soviet rule, so he is most certainly dead. She has a small son with her who must be about 13 or 14 years old, and she has a daughter aged 18. The daughter married a Soviet and went to Russia with him, leaving her mother with a baby who was then three or four months old, and is now more than three years old.

It is possible that I could make an impression on this Christian woman with money — but I have none. I wonder if I could sneak over to [our old home] and find the money that was left hidden there. But to do that I would have to risk my life, because a Ukrainian is living there, and I have no legal right to enter. Once again I thought about going to the apartment… but what about work? There are no jobs to be had. It is so bad, it is so terrible! Our Jagonia *Volksdeutsche* must leave Jagonia by the 12th of this month, meaning eight days from tomorrow.

God will help. It is possible that if the Christian woman [Mrs. Szczorowa] stays in the house, she will keep me here. There may be another couple who will need to live with [her and her young daughter]. The man is Maramasz, a fanatical Ukrainian patriot. There is no doubt in my mind he would hand me over to the police in a minute. Besides, I would not stay [if they moved in].

Mrs. Szczorowa's elder son served as a volunteer in the Ukrainian SS. That is what these people are like: the Germans liquidated his father because he was loyal to the Soviets, and the son serves the same Germans who were fighting the Soviets.

A Jew cannot do things like that. He always has to remain a Jew. I have found myself in very difficult situations, but God has helped me. My situation is very difficult now, but God will help me.

On *Yom ha-Kodesh* [Yom Kippur, September 21, 1942], there was a new and dreadful *Aktion* in Kaminke, so that once again we walked around despondent and worried. However, once more our parents survived the storm.[17] Then came the real blow, the day the Kaminke Jews were "liberated."

At dawn on that day, they [the Germans] came to the representative of the Jewish organization [the Judenrat], Friedman from Brisk, and told him that [the Jews of] the town would have to resettle in Radechow. The whole ghetto was already surrounded by SS men, police, and Sonderdienst.[18]

All the Jews together were dragged to the sports ground and from there [they were put into] railcars to Bełżec. My current landlord [Streker] saw my dearest parents, the poor things, both my father and my mother, standing in the street that day, with small bundles in their hands.

This, my friends, was the last road for them. They were murdered in the most horrible way — and holding small bundles!! My dearest mother, how many nights had she gone without sleep? How many cubic meters of flour had she worked on with her ailing hands, only to be snatched away now from the stream of life, while she carried a small bundle? This cannot be forgiven. The murderers must also receive their punishment, and it must be still greater. No trace must be left of them, just as none is left of us.

17 On that day the Nazis shot approximately 600 Jews outside Kamionka. The ghetto was liquidated five weeks later, on October 28, 1942, as described here by the author.

18 The Sonderdienst were units of local *Volksdeutsche* that were under the command of the German police or the German civilian authorities, depending on the place and time. They were often extremely brutal.

CHAPTER 14

New Aktions in Lemberg

I want to hurry up a little bit with my writing. If I survive, I would like to tell you about my experiences in greater detail and take my time. Right now, I just want to give you an overview of what took place one night in 1942. It could have been between eleven and twelve o'clock at night. A man knocked on the only small window we had in the apartment. I heard him right away, and Mechel went outside, because he recognized the person who was knocking. It was Mechel's brother, Yosl [Eisen]. From September to December, Yosl had been in a forced labor camp. A few days earlier he'd gotten sick with typhoid fever. For a certain sum of money Chaneleh was able to get him out of the camp; otherwise he would have been shot immediately.

On this particular night, Dr. Jakob Heim brought Yosl to our small window. He left him there and went on his way. They had learned an *Aktion* was due to take place early the next morning, and where [Yosl] was [staying] there was no hideout at all. So the doctor, who was also Yosl's friend, brought him to us. We also knew that tomorrow there would be new "fun and games."

Yosl came into the apartment with Mechel, and fell onto the bed. He had a fever of over 40 [degrees Celsius — 104° F]. We laid him on our bed and fed him some milk to restore him.

At dawn we prepared to go into hiding. The most difficult problem was Yosl. He was sick and weak, and in addition to having such a serious contagious disease, he had to stay with the children. But [under pressure], who had time to think of such things? For the moment, the main thing was for all of

153

us to hide ourselves. We had the double-wall hideout. After putting a light in there, the first thing we did was pull Yosl into the space. More than anyone else, he had to hide because he was a fugitive from the camp.

After that, Zlateh crawled inside with Abish and Elish. [They were followed by] Motek, Sima, Eti-Gitele and her only surviving son, Hertzl; Vilek, Klare's husband — Klare and her child were already gone — Mondik, the son of our neighbor Pasternak, and me. We also had the neighbors who lived in the other two apartments: Feder, a man from outside the city limits and his wife, a member of the Lempert family; their daughter and her husband Shvayder; Shvayder's sister and her husband, Prager, who was a butcher and his sister's two children: a boy and a girl, between 15 and 17 years old. Their parents and siblings were taken in the August *Aktion*.

[The Pragers] owned the two other apartments in the building. They took in other families, who counted on them to help them survive. They built a hideout which consisted of a hole in the floor, covered by a table. We were afraid that if they were found, they would find us, too, because many mishaps of this sort occurred. We wanted to pull them into our hole, but they could not stand the heat and were afraid that Yosl would make them sick.

I was always the last person to go into any of our hideouts. In the meantime, I blocked the trap door to the hideout by dragging a sack full of old rags under the bed. When we were all inside, Mr. Pasternak locked the door of our apartment from the outside. Following my advice, he hid in a baking oven in the hallway. Pasternak's father, an old gray Jew, had shaved his beard off — which did not improve his appearance — and stayed in the apartment, which his son locked from the outside.

The *Aktion* that took place then was dreadful. Small houses were set on fire with their residents in them. It was the first time that this happened. The area around our house was surrounded by Ukrainian police. I kept crawling out of the hideout and looking out the window to see what was happening outside in the street — if it could be called a street. From the Peltew Bridge to the fence, it was still unfinished. Moreover, I had to keep emptying the chamber pot because Yosl kept using it. We stayed in the hideout like this for two days.

On the evening of the second day, Chaneleh knocked on our door. Through the door, I told her where the key was hidden. She told us what was happening in the ghetto. It was horrendous — they were shooting, burning, beating and killing old and young, children and mothers. At that time Chaneleh was [still] working for the Schwarz factory, living in one of the factory buildings. That meant she wasn't home when the doctor brought Yosl to our apartment. It was by chance, when she went to see Yosl that she found out that he was at [Mechel's] place. She brought us a can of water, and we climbed out of the hole, laying Yosl down to sleep.

We were all ready. Zlateh, with the children and Sima, climbed back down inside. They sat on top of the potatoes all night long. We asked to be locked into the apartment from the outside, and Chaneleh did that immediately.

On the second day of the *Aktion*, the Germans forced their way into Pasternak's apartment and took his father. Then they entered Lempert's apartment but found no one there. On the third day the *Aktion* ended. Yosl stayed with us and Chaneleh came to see him every day after work. For the next few weeks Yosl stayed in bed until he got better.

I must also note here that before we moved into the apartment on Ordona Street I had to get a permit, so I went to the housing organization every day. At that time, Zlateh was still working for the Schwarz firm, and since the permit office was very close to where I worked, I made my way over there every day. There were thousands of people trying to obtain apartment permits. One day [in September, 1942], I happened to be standing in line, waiting, when SS men suddenly drove up and opened fire on the people. Many were shot. A young Jewish lad who happened to be transporting timber in a horse-drawn wagon was also shot.

Then they [the SS] entered the housing office, took the Jewish policemen and hanged them. I do not remember how many they hanged, but I believe in any case that it was about thirteen men. That included the president [Dr. Henryk Landsberg] of the Jewish community [Judenrat]. My sister knew that I had gone to the housing office, so when she found out at work what had happened, her strength deserted her.

After the second *Aktion*, all the residents of the building, and Eti-Gitele, who lived not far from us decided to build a hideout for everyone in the building. We all contributed some money, and bought wooden planks from Krajewski. Under my direction, we began the construction. I asked Pasternak, his son and sister, to leave their apartment so that I could tear up the whole floor. Every floorboard was marked, so that we could nail it back in the same pattern. Then we began digging, and carried the extra earth out in [cooking] pots. We worked only at night, [and during the day] we kept the apartment closed so that no one would see what was going on.

The biggest problem [we had was disposing of] the large amount of earth we dug up. We threw a mass of earth into the small courtyard underneath our window. Once we got the dirt out, I laid down wooden planks [in the hole we built], with more boards over them, and covered everything up with sand, half a meter deep, so that there would be no echo. Then we put back the apartment floor.

The entrance to the hideout was in our apartment, next to the stove. The trap door was covered with a sheet of tin, just like the areas next to the stoves in the other apartments: the tin was meant to prevent a fire from hot coals that might fall out of the stove. From the trap door, there was a narrow tunnel that led to the periphery of the main hideout.

Inside, we constructed a [ventilation] flue that went down to the hideout under Pasternak's kitchen. We built another flue to the outside, in order to [better] ventilate the area. We put a special kettle full of water in one corner, and put another kettle in the other. The walls were lined with benches that could hold up to fifteen people. It was a first-class hideout.

No sooner did we finish the hideout, when there was a camp *Aktion* early the next morning and we had to use it. We barely had time to get inside, especially Yosl. Guards from the camp were on their way, and they would recognize him and shoot him on the spot. Zlateh ran to the front door, and did not let them into the front hall until everyone had gone down into the hideout. She shouted that she did not have the key and [could not let them in].

I do not know, I do not remember, how many *Aktion*s and troubles we experienced. It is hard to remember. One thing I must repeat: "Another week has passed and nothing has changed." I hope from day to day, week to week and month to month that something will change. I can say that from year to year I have seen no change in my situation. It is so near, yet so far. May God help me!

CHAPTER 15

My Dreadful Experiences in the Hideout

The fires burning in Kobel, the area surrounding Jagonia, lit up the night. As usual, the Ukrainians set fire to many homes, putting even more pressure on our landlords to get out. Our landlords [the Strekers] certainly would have preferred to stay where they were, but they were afraid of fire and murder. They knew that once they left this place, they would not be as well off anywhere else as they were here. I remember how we lived a year or two ago—how happy we were just to have a piece of bread; and I realize that even now, the Christians live much better than the Jews did in the good times. They drink and eat the best of everything and get drunk every day. They have learned to make liquor, and the illegal stills are in constant use. As they say in English, they make "moonshine."

It is Friday [May 5, 1944]. The time is about seven in the morning. I have begun writing today, because I want to relate some more of our experiences. Yesterday, Streker told me that on Monday an SS commander will come here and assemble all the landlords of Jagonia to inform them about the evacuation and transportation. I asked Streker whether the whole thing could be delayed for another four or five weeks. Maybe there will be a new Soviet offensive, or maybe the long-awaited second front will open. The local population would prefer to see the Soviets enter the town, rather than leaving their homes and everything that is in them behind. But it is not up to them.

May God help us!

One day, when people were on their way to work, a mass of SS men stood next to the gate and stopped people. Some people had already received their new "R" and "W" identification cards.[19]

It was understood that all workers would receive these identification cards. That morning, workers who had no identity cards were taken and moved to one side. The marching columns did not know what was happening in front of them at the gate. By the time the workers found out that anyone without "W" and "R" cards were being moved to the side, more than 1,500 men and women had been stopped and were being guarded by Ukrainian police and SS men.

Some workers had explosives with them and were ready to blow up the fence near the place. Many people were shot then and there. The whole ghetto was in an uproar. People were hiding in every possible nook and cranny.

At that time, Mechel was still working in the slaughterhouse, and I was working in Krajewski's workshop. Neither of us received a "W" card. All Mechel's friends, who worked in the slaughterhouse, and those who came to work that morning, were taken to the camp. The night before the "incident," Mechel had a premonition and that night sent me to Blank, to see if I could get him a "W" card for a hundred *zloty*. The workers in the slaughterhouse collected money to pay a large, collective bribe to get "W" cards.

[Krajewski's] company, however, did not give a "W" card to a single Jew, and handed all the Jewish workers over to the police. The stronger workers were taken to the camp, and the weaker and older ones were taken away. As a result, both of us [Mechel and I] became unemployed on the same day, and could no longer show our faces in the street.

---

19 According to David Kahane, in *Lvov Ghetto Diary* (Amherst: University of Massachusetts Press, 1991), there were two new identity badges, marked either with a "W" or "R" issued in November 1942. Workers for Schwarz and Company, which made uniforms for the German Army, wore the "R" badges. The "W" badges were distributed to Jews who worked for companies that made supplies for the Wermacht. These Jews, who essentially worked for the Germans, were the only ones who could possibly survive.

While one part [of the SS group] carried out an *Aktion* near the factory gate, the main force began a dreadful *Aktion* in the ghetto, using Jewish police. We were all in our hideout at the time, so nothing, thank God, happened to us. Soon afterwards, various refugees who managed to escape from the recent *Aktion* in the Kaminke ghetto, showed up.

They were: Dovke Mishel, Lole Mishel, Lipe Kobel and Sheyna's daughter; Avrom Federbush, son-in-law of Yoshi the baker; Eckstein, the wheat merchant's daughter, and both of the Tshari sisters, who stayed with Mrs. Frommer. Some Jews managed to escape and were hiding in Bisk. Moishe Holtzman and his children, Deyze and Rose; his brother-in-law Dr. Oyster, and Moishe Tenenbaum (nicknamed Columbus), and his wife and their two children, were staying in Lemberg, along with Yosl Zeigner, the barber, his wife and a boy. (The girl had been taken from him earlier in Kaminke, when it was made *Judenrein* and all the Jews were murdered).

The SS left eleven Jews behind, to clean up the ghetto — five men and six women. [Among] the men were: Lazer Zeigner, Bailachel's younger son; my friend Hersh Zeigner, the baker, and Peretz Shaindele who'd gone to gymnasium with Henia's brother and Itshe Kohl. The women, if I remember correctly, were: Zlateh Abes, Oyke the shoemaker's wife, and the baker, Itsyaleh Indik's daughter. I do not remember the other three.

One fine day, three people fled from Kaminke: the two Zeigners and Itshe Kohl. They brought a nice bit of capital with them, that they had picked up in the [now empty Kaminke] ghetto. Realizing that it would be impossible to survive after the ghetto was cleaned up they escaped and came to Lemberg. They found themselves an apartment, and searched for a way to get to Hungary or Romania. I saw them.

A few days later, one of the most terrible *Aktions* broke out. Every little house that was suspected of hiding people was attacked with grenades, set on fire and burned down with the people inside. But if the inhabitants noticed the fire and tried to save themselves, bandits were waiting outside, and [mowed] the Jews down with machine-guns.

Mechel, Vilek, (Klare's husband) and I managed to obtain new identity cards after the "W" *Aktion*. Juzek Reiter got us fake identity cards for 500 *złoty* per card. He was a "W" representative in Lemberg and worked for a German firm. We had to get fake cards because his firm received only 150 "W" cards and had distributed all of them. Now we worked for Reiter at the German firm,

Geber and Wolf. More than 160 Jewish women and men worked there, where our jobs consisted of hauling rocks or sand to the concrete factory.

We started out very early every morning, marching out with the whole column to the gate. On the far side of the gate a few trucks waited to take us to the factory, every day of the week. We even had to work on Sundays. There were a few cases where the company handed Jewish workers to the SS because they had missed a few days of work. One man missed one day of work and he was also taken away. None of those taken ever came back.

The company also used workers from the camp. Those people were weak and swollen from hunger and cold, and our German overseers killed a few of them in our presence. The people from the camp could not work as hard as the better-rested people from the ghetto, who ate better and did not have to look at SS men all day long.

One lovely, frosty night in November or December we discovered that an *Aktion* was going to take place the following day. A little later, Dovke Mishel was brought to us by his younger sister Lole. He was ill with typhoid fever. Under the German occupation, and especially in the camp, people walked around with a fever of 40 degrees [104° F].

Soon after that, Hersh and Lazer Zeigner and Itshe Kohl arrived. They had abandoned their apartment because it was too small to hide in, and they came to us. A Mrs. Rosenfeld (whose husband was in the Russian Army) and her unmarried sister came to Pasternak's apartment. Earlier, they had all lived with Pasternak on Kinge Street.

We had prepared water and candles in our hideout. We also bought two battery-operated flashlights and we all climbed into the hideout before daybreak.

It is seven o'clock on Friday evening. The official in charge of the *Volksdeutsche* told them to leave their residences before the twelfth of the month [May 1944], meaning a week from now. But as I have emphasized several times in the past, God is able to help — the same God who has helped me up to now. *"A gutten Shabbos."*

Sunday [May 7, 1944]. The time is about nine in the morning. There is no way that I can see Streker. The last time I saw him was on Friday. I would like him to take care of something for me in town, but I have not seen him. He was away from home all night. In the interim, a soldier with two horses came here yesterday to take up quarters [in this house].

In the past it was possible for me to slip into Streker's house [from the attic] at night and exchange a few words to find out what was happening, but now that, too, has become impossible. I have various ideas, but I do not know if I will succeed in evading the hands of the murderers.

Meanwhile I have no money, and without money you cannot do anything. I also have a plan to sneak into our home [in Kaminke], to get to the spot where our property is supposedly hidden and remove it. I do not know whether I will [succeed], but if I do, I will deposit a marker in that place. It would be good to put a bottle with a written note inside at the site.

You would risk your life. At the time, these were just thoughts.

The deadline for the Strekers to leave was swiftly approaching — Friday, May 12. The army had already confiscated their two cows. The [landlords] are getting everything ready for the journey. Yesterday they slaughtered a pig and a calf to take with them as food. I will certainly have to leave two days before their departure because it may happen that in the final days the army or the gendarmes will come to remove their household goods.

May God help me! I want to write a little bit more. I do not even have any place to hide this [my diary], or a secure place in which to leave it.

Twenty-four people entered the hideout. I will list them for you here: Pasternak, his son, and his nephew; both Rosenfeld sisters; Vilek (Klare's husband), his brother Hersh Zeigner, Leyzer Zeigner; Itsche Kohl and Lole [Mishel]. None of the neighbors wanted to let Dovke Mishel into the hideout because he was sick and they were afraid. The neighbors gave him a choice: it was he or his sister Lole. He told Lole to [hide], and he left. But Zlateh ran after him and called him back, and told him to hide behind the double wall [in our apartment]. People could not complain about it, since that section of the wall was not held in partnership with the others.

Zlateh shouted at the people: "You are worse than the Gestapo. You banished a sick person. And you want God to help. You wanted to be preserved from danger." Immediately, Zlateh prepared a package of food and a liter of tea in a bottle for him, and pushed him into our first hideout. He sat there all alone.

My dearest sister! Today, when I am in such terrible danger, I can see what she did for him.

You should know that Dovke had been in our apartment before. He did not have a penny, and my sister always used to give him something to eat. Later on, when the three people came from Kaminke and brought property with them, they supported him a bit.

Dear God, why did you punish my sister?

The others in the hideout were Sima and Motek, Hersh-Leib's wife Eti-Gitele; Shvayder with his wife and mother-in-law, his sister and her husband, and the two orphaned children; Mechel, Zlateh, Abish, Elish and I. The hideout was intended for 15-16 people. It could not take any more. It was dreadfully crowded, but what could be done? We had to do what we did. [ed. note: There is a miscount.]

All the doors were locked from the outside by Eti-Gitele. Then we went to the factory apartment, because it was understood that [there] the Germans would check only the "W" and "R" workers; women and children who were not employed were not permitted to be in those apartments. Mechel and I could also go to our new apartment because the company had a house for its workers at 17 Damarstinowska Street — but we did not want to leave Zlateh and the children alone. This meant that Jews could not live [outside] the smaller designated area of the ghetto. [The Germans began housing the workers for the factories.]

Meanwhile the *Aktion* began. We all kept very quiet, listening to what was going on in the street. From time to time I climbed out of the hideout, and through the small curtained window, was able to catch a glimpse of what was happening outside. The armed militia did not enter the homes. They guarded the ghetto, inside and outside. The Ukrainian police were grouped, closely together, near our small apartment house. Occasionally, I opened the trap door to let some fresh air in. Outside everything was covered with snow, so nobody was able to detect the dirt from the hideout that was dumped there.

The first day passed quietly. They came, but did not touch any of the three doors. On the second day things got dangerous. Every now and then we could hear shooting, and when I climbed out of the hideout, I saw fires burning. Small Jewish houses were on fire. I did not tell the [others] about the fires: I did not want to cause terror among the people.

That first night, all the men climbed out of the hideout, but the ladies and the children stayed inside, because if anything happened it would be better if they were inside and there would be no need to escape at the last minute. On the second day it was impossible to open the trap door because it was terrible in the street.

They broke down the door to Pasternak's apartment and turned everything upside down. In Shvayder's apartment, the lock was torn off and the apartment was trashed. They tried to break into our apartment, but they could not open the door. The time was about three in the afternoon on a December day.

Soon afterwards another gang arrived, or it could have been the same one that was there earlier, and they tried in vain to open the door in a number of different ways. We heard them sending someone for an ax, and then they began striking the door with [it]. We had a strong lock which did not give way like the others. In the meantime, everyone had to keep very quiet.

But as 24 people breathed at once, it created a suffocating environment, while the hacking sound from outside lasted more than half an hour. Everybody inside the hideout tried to be as still as possible — so much so, that our gasping sounded like a locomotive.

Meanwhile they ripped out the frame of the small window together with the bars, and one of them entered the apartment through the hole. A second man succeeded in breaking the lock off, and they all came into the apartment. They threw everything from the closet to the floor. There was more than a kilogram of Soviet tea, three kilos of Polish soap scented with Eau de Cologne, and half a liter of liquor that had been specially prepared for situations where it could save our lives. They drained the liquor on the spot, and took the tea and soap.

Meanwhile time was passing. Lazer Zeigner fainted. The children were scarcely bearing up, but Zlateh fanned the air for them a little bit with her hand. Prager's niece and nephew both fell down in a swoon. The same thing happened to Pasternak's son. The [candles could not burn] in the airless space. When Lazer Zeigner recovered from his faint [he was] unable to endure any more, and cried, "Let me out! I will ransom all of you. I don't want to stay here and choke."

But Mechel and Vilek held on to his hands and covered his mouth. Little Elish was also feeling worse. They moved him closer to me, thinking that near the trap door there would be more air. Meanwhile, though, the air was still bad. The small boy began to choke. I had to hand him back towards the inside of the hideout, so that no one, God forbid, [outside the trap door] would hear him.

I heard the men outside leaving the apartment, but I was afraid to tell the people, in case they all rushed [towards the trap door] at the same time. After a short time, when I was convinced that there was no one in the apartment, I told them to wait a few seconds longer. Very slowly I opened the trap door — and at once detected smoke in the apartment. I was afraid, thinking the apartment might be on fire.

I said nothing, but quickly jumped out, telling them to hand Abish and Elish to me. After that, all the people who had fainted were lifted out.

Our next door neighbor's house was on fire, and the smoke was pouring into our apartment through the knocked-out window. The roof of our apartment was made of wooden shingles, but, fortunately, it was completely covered in snow. Everyone panicked.

Zlateh was shouting: "Don't be alarmed! God will help us. Nothing will happen to us." When we saw the Ukrainian militiamen walking up and down in front of our house, we realized that the *Aktion* was still going on. Meanwhile a house across the street caught fire. It grew dark. Some people were still afraid. Hersh Zeigner, Leyzer Zeigner, and Vilek Prager went to Dovke's, where there was more air. He was alone.

We told the women to go back into the hideout, and some of them did, but Zlateh did not want to go back. She prepared white linen sheets so that when it got dark, we could wrap ourselves in them and no one would recognize us. Zlateh was always calm and never lost her head. This was true during all the *Aktions*. With her hopefulness she also gave courage to other people.

It was getting late. Soon Hersh came around with the news that the *Aktion* was over. We hurried out of hiding, boarded up the broken window with a sheet of wood, and then covered that with a shawl and pillow to stop the wind from blowing in. It was dreadfully cold. We went to the other side of the house and saw fires burning all around us. The house where the Rosenfelds were living was on fire, and the homes of all our other neighbors were already burned down to the ground. Shvayder, who was hiding out with us, lost his 10-year-old son — he was burned to death.

I cannot list all the terrible things that happened at that time. It is impossible to write all of it. There are not enough words to describe it all. Our home was still standing, and God guarded over us for now.

CHAPTER 16

On Wieszbickiego Street — Under Jewish Arrest; Or a Trip to the "World to Come" and Back Again

Immediately after the *Aktion*, we began working on the apartment given to us by the Wolfer Company. These apartments for Jewish workers were on a corner, at 17 Domarstinowska Street. Mechel, Vilek and I were given a small apartment to share with four other workers. There was no kitchen. The first thing Mechel did was build a kitchen [out of parts salvaged from other places]. I brought in a wide chimney-pipe from a burned-out house, a small kettle and an iron plate. We dragged all these items to our apartment on a bedspring, and then used the same bedspring like a sled, to drag other things to our apartment.

We used to live on Ordona Street, but since the last *Aktion* there was no longer a need for a large ghetto, and our particular area was trimmed off its edge. The rules were such that those who were not working had no right to live there, except for those with company authorization to work as cleaning ladies.

We were in no hurry to leave our apartment on Ordona Street, especially in light of the fact that we had a good hiding place there [but there was no choice]. As soon as we moved into the ghetto apartment, we searched for a place to construct a hideout. When we got there, we found other people already living in the building. During the recent *Aktion*, the Germans discovered the locked basement and removed 120 people: wives, children, mothers and fathers — the families of the working men.

With the closing of the ghetto, my flour trading came to an end. Moreover, we were no longer permitted to walk in the streets alone, only in groups. Later, each group had to have a Christian escort. Mechel stopped working in the slaughterhouse, so we no longer had any meat to eat. We did have a supply of potatoes, flour and wheat and wanted to ensure that the children would not lack anything. [We made sure that nothing was missing in our home.]

We began building hideouts for acquaintances, friends and strangers. We charged various prices: 1000 *złoty*, 1500 *złoty*, 800 *złoty* and 2000 *złoty*. We used our own materials — bricks and sand from a burned-out little house. We dug up sand and took it back in a wheelbarrow. We purchased a little bit of lime. We dug and we built. The most important parts of the hideouts were the trap doors which served as the entrances. We had to make sure that the trap doors would be difficult to find. We worked hard, day and night, and put a lot of sweat into our labor, but it was worthwhile. We built the hideouts at night, after work, because during the day we worked [at our assigned places].

We built hideouts when we could not obtain the "W" cards necessary to get work, and when we could no longer leave the ghetto. (That forced us to buy bread in the ghetto — which cost a few *złoty* more [inside the ghetto] than it did in the Christian part of the town.)

We were so well known as builders of hideouts that people dragged us from one job to the next. Any time [someone wanted us to build] a hideout that was not safe, we would tell them so, but they would pay us anyway. There were times we built hideouts only after people had exchanged their apartments for safer ones. And people were looking for a hideout builder they could trust. At that point, we had so much experience building hideouts that we became specialists. There was not a single case of anyone being arrested from our hideouts: none of them was discovered.

Zlateh and the children continued to live on Ordona Street, and we walked from [our new place] to work. The Gestapo at the gate checked everybody who went by. I was with Mechel and another man: we were the last three in our work column. At that moment — as on every day — there were more than 120 people marching to work. I did not know what was happening in front of me. I reached the Gestapo man, whose name was Zieler, and was the only person he stopped in our group; he checked my "W" card with the aid of a flashlight. (The card was a fake.)

The German handed me over to the Sando [Jewish] police. Soon after that, they moved us — 68 men and women — to the Jewish prison on Wezbicki Street, inside the ghetto. More than 400 people were jailed there: young people, old people, women, teenage girls, children and infants. Later on, I always saw Zieler in the Janow camp.

The next day, SS men arrived and surrounded the jail.

They began to load the people onto trucks. Some people struggled and were shot on the spot. I kept pushing my way into a corner. Six trucks full of people had already been driven away. Enough people remained behind to fill yet another truck, [the one] in which I would certainly have been taken away. They began to load us into this last truck. When twelve people were already on board, a motor car arrived and something was said to the other murderers. The people [who were already in the truck] were then harassed as they were rushed back into the jail, as they were beaten over the head or across the face with riding crops.

These "returnees" told us that they were taken to the sands, but there were no more graves left, so they had been brought back. All the graves were full of murdered people. Dozens of bodies were lying on the edges of the graves, because there was no space left for them inside.

That is how I was saved.

Later we found out that the workers from the camp had not been able to dig graves, because the ground was frozen solid.

I stayed in prison for another two nights and a day. There was an *Aktion* in the ghetto on the second day. The police searched all the houses, and whoever was caught was brought to the jail. Within a few hours the jail was again filled. Two of the cells had several people with typhoid fever. Lice crawled over them as they lay burning with fever. From time to time, someone died.

Imagine what my sister went through when she heard that I had been pulled out of the [marching] column, and that the Germans were "cleaning up" Wiezbicki Street. That was how they described the process of taking people from the Jewish prison to the sands.

There was no place to stand: one person was crowded on top of the other. I quickly informed Mechel and Zlateh that I was still alive. They drove or ran to all our acquaintances to try to save me, but nothing helped. To make things worse, I had no more than $300 on me. Mechel came to the window and saw me. I had $160 that was easy to get at, so I threw the money out the window, to where Mechel was standing. I kept more than $100, because I made deals with the Jewish police in the jail, and I was hoping that for $50 they would let me go free. Meanwhile the camp commander, *Untersturmführer* [Gustav] Willhaus, and a couple of his assistants — later I found out that their names were Bittner and Webke — began a selection process. Everyone was examined separately; everyone was asked his occupation. I said I was a carpenter. The camp commander did not understand me, so the Jewish policeman translated the word "carpenter" into German. It was God Himself who sent me to his side.

When he saw a weak person, Webke said: "He belongs to me." Later I found out that Webke was an expert exterminator of Jews. When he said: "He belongs to me," it was the equivalent of a death sentence. He selected 62 strong, healthy people from about 200 men.

Not much later, an armed escort arrived from the camp. They lined us up in a courtyard on Wierzbicki Street, and Willhaus asked everybody if he had good shoes and a coat. Several men replied that they did not have good shoes. Willhaus led these men back [to the prison] and told those who were left inside to give those men their shoes and coats. He told those who were going to the camp to put them on, because they would need them. Then we were lined up five abreast, and led to the bathhouse on Balonowa Street. There everyone was searched, and if anyone had money or a watch it was taken away. And if anyone had a pair of good gloves, the guard took those away, too. As far as a good coat or boots were concerned, they ordered the wearers to take them off, and exchanged them for their own, (which were in worse condition).

After the bath, we were again lined up, five abreast, and led into the camp. We were told to watch one another very carefully to make sure that no one escaped, because if one person escaped, ten people would be shot.

At about eight o'clock in the evening I found myself in the camp. Until then I had only heard about it; now I was actually seeing it with my own eyes. I do not want to describe it because now is not the time. I am writing now about what I should do next. I must be made of iron to endure this. It is terribly difficult to survive. I hope that God will help me.

CHAPTER 17

In the Camp and in Roker's Place

We were taken to the camp reception office. Everyone was registered and had to sign the registration form. From that time on my name was no longer Mordche Taksel (for I had signed my name as Taksel the whole time, in the course of my jobs, and not as Stromer. It [the name Taksel] was very useful to me). I received a number, and a yellow patch, which I had to sew [onto my jacket]. I became Number 36-382.

We were held in a barrack, all together, for about two days. We were then divided up into various work groups. I, as a carpenter, stayed in the camp to work. This was the worst work — not that we were overworked, but it was dangerous to stay in the camp all day. There was always some drunken SS man who would beat up or shoot the workers. The camp commander himself used to take shots at people all day long from his window at the workers down below; he aimed at their heads, or more exactly at their eyes, using his automatic weapon. After 50 or 60 people were shot, camp workers loaded them [the dead bodies] into trucks. And when railroad cars filled with timber, bricks and cement arrived, the workers unloaded them.

The rest of the workers, who worked in the town, could stash away many supplies. They could meet everybody and buy a loaf of bread, while the people in the camp were dying. I was lucky to work with a group of Christians. There was only one other Jew in this group, and as a result [we were] not tortured by the Germans and did not add to the numbers of the dead.

Every day there were deaths, sometimes more and sometimes less, be-

171

cause of the daily wakeup calls in the camp at three or four o'clock a.m. at night. After the wakeup call, the bunch of bandits would come out and brutalize everyone. There were several thousand people. They [the bandits] led their "customers" and had fun. Some of the bandits ran through the crowd, beating and shooting as they went.

I want to abbreviate my account of these events because I do not have the necessary concentration for it. It is enough that several thousand people had to march through a gate, where a whole bunch of SS men stood. Each group leader reported the type of work group it was and how many people were with him. Only then would the group leader receive a permit for the company from the guard in the [sentry] booth — which also served as an office. Then [the SS men] looked over each person as he marched past. Whoever did not please them was pulled out of the rank of people who were marching five abreast and placed next to the wire fence to be shot. You were shot immediately, or else, when the entire column passed by, all the people set aside were shot. This happened every day.

Sometimes, they livened things up with a run. Every group of five marching abreast was forced to break into a run as they approached the gate. Anyone not in condition to run was stopped. There were sick people who summoned up their last bit of strength, just to march a short distance, but when [they were forced to run, they could not do it].

Some people walked around with a fever of 40 degrees [104° F] because they could not stay in the barracks. If anyone was not present at the gate, a guard was sent to the barracks to shoot him. No one must report sick because anyone who did was shot on the spot. There was a hospital, and each group had its own doctor. There were plenty of doctors, lawyers and engineers there. There were enough Jewish doctors for each group to have its own doctors.

I worked in the camp for several weeks and was forced to sustain myself on the camp soup because I had given my money to Sender Podhoretz/Kuhos to hide it for me, and I could not find him right away. Later, he escaped from his workplace — with my money — into the ghetto. It took me some time to ask Mechel to get my money back for me. At any rate, I lost some of it.

The big leader in the camp, the one who was always present when the work assignments were being distributed, and the one without whom nothing at all was done in the camp, was a certain Akser, a Jewish lawyer from Lemberg. I plucked up my courage and asked this man if he could save me by sending me to work in town because I just could not cope with life in the camp.

I had let Zlateh know that I was all right and that I did not, God forbid, lack anything. I did not want to share my problems with her for she had enough problems of her own. She had barely made it to the new apartment on Ordona Street. They built the fence while she was running [back and forth] with her packages of food, and she had to leave the timber planks behind because she simply could not carry anything more. (It should be noted that firewood was vitally important.) I would bring home every scrap of wasted wood from every job I had constructing hideouts — so that my sister would not lack firewood.

The first time I asked Akser for a favor was after I had worked as a carpenter in the camp for two weeks. Then I approached him again during the third week. He told me that he remembered [me]. Do not think that Akser was just anybody! He was able to do someone a favor, and he always helped the Jews who were in trouble and saved them.

A few days passed by, and then he assigned me to another job — in town. As luck would have it, the work group I was assigned to consisted entirely of people who were with me in jail. As it happened, a group of men from the prison were brought to the camp. Out of this group, fifteen men were sent to work in town, including the foreman, who was a friend of mine from the Jewish prison, a man named Dalf. For a few weeks, while I worked for the carpenters in the camp, the group from the prison worked for a company in town. Later on, that company no longer needed workers; but another firm asked for twenty workers to be sent to them. Akser took that [first] group, three other people and me, put us together and sent us to work in town.

The first time our group came to the gate, the foreman told the guard that twenty men were reporting for work. The guard did not know where the foreman got the permit. The SS man standing at the gate told us that we must not run away, because for each man who escaped he would shoot five other people from our group — and this was not an empty threat on their part. They were also capable of shooting ten men for one escapee, and I saw that [happen] more than once. The SS man also told us: "Make sure that they are satisfied with your work because you are going to work for the army."

Then he ordered us to move to one side and wait...wait and wait, until a soldier came to take charge of us. Soon a military truck drove up. We were told to climb into the truck, and were driven to the Czerniowice train station. There, at the main rail station, all [sorts of] merchandise was arriving. One of the men in our group happened to work for the firm earlier, when he still had a "W" card. He was caught at the gate on the same day that I was and had been sent to jail even though his "W" card was genuine. In jail, he was told that his "W" card was a fake. So when the soldier told us that we were going to the company where he used to work, this man on the truck began to dance for joy. He hugged and kissed everybody. Imagine: he had worked for them for a long time, and had done very well.

When we arrived at the train station we were put to work carrying boxes of coal from near the main railway station to the coal warehouse. Once I had left the camp and I found myself in the street, I began to work. I was happy. I saw human beings around me. I stopped being so cautious because now I was in a new world.

On the first day, we received food from the military kitchen. The food was quite different from what we were fed in camp. In camp, the food consisted of unpeeled potatoes and water. The cooks would cook the meat and flour for themselves. (But we did not lack bread or butter at work.)

The company was a military one; it was called the "First Aid Station for the Wounded." During the Battle of Stalingrad, when the trains came from the front loaded with wounded, the Red Cross unloaded the wounded and we did the rest. We removed the linen covers from the straw and the ovens, and folded the blankets. The blankets and linen sheets were taken on a truck to the assembly warehouse, and the straw cover was deloused. Under the straw coverings we found full and partly-filled cans of preserves and whole and half loaves of bread. We also used to buy cans of preserves, bread, sausage and anything else they had to sell from the Red Cross soldiers. We would take whole sacks of foodstuff back to the camp and sell it. We also would find socks, watches, pocket knives and straight razors.

I found Santshe Grinberg, [who was] working in the ghetto. Every day, he took things to Zlateh for me: We would find whole boxes of candy and I sent them to Zlateh's children, [along] with bread, cans of preserves, butter. Everyone was astonished, because most people were sending packages from the ghetto to the camp, whereas I was sending the same kinds of packages from the camp to the ghetto. I was glad to be able to help my sister and her children, [and in this way], she did not lack any food.

We also loaded wounded soldiers into freight cars bound for Germany. Before they left the station we outfitted each car with boxes of firewood and coal. All of us had a song ready for each train car: "Maybe you have a piece of bread?" [The soldiers] responded in various ways: some gave us a whole loaf of bread, some a piece of bread and some nothing at all. We carried bread-bags and tried to pack everything into them. Sometimes we wore sweaters or short fur jackets [and stuffed goods inside]. Then we sold the foodstuff in the camp. People like me, who went into town to work, did not go short of any food. Occasionally, we would take blankets and sell them for almost nothing, so that others could make a living, too. We were not short of money.

For a few days there were only twenty men in our group. Later, more and more wounded arrived, and ten other men were added. There had been an *Aktion* in Greiding, and a few men were brought to Lemberg. Ten men from that group were assigned to us. However, on the very first day, four men escaped. We were horribly frightened. We were afraid that as a punishment for the escape of the four, we would all be shot. We walked around, terrified to return to the camp. This took place while the ghetto still existed. The soldiers were angry and ordered us to get into the truck. They were responsible for us and had to return us to the camp. We asked them not to report the four escapees when we got back to the camp. Workers were not counted when they returned from work. The work foreman had a friend in the office, a Jew. (All the people who worked there were Jews.) He told him that four people were missing, and his friend gave him advice. Since men were being brought from an *Aktion* into the ghetto, [he told the foreman to] take four of these men. In the morning we walked together with these four strangers.

We let two men go home, a father and his son, and replaced them with young lads from the ghetto, volunteers who no longer had anyone and no place to hide. They were afraid that if they were caught in an *Aktion* they would be taken directly to the sands. Here, at least, they were in the camp and in a good workplace. There were many volunteers of this sort. But when those four men escaped it was impossible to enter the ghetto, because it was late at night. In all the time that I worked in the camp and for the army, I did not go to the ghetto.

During those weeks, Mechel and Abish became sick with typhoid fever. The apartment they lived in was very cramped, and two people had the disease; Mechel and Abish caught it from them. This drove me crazy. I was constantly afraid that Zlateh might, God forbid, catch the disease. Mechel was taken to the Jewish hospital, and the child stayed home. I still could not enter the ghetto. Mechel and the child got better, and then Mechel came home. Two days later there was an *Aktion*, and all the people in the hospital were taken to the sands. Anyone found lying in bed in an apartment was shot right there.

Soon this work assignment ended and ten of us were assigned to Roker's canning factory, near the city limits. Every day the trolley came to the camp, and we would travel to the slaughterhouse, and from there we would enter the Roker factory. I was, as they say, green: I could not get anything done on the new job. However, I quickly grew accustomed to it. I began buying all kinds of things in the camp and selling them in the factory. I earned good money every day, sometimes 500 *złoty* or more.

These items came from *Aktions*. The people who worked in the stores brought these things into the camp and sold them there. One person brought a jacket, and another brought a pair of pants, a whole suit, women's garments, coats. It was very sad: all of this was Jewish property, and the owners had already been sent to the Next World.

While I worked for Roker, I went to the ghetto every Sunday to visit the children. Poor creatures, they counted the days until Sunday. I did not begrudge them anything. And every Sunday I left 500 *złoty* with Zlateh to live on. I would buy several loaves of bread and other things. All week long, I lived with the hope of seeing them on Sunday. I had a good suit made for myself, [a decent pair of] shoes, and dressed myself well. I also had food to eat in the factory. The cooks sold various items, so I was able to buy good pieces of meat.

I would send Zlateh foods with the people who worked with "W" [cards] and went to the ghetto every day. I would buy and send meat, butter and bread. Mechel was still working for the same company, so he went to the ghetto every day and was also able to bring home various supplies.

But the fear Zlateh and her children experienced every day cannot be described. Not one day went by without an uproar, fear and the need to hide. The children would hide in the wooden base of the bunk bed because Mechel had made a double base out of boards, creating a false bottom [where the boys could hide]. Zlateh and Elish slept on the lower level, while Mechel and Abish slept on the upper part of the bunk bed.

Some time later, a new ruffian called Zimek[20] appeared in the ghetto and created chaos. Once he burst into the house where Zlateh lived and caused a hideous panic. Little Elish leaped out of the window into the street. Unfortunately there was no one in the house next door, where he wanted to hide, and the door was locked. So he climbed back into his own home. They lived on the ground floor. Zlateh and the older boy were hiding in the basement. The small boy went inside the house, closed the door and hid in the double bottom of the bunk bed.

My dearest ones, I am going to end the story now because I think I may have to move out of here by tomorrow. I do not know when, or where to. They [the Strekers] are moving out and the new landlord will certainly want to check out the whole of the house, and will also climb into the attic.

I wish to emphasize once again that what the children lived through cannot be described. Things kept getting worse. The Christians informed on the Jews whom they were hiding, and they [the Jews] were all taken immediately to the sands.

Meanwhile Roker provided us with room and board. There was one good thing about this: we did not have to return to the camp every day and report or witness all the suffering. Neither did we have to walk through the camp gate and tremble with fear as we passed the SS men.

The company's quarters for us were on Zbojowska Street. Our rooms were furnished with iron spring beds. We lived with 32 men and a doctor. We were in a much better situation than all the people in the ghetto. We could go to sleep whenever we wanted to. By then it was springtime, and we were getting up very early. A few of us, friends, would go to work and come back from work earlier or later, not with the rest of the group.

20 The reference is apparently to *SS-Hauptsturmführer* Josef Grzimek, who succeeded Willhaus as camp commandant.

My trading days came to end, because we no longer went back to the camp — but it was all worth it not to have to see the faces of the SS men. Each day, twenty Jews from the camp would come to work with us. Some of them brought all kinds of items for sale, and I would stay around them because I had connections in the factory. From time to time a truck would arrive from Kaminke to pick up marmalade. At such times, I saw to it that I was not seen or recognized.

The work in Roker's [canning factory] was not easy. Fourteen men carried beets up to the second floor, with two men carrying each crate. They made marmalade out of the beets. The rest of the men carried bricks, mortar and planks. We worked very hard until four o'clock in the afternoon. The work was so hard that on some nights I could not straighten out my fingers — but after four o'clock we were free men.

Every Sunday we continued to visit the ghetto. I would prepare a package of bread, sausage, chicken fat, sometimes a chicken, and several liters of milk for Zlateh. In the ghetto a liter of milk cost 8-10 *złoty* or ½ a liter for 5 *złoty*. I would give Zlateh 1000 *złoty*, to get work permits so that she would not be afraid of the SS and the Sonderdienst. I would also buy cans of marmalade, weighing 12 kilo each from the factory, and take them the ghetto on Sundays. I would leave half of the cans with Zlateh, and would sell the other half. Since I paid 250 *złoty* for 10 kilo, it was possible to make 60 or [at least] 50 *złoty* on each 10 kilo in the ghetto. Every Sunday I would also buy 20 liters of gasoline. It was terrible to carry this heavy load, but I had friends who would help me with the carrying and I would pay them. If I brought 20 to 30 liters of gasoline into the ghetto, I paid 15 *złoty* or less and made 30 *złoty* or more. I would leave the merchandise with Zlateh and did not take any money from her. Zlateh sold it gradually during the course of the week. That was how we managed.

All our efforts, however, were in vain. Once again there were *Aktions* in the ghetto. Whole groups, hundreds of people in each one, were exterminated. Every day, people fell victim. No one was taken to the Bełżec concentration camp any longer. Instead, people were immediately shot to death in the camp and burned.

We shook with fear as new groups were taken from the camp barracks every day. We worked in extreme terror. After work we were afraid to go directly to our quarters. We wandered around in small groups until darkness fell. We did not sleep in peace as before. We shivered with dread every minute and every second.

When there were no more beets to be had, I switched to doing construction work. There, on the second floor, we had plenty of rope that we used to pull up roof-beams. If we saw something [happening], we would move to the other side of the factory, and lower ourselves to the first floor. On a few occasions the bandits dropped in on us, but we didn't even notice them. Our director, Ulier, saved us and earned 30,000 *złoty* [for doing it.]

Once, the camp truck, full of soldiers, came to Zbaweski Street, but they didn't come for us. They came to take people from another factory, but did not have the correct address, [so instead] they took all the women: Aunt Rivkele's Chana and her two daughters, and Sorele the daughter of bandy-legged Leah. They were working in Leather Factory Number 8.

Nossin, Leibish Grinberg's daughter Pepe, and Altkoren's sister-in-law were let go. The situation in the ghetto also worsened. Working people were being taken away: whole groups, half groups, ten people at a time, twenty people. At times, even more people were taken away. We sensed that the end was near. [Once again] trains were loaded for Bełżec.[21] Naked people jumped from the train taking them to their deaths, trying to escape, and returned to the ghetto they just recently left. Yosl Eisen was one of the train jumpers who went back to the ghetto. Chaneleh Eisen and Leytshe Barits were gone. They were taken from the Schwarz factory. Shloime Barits was gone, as well.

Every day, a few of us who had wives and sisters in the ghetto ran to see our loved ones — right up to the dawn of that horrible day, Wednesday. On Tuesday evening we went to the ghetto. I said goodbye to my only, dear sister and her two children. Little Abish, weeping, said to me: "Don't leave me!" Zlateh asked me if it was possible to carry Abish and Elish out of the ghetto in baskets. I could have taken them out, but what would I have done with them after that? My lovely sister told me that their graves would be ready by Thursday. It was true: the graves were ready on Thursday.

21 By this time, the Bełżec death camp was no longer functioning. During the liquidation of the ghetto, the Jews were sent to Janówska and other camps to be killed.

Oh God, why didn't I take them out of that fatal ghetto? Next month it will be a year since the day it happened. I think that Tuesday was June 2, 1943. I searched for the little boy [Abish]. I wanted to see him one more time, but I did not find him. I left my only sister in a living grave and the cruel beasts destroyed their lives. Could I have taken a woman and two children with me? Where would I have hidden them on the first night?

My heart had led me astray. I did not believe it was the end, that they had reached the end of their lives. Who would have expected it? I could at least have taken a good look at them. But I did not believe it. I thought that it was only a kind of scare, and that nothing would happen to them. She always used to yell at me: "Motenyu, save yourself! Don't look at me. I have two small children, and I must go with them. Save yourself."

And now she — my sister and those small innocent souls — are no longer here. I will never again see them, or hear the word Uncle from their sweet mouths. They were shot in such a way so that there would be no trace of the murderous deeds, and their sweet bodies were burned.

On Wednesday they lay hidden all day. It was not until Thursday that Zlateh was led away with both her children. Zlateh held little Elish in her arms, while Abish, barefoot, with no shoes, followed as he held his mother's hand.

Nossin [Hoyzler, a cousin], Chana[Stromer]'s husband, told me about all this. We both cried. She cried out to him: "Nossin!" I can imagine how the two souls yelled "Mama, Mama, I am afraid."

[Zlateh] always said she would have to go together with the children, and that is just what happened. Like a heroine, she walked the last road with her children and went to meet the murderers.

I hope to God that [the murderers] will pay for all the suffering of the Jewish people. They must have a terrible future, a terrible defeat. May God pay them for their acts of murder.

CHAPTER 18

[Untitled]

I want to keep this short. If God helps me, I will find myself in a place where I will be able to continue writing, although it is impossible to describe everything. I reckon that tomorrow, on Thursday, May 9, [1944] I will have to leave the nest. There is a possibility that I will try to slip into our house [in Kaminke] and perhaps find hidden property. I know the hiding place, but I am not sure whether my parents removed the property at the last minute or not.

[I was concerned] especially after the *Aktion* that took place on that Shabbos in Kaminke. I asked them [my parents] to make sure to join us in Lemberg, so that we could either live or die together, but I am not sure whether there is property there or not. [Besides] trying to get to our house would mean exposing myself to great danger. Just walking out into the street is risky.

On that Tuesday [June 1943], Mechel and Yosl [Eisen] left the ghetto with me. We were missing two workers who escaped to the ghetto a few days earlier, for they were afraid that they would be taken from their quarters. By the time we got to the little door, more than 28 men wanted to leave the ghetto with us. All of them had fake numbers and yellow patches. I gave Mechel a yellow patch, too. The others, like Mechel and Yosl, had nowhere to go. Secret agents and Ukrainian SS were standing around the [ghetto] fence. We walked briskly toward Balonowe Street, then along Panienska Street, and ran almost as far as the slaughterhouse. We asked the other people to separate from us, and some of them did. From the moment we left the ghetto gate, two secret agents followed us. Ekerling, a friend who had been with me in the Jewish prison, and shared sleeping quarters with me, recognized them.

When we split into two groups, the secret agents followed the other group. Our group was not a small one — there were thirteen people in it. Everybody brought along a friend, a brother-in-law, a brother, to fill only two possible slots. I also brought along two friends. A set group of people were coming from the camp, and we could not exceed the allowed number because we could be inspected at any time.

When our whole group arrived in Zbojesk, we were greeted by our foreman, a man named Goldstein, a former Polish railroad worker and his assistant, Bilewicz, a former director of the Okocime Brewery. Both had converted to Christianity while Poland was still independent. They began shouting [at us]: "You want to bring a disaster upon us!" and they were right. Meanwhile an uproar started among the Christians when they saw a bunch of strangers. They already knew us, more or less. We just could not cope with the situation. There was a small hideout [at the brewery], a basement, and for the time being, I pushed Mechel into it.

Yosl and about ten other men stayed near the ghetto gate. Now they screamed: "Take us away from the gate! Once we're away from it, we'll find somewhere to stay." In the meantime the foreman took two more people. The he went to the Roker factory and brought back the guardpost commander to disperse the crowd. The commander was, however, a very good young man — a Viennese. He understood the troubles of the unfortunate Jews, so he told them that if they wished, he would take them to the ghetto. It was already dark, the middle of the night. Yosl and two other men walked into the Bzochowice forest and then walked further. They wondered where to go from there. One needs a roof over one's head.

Yosl knew the way because he had been there once before — when he was taken to Bełżec. While on the train to Bełżec, Yosl and others used a knife to cut a plank out of the floor of the railroad car and lowered themselves to the tracks between the wheels. Once out of the train, they returned to the ghetto.

The next day I took Mechel with me to the factory and arranged a job for him [as a painter]. Meanwhile the director wanted to help several children with special pull, among them the sons of Lislipl and Kotlarski, who worked in the factory. Once, the director gave the foreman a letter they could show to inspectors to protect the three new workers,

In the ghetto, life was becoming hideous. Houses were burned with the people inside them, until the last Jewish soul was gone. A few days later, at dawn, Yosl returned. He hid in the outhouse. One of our men went to the toilet very early in the morning and found Yosl hiding there. Yosl asked the man to tell me where he was.

I hurriedly got out of bed, and took Yosl down into the basement where Mechel had been hiding. Yosl stayed in that basement for the next 25 days. He was glad to have even that one little basement, because he had been beaten by a Ukrainian gang on the way [from the forest] and everything had been taken from him. After he had been in the basement for eight days, two youths who had also started out on the road came back. One of them had a brother among us. We hid them in the basement too, and every night, when everyone was asleep, I would hand food and drink down to the men. I also provided them with a small shovel, and they dug another hole in the basement to hide in. After 25 days, very few people knew about the people hiding in the basement. The foreman or his assistant didn't know about it.

One person in our group died. Then the foreman found out about the hidden men because Schupo people and Ukrainian police burst in to conduct a search. We were all at work at the time, and the men in the basement were not discovered. I realized, however, that the men would be better off above ground than hiding in the basement. Meanwhile the two friends [that we hid with Yosl] had good pistols with them and decided they would not be taken alive.

There were 55 of us in our quarters. If, by chance, an unauthorized person were to be caught in our quarters, all 55 of us would be shot. I bribed the director with a thousand *złoty*, and Yosl worked in the factory as a glazier, but the arrangement did not last long.

There was no one left alive in the ghetto. Jews from the camp went into the ghetto to clean it up. With their own hands they gathered human livers, intestines, arms and legs. They searched all the hideouts [and blew them up] with grenades and then burned everything, including the bodies of all those who had poisoned themselves — hundreds of people carried cyanide. The wife of one of the men in our group hid in a hideout. When she came out to say goodbye to her husband and their 13-year-old son in the ghetto, she was shot.

When Yosl went to work on that first day, he told me that one day [of life] was worth any amount of money. I know, today, what freedom means. But I would be willing to settle for being arrested, if only I can survive the war.

After the liquidation of the ghetto, Mechel walked around like a man without a head. He did not eat or drink. He was like a lunatic, which was no surprise. In the course of a single day, he ceased to be a father and a husband. We had $92. I gave him $42, and hid $50 for myself.

One day Mechel was sent to Jagiellonska Street on a chore for the director of the company, who owned a business in that neighborhood. On the way home, Mechel and the Christian escorting him were arrested and taken to the police station on Podzamcze Street, and his $42 was taken away. They wanted to send him directly to the sands, but the [Christian] worker returned to the factory and went to see the director immediately. The director happened to be away, so when he [the Christian] saw the [factory] engineer, he told him about Mechel, [and the engineer went to get the director] — who did not yet know about the dollars. He liked dollars — but only golden ones. The director rescued Mechel [anyway] and drove him away in his car.

We were in that factory for six weeks, from June 2 until July 15, 1943. Then suddenly, on Thursday, at seven o'clock in the evening, two trucks and a light half truck drove up, and [the people in them] surrounded the whole building. There were at least ten guards with them. Mechel, Yosl, a man named Shatan and I were sitting together in our apartment, when I looked out the window and saw our people suddenly begin to run. I quickly stepped outside, and saw SS men from the camp, with machine guns in their hands. They were shouting "Hands up" in German and they were shooting into the air.

I recognized Schoenbach, that bandit from the camp, who was familiar to me. Without thinking twice, I jumped down into the basement. Shatan wanted to jump after me, but I told him: "You know that we all have pistols, and if we meet them we'll shoot on the spot." Only then did Shatan cover the opening with a box. I pushed myself into the second hole, because the small basement already held the two men and one of their brothers, a man named Welger or Weiss, the son of a wine merchant. They unplugged the hole that was covered with straw, and let me in. Soon an SS man came down to the basement and conducted a search, but he did not have a flashlight. He groped [around], right next to my hand, but he did not detect me. Then he left.

It was horribly cramped, but I calmed the [men] by telling them: "Just a little longer!"

The [Germans] allowed the whole group to go back into the apartments to collect their belongings. We heard the sound of their feet. Meanwhile the commander asked — and I heard him because the entrance to the basement was open — if anyone was hiding [in the basement]. It seems he was asking the man who had already made a search, [and he] answered: "No."

Until we heard that, our souls almost left our bodies. Soon the whole bunch of them boarded the trucks and left. I quickly went up to the attic where I had hidden my pistol. I was lucky they left me a pair of slippers — everything else had been taken. I found an old hat that I took with me, and held on to a tattered vest, because the only clothes I had were a pair of pants and a shirt. I put the clothes on and went back down to the basement. There I waited until dark, so the four of us could leave. We all had guns.

Meanwhile a soldier, accompanied by two Polish men, came from the factory. They were supposed to watch the apartment. They searched the rooms and then left, leaving one man, a Ukrainian, on guard. Later another man arrived, a village watchman, a Ukrainian — a civilian bandit who used to cause trouble at night on Zbojesk Street; and there was another man, called Gerczok, who used to work with us in the factory and who lived on Zbojesk Street.

The night watchman began searching in all the corners, pointing his flashlight to illuminate them. And he spotted me! When he saw me he let out a dreadful holler: "You Jew, you've hidden yourself!" I shuddered. Zbojesk Street had a Ukrainian police station where they could have finished me off in a few minutes. I started pleading with him, but he began to shout very loudly, pulling me along with him.

At that moment, I sprang out of the basement, went to Gerczok and begged him to rescue me. The other man said that he was not doing anything to me. With all my strength I wrenched myself out of the bandit's hands, jumped off the porch, and ran into the fields. The [Ukranian] ran after me, yelling "Grab him, the Jew!" and called me other names. I ran for some distance and then fell. Realizing that I would not be rid of him, I pulled out my gun. As luck would have it there was no bullet in my firing chamber — and the man did not shoot.

He continued to chase me, but it was getting dark and I was able to escape through the meadow. I could still hear his voice, and kept running for quite a distance, until I felt it would be safe enough to rest for a while among the [fields of] grain.

After I rested in the rye for a while, I continued on my way. I don't know what happened to my friends, whether they ran away or whether they stayed behind. Nor do I know what happened to Mechel, Yosl and my other friends.

I walked toward Kaminke, bypassing the Jewish police station, now manned by Ukrainian police. I also avoided Remenow. I jumped over two streams. At dawn on Friday I came to a small forest near Zwertiw, where I hid among the bushes and rested. Later, I crawled into a rye field where I let the sun dry me off. I was wet from having to swim across [a river]. I rested until five o'clock in the afternoon.

Then I saw someone walking and came out to meet him. I was dreadfully hungry. The last time I had eaten was Thursday morning because I didn't feel like eating lunch that day — that was the same day we learned that the hiding place on Pogodna Street was no more. We'd sent the assistant director of the Roker factory there, but it was empty. The only people who could take things out of there were people who lived there.

The man I saw walking said he didn't have even a small piece of bread with him. I spoke Ukrainian to him. I found out from him where the road led, and I started walking. At first I thought I would go to the Warszawskis, but I changed my mind. I decided it was not right for an acquaintance to see me after such a long separation. Moreover, he might talk to someone in Kaminke, and that would cause trouble for me later.

It wasn't long before I passed by his place and continued along the main road. I stopped at a ditch and drank some water. Then I walked on in the [moonlit] night. When I reached Sabiszana, I turned off near the mill, where the railroad runs to Sokal. From there, I walked for a stretch until I reached Jagonia, where I turned off, into the suburb of Belz.

I went into Olnicki's courtyard, knocked on the door and called out for Heranka. A dog barked furiously and they switched on the electric light. He [Heranka] looked out the window and did nothing! They did not let me into their home, though they surely recognized me. In the meantime, Razdewinska woke up and raised an alarm. Prokopowicz, and his son Jendroch, went outside to see what was happening. At first I hid in a small room at Olnicki's, but I realized at once it was a bad idea.

I saw some people walking, and one of them held a flashlight in his hand. I quickly went outside, jumped over the fence, and crossed the fields to Jagonia. Day was beginning to break. I planned to stop at Sztopl's, but I was not sure where he lived. Realizing that I was near Józef Streker's house, I went and knocked on his window. He opened the door and came out.

At first Streker did not recognize me. After my recent experiences, that wasn't surprising. He invited me into the house, and when I asked for a drink gave me milk and bread. Then I asked if I could rest for a while and asked for something to cover me. They gave me a big coat. Then I asked the Strekers not to tell anyone, including their children, about my visit. There were only three people in the house: the man, his wife and his daughter. One son was serving in the Sonderdienst. Another son was married and lived apart from his parents. Their married daughter also lived somewhere else.

The Strekers brought me food twice a day, every day. While I was under their roof I did not, God forbid, suffer from hunger. After seven months they told their younger daughter I was hiding in their house. She recognized me at once, and so here I am.

I have been hiding in the attic for ten months. When I first arrived, the Strekers would ask me to come down on Sundays so I could shave and wash myself. A few months later, when it became extremely cold, I would come down every day and stay for half an hour, and sometimes for a whole hour.

What I want now is to hold on to this attic until the end of the war. But [Streker] is loading a wagon, and leaving this place now is far more difficult than it was when I first arrived. There are [German] army units in every village now, and they [the Strekers] are afraid of the partisans. God alone knows what I will do. I have no opportunity to speak to Streker. Yesterday, his daughter and her husband left. May God help me to get out of this tragic situation, and put me on the correct path.

I do not even have anything to wear. Meanwhile it is very cold, and it has been raining all day. Tomorrow is Tuesday [May 9]. I believe that Tuesday is a good day, an easy day. Maybe the best place [for me] to go is Riznik's. He lives in our house [in Kaminke], but I am very afraid of the Ukrainians.

I am not finishing the chapter. It happens to be the 18th. God willing, it will be *Chai* [the numerical value of this word's letters add up to 18, meaning life.]

Mordche Stromer, May 8, 1944.

It is Wednesday evening. I have yet to see the Strekers. They finished loading everything onto the wagon and are leaving tomorrow. I remain stranded. May God help me!

During the whole time I have been here, Thursdays have been unlucky days. Not, God forbid, every Thursday, but several. Now it is also the day on which I fast. However, nothing has actually happened as a result. May God help me now, so that when I leave this place I will not, God forbid, encounter any obstacles

Mordche Stromer,
Wednesday, May 10

I was ready to write about the whole family, about all our friends and acquaintances. However, I must break off for the time being. It is possible that once I am in a new place, I will continue to write about them.

Mordche

[Editor's note: The list of people to be remembered has been consolidated and moved nearer the end.]

May 21, 1944

Thank God, I am in the same place and in the same attic. So far, I am writing in the same place I have been writing in until now. May God help me to survive all this without any hindrance. I have been utterly devastated because the Poles are moving away from here; but is there anything I can do about it? I hope that God will not abandon me.

Streker moved to Krakow with his wife and daughter. The house was supposed to be left to someone called Szczor. But God helped, and Streker's sister stayed on. Like her brother, she is a *Volksdeutsche*. Her husband, though, is a Ukrainian, so she and her husband remained. All this happened at the last minute on Thursday, May 11.

[I was so worried], I did not sleep at all on the night between Wednesday and Thursday. Very early in the morning I was waiting to see Streker. His sister was in the apartment. He called me down from my place and took me to his sister. I know them. He'd already told his sister about me and she agreed to hide me, but with great fear. However, she was not willing, for any money, to let her husband know I was staying in the house.

Imagine my situation! Is it possible to stay in an attic without the proprietor knowing about it? The situation would be different if the attic had a hiding place, at least. The attic is completely empty, except for some straw. I asked that the husband be told about me, but his wife won't consider it. I have no alternative. I have no other place. That Thursday, I wept bitterly all day long.

The Strekers left in the afternoon, and I stayed behind. On Thursday, just as on every Thursday, I fasted. Early on Friday morning the new landlady brought me food. I was hidden under the straw. On Sunday she visited her old home on Zaborze Street, [and while she was gone] her husband lit a lamp and came up to the attic. He visited the attic three times, searching in all the corners.

And God helped — he did not see me.

You should know that there were German soldiers downstairs, soldiers from the front. If the husband would see something and go downstairs to raise an alarm, I would have been shot at once.

When his wife came home I told her [what happened], and we agreed the situation was impossible, since her husband did not know I was there. We agreed that on Monday she would go to town to take care of some business, and that when she returned home she would tell him she'd met me. Then, on Tuesday, I would come to visit. She would tell her husband that I had been hiding in his brother-in-law's house, and that he should not worry.

On Tuesday at daybreak I went downstairs. He was still asleep, [and when he got up] I met him. I did not know him from Adam, as the saying goes. Under Polish rule, he'd been sentenced to prison for several years for committing a murder. But everything will be fine if he agrees to keep me. He is terribly afraid.

Then his younger brother, who was helping him work in the fields, showed up, and God forbid, he finds out I am here. Meanwhile we agreed that we would wait for Streker, who was supposed to come by any day now. It is possible that he will resolve the difficulty.

May God help me! The worst thing is that I do not have any money. However, I hope that God will not abandon me. I have had a dream about my saintly, holy, dead grandmother, and she comforted me, saying that she would watch over me just as she did when she was alive. I have had dreams on more than one occasion, but when my saintly grandmother appears to me in a dream, I am certain that no harm will befall me. God help me and protect me in all my ways!

[Editor's note: The following section has been consolidated from other parts of the diary]

Continuation about Hitler's murders and our close family. First of all, I will provide information about members of the Stromer family according to age:

I want to provide a very brief account of what has happened to our nearest family:

Our dear father and mother were taken away during the very last *Aktion* in Kaminke, and taken to Bełżec.

Uncle Chaim-Hersh and our late grandfather were both murdered on the first Wednesday in the store next to the bath house. His daughter from Kaminke, Rochel, had a young daughter who was taken to Bełżec in the first *Aktion*. Later on, I believe, all of them were shot at Zabode.

Our grandfather and aunt from Narajew died. They did not have any medications, and Jews could not travel from one place to another. They were "lucky" in one way: they died in their own beds. I would send them one-kilo packages of sugar, medications, and money, by mail, from Lemberg. But I do not know whether the packages were ever delivered to them.

I do not know what happened to Mechel and his brother Yosl — whether they were shot on the spot or were left in the camp. A few weeks later, [Streker's son] who was in the *Sonderdienst*, wrote that on that day [i.e. the day when he wrote] they had shot all the people in the camp.

Kver was the first to die. Izzy was murdered on Damarstinowska Street while under military arrest; the body was brought home in a sack and set down near the door. Monye was [murdered] on the first Tuesday, when the Germans had just entered Lemberg. They left him there, naked. Later, in an *Aktion* before the one in August [1942], the uncle and aunt, and then in one day, Monye and Klare [Vilek's wife] together with her little boy [were shot]. The SS carried out a special *Aktion* against the workers who were employed by the SS; Monye worked for them, and Klare was supported by him. They were shot in Lemberg, on the sands. Vilek was in the camp.

[Chaim-Hersh's] daughter in Lemberg, Eti-Gitele, who lived in Zlateh's house with her husband and their two children, were taken away in the August *Aktion*. At the time, they were dying of hunger, and Eti was swollen. Zlateh used to help her a little bit, but they [Eti's family] consisted of seven people. One boy was taken out of the factory and driven to Bełżec. The fourth son was caught and taken to the Winiki camp, and murdered there.

[Eti] was left with just one [son], Hertzl, a tailor. On one occasion he took a small piece of leather from the shoe factory. At the end, when we lived on Ordona Street, she was not doing badly. She had food to eat, as she herself used to say. But when she had food to eat, as she said, there was no one there to eat it, and when someone was there to eat, there wasn't any food.

[In the factory,] Hertzl was caught with a pair of [leather] soles and was later hanged in the Janow[ska] camp. I was there when, by chance, I saw him imploring them to spare his life. They responded by beating him even more.

There is a whole story about this incident. However, it is enough to say that when Hertzl was caught in the factory, he managed to escape. The ghetto was still in existence at that time, and he went there. He was caught with another Jewish tailor, who was immediately hanged in the factory. As for Hertzl, who escaped, Wilhaus, the Janow[ska] camp commandant, ordered 25 Jewish policemen to bring him back by seven o'clock the next morning, or all 25 of them would be hanged.

Zlateh let Hertzl hide in her apartment, but in the end he was captured and hanged. Eti-Gitele remained all alone. [I am sure she died] at the same time as my dear sister and her children. Uncle Chaim-Hersh had another daughter in Lemberg. Her husband died of natural causes, but she and her daughter and her sons-in-law were deported.

Uncle Meyer-Leibish Stromer and his wife, Aunt Basye, were deported from Kaminke to Bełżec. The eldest son, Shloime, [husband] of his daughter Bintshe Gever from Kaminke, was taken away. As I mentioned earlier, her husband escaped with me and was murdered in cold blood in Lemberg. Bintshe and the two girls were able to hide in Kaminke during the whole of the last *Aktion*. Then they left the hideout and tried to escape to the ghetto in Lemberg. The militia shot them in either Remenow or Zoltanec.

Uncle Meyer-Leibish's daughter Shaindele was taken away in the August [1942] *Aktion*, when she was in the camp with Zlateh. Later on, her husband Shaul, and their three children, went through very difficult times until they were all murdered. His son, Moishe, and his wife Pinah were deported in the August *Aktion*. Another son, Shaya, and his wife and children were deported. His son Herman and his [grandson] Kobe worked at a construction site, carrying bricks. Herman was deported in the first *Aktion*, and Kobe became a Jewish policeman.

From the police force, Kobe was taken to the camp, where he was certainly murdered. His sister Lusia worked as a nurse in the Jewish hospital in the ghetto and later worked in the camp hospital. She surely met her end when all the Jews in the camp were shot. Salke, Herman's wife, would stand in the ghetto streets with her mother and sister selling *pletslekh* [flat cookies]. In an *Aktion* in the winter of 1942, they were deported to Bełżec.

On the Friday of the August *Aktion* [1941], Uncle Yude[l] Stromer, his wife and his daughter Dina Apfel were with Zlateh in the camp. Whoever knew Uncle Yudel always saw him with a beard. Poor fellow, [he was forced to shave it off] and we were all disconcerted to see him without it. Until the end, he and his two daughters worked at the leather works. The factory, LPG, employed hundreds of Jewish workers, and the German director helped his workers quite a lot, but in the end all of them died. No one was left alive, not the daughters, not the son, not the daughter-in-law, not the sons-in-law.

I have already written about the daughter of Uncle Yudel's oldest daughter, whose children were raped on Dnieszenia Street. When we arrived in the ghetto, she, her husband and children were no longer alive. The other continued to suffer for some time.

I do not know what happened to Uncle Shmuel from Greiding, nor do I know what happened to the family of my dear brother-in-law [Zalman] Edelstein from Strelisk.

This is what happened to the children of our late Uncle Yankel: Mirtshe and all her children were gradually murdered in Kaminke and Lemberg. The first to be murdered in Kaminke was her son-in-law, Pantshe's husband, Avramtshe Shprotser. He had been in a Soviet prison, and came home one Tuesday. On Wednesday he was murdered. Pantshe, [who was with] one of their daughters, was shot on Zaboda Street. The child was thrown alive into a ditch. Her [other] son and daughter would roam through the streets of the ghetto, begging. Dania and her husband and her children, Gusta and Baila, and her husband and children, are not alive any more.

Taube, Abe, Mirel and her husband and three children, Sorele who married Palpe Dikes: all of them died in Kaminke. Zelig was a political prisoner under the Soviets and did not return from prison. Zlateh Abes's children, together with Taube, and Mirel with her children, were all taken out of the hideout and shot on Zaboda Street. Mirel had a small child in the hideout. While a search was being conducted overhead, the child began to cry, so its small mouth had to be kept closed, and the child suffocated. There were many people in the hideout. I was told that our saintly mother asked to be allowed to enter the hideout, but was turned down.

This happened during the very last *Aktion* in Kaminke, when the town was made *Judenrein*. Zlateh Abes stayed alive until the end, working as a ghetto cleaner, and was shot near the ancient cemetery.

The late Chaim Itshe's wife and all their children, two of them in Kaminke and the rest in Lemberg, are all dead, except for the one who is in Palestine. Their youngest son would wander through the ghetto, just like Pantshe's son, selling cigars. I would meet the boys and give them a few *złoty*. Moteh Mendl and his wife and children were swollen from hunger. His oldest son died of hunger. Not one of them is still alive. I do not know what happened to the lame Leah. However, her children, Tsalke with his family, and Sorele, are not among the living.

Chana and her husband Nossin Hoyzler were the last to see our poor dear sister with her children being led to the place of murder. They were taken from the factory to the sands. Nossin and one of his sons, and the son of lame Leah, remained alive in the camp, but they certainly died when the camp was liquidated.

The following people were taken to the sands from the factory: Chana, Sorele and Chana's two daughters. This took place when the Germans were already liquidating the ghetto.

I could tell various stories about each person; but this is not the right place, the state of mind or the time. I hope that I will live through these terrible days. I think that at any moment the Soviets will arrive, knock, and my door will open, and I will be able to see the sun. May God help me, and may I live to the day when I can see my dear, only brother.

If I were to write everything down — it is horrible! I recollect the time when I was returning to work from the camp, and I saw Jews being brought to the camp from the Christian quarter. There were a few women among them. One of them had two small children, little girls, nice twins. As soon as the people had been taken off the trucks, the SS camp-murderers went up to them and began to beat them, screaming: "You are Aryans!" It seemed that there was some reason why they were hiding in the [Christian] quarter.

Suddenly, one of the SS men spotted the mother with the two girls, who were beautifully dressed. He grabbed one child, called to another bandit, and tossed the child in the air while the other bandit shot the child with a machine gun. She [the mother] fell to the ground in a faint. They did the same thing with the second child, but this time the two SS men switched roles. The second one threw the child [in the air] and the first one shot her. Both of the girls fell to the ground, pierced through with several bullets. The children were about two years old. The whole episode lasted about ten minutes. This was done in front of all the camp Jews, so that they could all see it.

Do you think that anyone from that group was left alive? Part of the group was lying naked, piled in a heap, shot to death next to the kitchen. I saw with my own eyes how a camp SS man named Bittner held a baby by one of its small legs, and slammed its body against the frozen snow until the baby's head was smashed. On the same day, the same SS man shot eleven camp workers who were waiting to exchange their shoes. It is better not to talk about things like that.

The Eisen Family: Shaindel Eisen, my brother-in-law's mother, was with Zlateh in the Janow[ska] camp on that memorable Friday. As I mentioned earlier, she was hidden for some time in the attic of Esther's apartment on Marczina Street. I do not remember whether the number of the building was 40 or 41. In the same courtyard, across from Dworowska Street, there was a blacksmith's workshop. I clearly remember the location, because I am sure that one of the sons [Levy] lives in Palestine. He may want to see the place in the future.

The elderly Eisen, who always held on to her *Korban Mincha* prayer book, poor woman, suffered a lot. During her lifetime, Esther and both her children were taken away, her daughter Chaneleh died, Rochel with the two smallest children were taken away, Yosl's child was taken away. Yosl and Hersh-Leib were in the camp. I will not write again here about all the troubles which the elderly mother had lived through. It is enough to mention that the place where they were hiding was discovered. Someone said that it was the blacksmith who informed on them, while someone else reported that the landlady did it. When the group of bandits entered the courtyard, they had no ladder to climb up to the attic. They started shooting, and at that point the ladder was lowered from the attic. The bandits climbed up, and ordered everybody in the attic to jump down.

The oldest daughter, Rochele and her two children, were taken away in the August *Aktion*. At that time, Hersh-Leib found his way into the camp as a glazier. Later on he escaped and worked at a job outside the ghetto. When the ghetto was liquidated, he and his son Motek and his young daughter Sima, who were hiding with him, were all taken away.

All this happened at the very end. His two older daughters, Chana and Feyge, who saved Zlateh's children from the ghetto, were working in the Schwarz factory during this whole time. When Schwarz's Jewish workers were liquidated, the two girls — because they were girls — entered the women's camp as seamstresses. They remained in that unit until the entire labor camp was liquidated. That meant all of the workers, male and female, were shot.

My landlady's [Streker's] son wrote to his mother: "Today we shot all the Jews of Lemberg in the Janow camp."

He was in the *Sonderdienst* in Lemberg. I mentioned this before; however, I want to repeat it because I read his letter. He began his letter with the words of a religious Christian:

"Let us praise Jesus Christ.

"Dear Parents,

"Today we shot all the Jews of Lemberg in the Janow camp, men and women. The young women walked to their death with their heads held high, singing Yiddish and Zionist songs. (The landlady's son [understood] Yiddish well because the lame Hersh Driker taught him how to be a tailor in his workshop.) *Some of the Jewish men had revolvers in their pockets, and they shot seven comrades from our Sonderdienst unit."*

These are his words. I am citing them because I do not want you to think that the Jews were afraid to die. On many occasions they hurled themselves [on the enemy]. But it was not noticed. I believe that at the time when the camp was liquidated, Mechel, his brother-in-law Yosl from Dorosziv, Yosele, Klare's husband Vilek, and some of my other friends were killed.

This is the tragedy of the Hersh-Leib Strassler family.

Yosl Eisen's wife, Chaneleh, was taken away from her job in the Schwarz factory. His only child, Renye, was taken away in the August *Aktion*. Yosl found his way into the camp during the big August *Aktion* and then escaped from the camp. He was caught again in an *Aktion*, and loaded onto a train that was going to Bełżec. People were being loaded naked onto the train, and the camp Jews were closing the doors of the train cars. At that moment one of them threw a knife into the car. Later on, the knife was used to cut a wooden plank out of the floor. And so, near Rawa Ruska, he [Yosl] escaped from the [moving] train, and fled naked to Lemberg.

Eight days later, in the last *Aktion,* he left the ghetto with me, as I mentioned earlier. Then he had to leave the place where I was staying. The Ukrainians caught him, beat him mercilessy and took his money. Later he returned to me and stayed lying in our hiding place for 25 days. He was later deported together with all my other friends and Mechel.

Mechel Eisen. I have no idea what happened to my brother-in-law. Seeing that I have already committed to writing everything that there is to say about my sister, what remains to be added is that she died as a real Jewish heroine with both her children on June 4, 1943 [the first day of Sivan] in the Janow camp. The victims were cremated, while the children were thrown alive into a burning fire. Not all the adults were shot to death. Some slightly wounded victims were thrown alive into the burning fire.

Esther Eisen, or Krantzler/Katz: she was deported with her little daughter, in the first days of the August *Aktion*. Later, also in August, her little son Abele was hustled onto the truck together with Renye — they were holding hands. A few months later, her husband Chaim Krantzler/Katz was captured in an *Aktion*. He had a lot of trouble. We had been neighbors when we lived on Ordona Street. Zlateh was always giving him food to eat. When Esther was still alive, she would make sure they got by. She would buy a can of oil or benzine to sell and look for a penny, enough to buy a piece of bread. The children would eat with the elderly Mrs. Eisen food sent one day by Zlateh and the next day by Chaneleh from Dorosziv.

More than once, our Abish carried the little basket of food to his grandmother. He was afraid of the Christian children, but my sister used to persuade him: "Abish, go to Grandma. Nothing, God forbid, will happen to you." When we lived on Bilinkiewicka Street, we were not far from Grandma's apartment. Esther and [Shaindel] her mother lived on Kardinal Trojmbe Street. The elderly Eisen was asked to stay with us or with Yosl, but she did not want to, and she could not leave Esther with the two children.

August, or the Jewish month of Av, have been the worst months for Jews throughout their history; and during the Hitler period this month was especially distinguished.

Chana Eisen, or Pardes, died. Her husband Shaya, a terrible egoist, played a major role in her death. He did not want to rescue her. His son Mondze was deported in the August *Aktion*. I remember that when we lived on Bilinkewicka Street, my brother-in-law [Mechel] would have a minyan every morning and evening, and that he [Shaya] with his little son Mondze would come and say *kaddish* [for her]. It made one's heart sore.

Later, Shaya moved in with his [Shaya's] mother and sister. And when the women were deported with the children, Shaya was left all alone. He was probably killed in the last *Aktion*, when Lemberg was made *Judenrein*.

The Yosl Haberkorn Family: I have no idea what happened to Yosl and his son Lonek. At the time, we were living in the company quarters supplied by the Roker factory. When there were no Jews left in the ghetto, Mechel and I inquired whether they [Yosl and Lonek] were still alive. We were told that they were alive and hiding somewhere. It is possible that at the last minute they removed the hidden items from the small attic, and in this way saved their lives. It would be wonderful if it was true.

Sheyve was killed that Friday, during the month of Av. According to what Zlateh told me, when she returned from the camp, Sheyve was not taken to Bełżec because she could barely get out of bed and could not stand on her own feet. Pepe was also deported in August. As I said earlier, such pearls are not born every day; she was a dear, saintly Jewish soul.

Shloime Barits's Family: Shloime hid all his property, except for a few items. He suffered a good deal during the German occupation, so much so, that he was forced to sell candy and lipstick to his co-workers, where he worked as a furrier in the LPG fur factory on Zborowski Street. From there, he was taken to Bełżec. Leytshe, his wife, worked for Schwarz and she, too, was taken away from her workplace. I do not know what happened to their parents in Zloczów. However, as long as Jews were able to write, they corresponded with us. Later on, Jews were not allowed to write letters. Their fate was no different from that of the other Jews under Hitler.

I know that Shloime had property in the stable where Leytshe's parents lived. If it is still there, it has surely rotted away by now. I also know that Leytshe's older brother was in Zloczów, staying with an engineer named Diner. And another [brother], Avrom, worked at his profession as a dental technician. I believe he ran his own workshop.

Shloime's parents, his father Chaim-Wolf Barits and Sheyve were taken away on Friday. His mother — Chana was her name — was killed earlier than her husband; I have already written about this. They always hoped to live long enough to see their children: one son, Shmuel, was in Argentina, and another son, Neshe's husband Moishe, was in London. Shloime had one sister in Zloczów. She, her husband and children were exterminated.

Because I know that Moishe Hochberg from Dorosziv was in the Soviet army and may return, I want to write for him about his close family:

Hochberg from Dorosziv: Moishe Hochberg's parents were deported in the August *Aktion*. They were hiding and were driven out because it had become too cramped in that hideout. I remember how, during the month of Av, those unfortunate people ran [for their lives] between four and five o'clock in the early morning of a holy Shabbos.

They ran as if crazed, trying to hide in the fields among the sheaves. But it happened that on that Saturday, Christians saw them lying in the field and informed on them. They were taken away.

The following experienced tragedy: Yosl Eisen, their son-in-law, Renye, their only grandson Yosele, their son and their daughter Etele — all were deported. Yosl Eisen, Yosl Hochberg and Etele were all working on Dnieszenia Street, in the Lona coffee factory, and were taken away from there. Etele was taken to Bełżec. Yosl Eisen, meanwhile, entered the Janow camp, and Yosl Hochberg was taken to the camp in Wielki Most. Eventually he, too, was brought to the Janow camp in Lemberg.

Yosl's [Hochberg] wife was taken away at the same time as Zlateh, on that Friday. She had a tiny baby boy. She wanted to save herself and the child, so she proposed to the SS man that if he left them alone, she would give him her possessions. The SS man went home with her and took her possessions — along with her and the baby. When they were all brought by car to Podzamcze, a man came and shouted: "Where is the Jewish lady who gave me gold and foreign currency? I want to let her go home." However, there were thousands of people at the collection point at Podzamcze, and she was lost in the crowd.

Moishe Hochberg's wife always carried packages for the community. She had one brother in the Korowic camp. I do not know what happened to her.

Today is Wednesday, May 24. Tomorrow, Thursday, I will fast. My former landlord's [Streker's] sister hands up food to me twice a day. It is hard to get used to her food. My former landlady was a well-to-do woman and was better able [than this one] to cook something. This one is poor and has nothing to cook. I would be willing to accept one dry potato if only I could be sure of this place.

Meanwhile, she told me today that the army is supposed to be leaving tomorrow, and they are afraid that they [the army] will set fire to the village;

but I hope to God that nothing, God forbid, will happen, because all bad things which happen on Thursday[s] must turn to good. Today I wanted to give her five dollars. In the meantime I am holding on. If I live until Friday I will give her the money. Meanwhile, tomorrow, I will not see her, but I will on Friday morning. If I get lunch on Wednesday, I do not eat until Friday morning.

Since I changed from one kind of cooking to another, I have had problems with my stomach (diarrhea), and this is a very heavy blow for me because I am restricted in how much I can move around.

God forbid that the soldiers downstairs should see me! What disgusts me most of all is the attitude of my landlady's husband, the Ukrainian, Zabawka. He does not want to know about the whole thing, and he is not interested in whether or not I get food. When she gives me a slice of bread and a bottle of water, she is very careful around him. If I got bread it would be great — but what I actually get is sour potatoes and sauerkraut. I will be thankful to God if they only want to keep me. Imagine: I have to be afraid of the landlady's brother, as well as of the soldiers. I am lucky that I do not sneeze or cough. I thank God alone that I am healthy, praise be to Him.

Meanwhile the May nights are extremely cold, and on account of the cold it is impossible to sleep. At the same time my anxiety is terrible now that the army is leaving. I cannot sleep nights because if, God forbid, they set fire to this old place, which is as dry as pepper and has a straw-thatched roof, and I fall asleep, I will not have a chance to save myself. However, I hope that God will command the right angel to watch over me — that same God who has protected me up to now will continue to do so in the future.

Dear God, help me!

I also want to write about our neighbor, Mrs. Tepper. Her maiden name is Fekh. One of her father's brothers was Yosl Fekh, Blume Shardes's husband from Kaminke. She had another brother in the Soviet army, where he served as a driver, and a brother in Belgium. Maybe they are alive.

Her husband was in Korowic camp and stayed there. She was a heroic woman — she and her two small children. The elder daughter was called Grete, but I do not remember the name of the younger daughter. On that memorable Friday she [Mrs. Tepper] was in the camp, and [was taken] in a transport to

Bełżec. One of her sisters, and her parents, were deported earlier from To-kadewska Street. The only two people who remained were a disabled brother and a sister who wore glasses. They suffered and went hungry in the ghetto. They worked for the air force in Sknilow. More than once, my dear sister brought happiness to them by giving them a bowl of soup. They were deported before the very last *Aktion*.

Mordche Stromer

Blessed be God: It is May 28.

I thank God that I am alive. It is very difficult to survive. My new landlords are terribly afraid. Every day we hear news. The army unit stationed in Jagonia has left, so there is no one in the village. They [the landlords, the Zabawkas] are afraid of the arsonists, called *banderovtses*,[22] who could come and burn down the village. Can you imagine?

Zabawka removed the threshing machine from the barn, so that if the barn is set alight the machine will be saved. I do not have a hiding place. I lie in the attic, quite exposed. I hope that God will go on protecting me. Yesterday, one of the new residents began moving out because he was told that they were going to burn down the village. Meanwhile they [the villagers] ran to the city, to the city council, and he [the man who was moving out] was ordered to remain. If he would have moved out, the Zabawkas would have moved out too.

May God protect me and lead me on the right path! I still have hope that I will endure all these troubles. I would already have hidden my book in the ground somewhere, but I am reluctant to part with it. I can spend several hours writing. I know that I am writing with many errors, but I cannot write in Polish because everybody would be able to read it. If God only helps me

---

22 These were Ukrainian ultra-nationalist units led by Stepan Bandera, a pro-German prewar Ukrainian activist. They fought the Soviets and murdered large numbers of Jews.

to live through this terrible period, I will, together with my brother-in-law in America, publish this whole experience as a separate work.

If it was not for the fear, I would be able to tell of all the things that I have seen with even greater precision and detail — if I had a clear mind. I would tell about the biggest bandits in the world, who are called *Hitlerovtses* [followers of Hitler].

The book would be a memoir, the diary of an unfortunate person. Is it possible to describe everything I have lived through up to this very day? Can anyone understand what I have been going through in this place, all the time, through the whole summer of 1943, in the attic, without seeing a living soul, and always in the dark?

Many months went by before I made a small hole in the roof. I spent the cold winter in this same attic and I was lucky that the winter was not too cold. However, for a man who constantly has to lie in a cold attic, there have been plenty of days and nights when I was completely chilled. I do not even have a pair of underpants. I wear a shirt, and instead of underpants, a pair of short sports pants. No sweater; no undershirt. When I escaped it was in the month of Tammuz [June/July]. On my feet I wear a pair of socks and old slippers. No jacket, no hat. Just recently Mrs. Streker gave me, as a present, an old torn suit of her son's, of the kind worn by the Polish army; and for my head, a ripped hat.

But this is foolish. The main thing is that God has not forsaken me. Fortunately, during this whole period I have not been sick. What would I have done if I was, God forbid, sick, and needed a doctor? Would they call a doctor for me? They would be afraid to. God makes me strong so that I do not need any help.

Since the Strekers left, I realize for the first time what it means to eat. With [my old landlady], everything was on time. I knew in advance that in the morning and at lunchtime I needed to watch [for her], and she would hand me up food. I more or less oriented myself with regard to time: after the cows were milked in the morning and at lunchtime when she was feeding the horses and cows, I knew she would be sending up food. With them [the Strekers] I never went hungry.

After many months, Mrs. Streker would, when possible, call me down to eat breakfast in the house, and to warm myself up a little bit. This happened especially when we were hoping that the Soviets would arrive at any minute. During the months of February and March, their treatment of me was like a barometer that rose and fell like the stocks in the stock market. When the political situation became critical for the Germans, things went better for me. When the Soviets were pushed back, I was treated more coldly. There were days when Streker came and told me that he wanted to give me back the money I had given him, and that I should leave.

Several times there was talk that I should be hidden somewhere on Jagonie Street. On one particular occasion, very early in the morning, one of Streker's sweethearts came to see him, a woman named Barbara Erd. She called him aside and told him that a discussion had taken place in her house, where it was said I should be hidden somewhere in Jagonie Street. I happened to be standing near the attic door, waiting for his wife, who was washing laundry and was going to pass it to me so that I could hang it in the attic to dry.

Imagine my situation! I realized from her [Barbara Erd's] words that she knew that I was hiding in his house — though the landlord had never mentioned that anyone, apart from his wife and himself, knew about me. During [the first] seven months even their daughter knew nothing about me.

This happened on a Thursday, and God helped, and nothing came of it.

The [new] landlady has no fixed time for giving me my food, and I have to wait for her because I do not want her to have to wait for me. Meanwhile, it is not good to wait near the little door and also not good to wriggle back under the straw. Sometimes she brings me a few cold potatoes for lunch, and at other times she goes away and does not cook, and brings me no food. But I will accept everything in a loving spirit.

I am ready to go a little bit hungry, if God watches over me. I am not, God forbid, complaining about my landlady. The fact that she is keeping me is enough. It is enough when she gives me a potato. She has not taken any money from me, even though I offered her five dollars, because she is a very decent Christian. Yet she is a poor woman, and she herself does not have enough to eat. While her brother was around she would visit him, and he always gave her some food to take home to eat.

If he had known before he left that she was going to stay on as the landlady, he would have left some food for her. However, everything happened last minute. All this would be trivial if humanity could just survive, if the second front could be opened, or if the Soviets could start a summer offensive, in which case, maybe, the bandits who set fire to homes would stop doing it. And if it was necessary to hide, everybody would have to hide.

The days are long. My brains are shriveling up from thinking. Various ideas come into one's head. Every day since I arrived here, I pray those prayers I remember by heart, and every day I say *Kaddish*. I do not believe that I am sinning by doing this because the situation the Jews are in never happened before. It is terrible.

So I am saying *Kaddish*. I am now without parents, and without my sister and her children. Only a year ago, I spoke with them and could look into their eyes. It is now a year since my sister told me that by Thursday the graves would be ready, and indeed, on [that] Thursday they were murdered.

Eight days from this Sunday, I will have *yahrzeit* for my grandfather, from [after the Sabbath through Sunday]. I shiver when I remember. I do not understand all of my thoughts, after what I have lived through — neither [do I understand] my lust for life. All I know is that my will to live is frightful. I do not know why it is so. Perhaps it is because I can imagine how it would feel to clasp to my heart my brother and my beloved sister, how it will feel to weep and tell them all the particulars about our close relatives, how they lived and suffered under the Germans.

Maybe my heart would be lightened. And maybe I will live to see the defeat of Hitler. Or it is possible that I will be one among the many tens of thousands of Jews to be killed during this final period.

Today, I again hear cannon fire from far away. When will it all start? I know that it will not be child's play, but let it start! Perhaps they [the Russians] will succeed in breaking through. And when will I be able to be a free man? You can hardly imagine what freedom means. That can be understood only by someone who has lost his freedom.

My situation is much worse than that of a man who has been sentenced because he is secure, his life is safe, he has food and work, whereas my whole existence here is of no value. In normal times a serious criminal was sentenced to a dark cell, a hard bed, and had to go without food from time to time — but my situation is far worse. That man, apart from all those things, has only one concern. He does not have to tremble [in fear of] being caught and shot, or of being burned alive in the straw.

But the will to live is greater than all these troubles. You ought not to think that other Jews did not want to live. They struggled desperately to stay alive. It is terrible to reflect that one year ago today, I was still in the ghetto. It was a Monday, and on Tuesday, that last Tuesday, I was still bringing those poor creatures cans of cooked meat — but did the little pigeons [Zlateh's children] have a chance to eat it?

Oh God, have mercy! I will never hear another word from their sweet lips. Their mouths are closed forever. Poor things, they also wanted to live. And those unfortunate ones understood that they had to suffer for the name "Jew." My eyes are full of tears. In another eight days it will be a year. Will I live to see another Sunday?

And if to this day, there is still a Hitler and the suffering of the Jews has not yet ended — Oh God, punish him now!

I want to add a few details about the life of our mother's only sister, Aunt Peshele and her husband and children. I know that one child, Liber, went to the army in Russia, and it is possible he will return. Both of the cousins, Liber Kver and Meyer Stromer, are in the army. May God protect them so that they will return home.

As I wrote earlier, the first to be killed was Izzy, the youngest son. When the Germans arrived there was a tremendous uproar. Whoever wanted to was murdering and beating Jews. The janitor from Number 6 Gazowa Street came and took Monye and Izzy to work, bringing them to Damarstinowa Street. There the Jews were flogged, and were murdered. Monye managed to escape from there, completely naked. He saw his brother being murdered. He himself was badly beaten, so much so that he had to stay in bed for several weeks. His wounds were so bad that they wrapped him up [in bandages or sheets].

It is possible that Izzy was killed by his Christian acquaintances from the factory. Later they put him in a sack, brought him to Gazowa Street, laid him down next to his door and rang the bell. When our aunt came to open the door, they said, "Here is Stalin — take him!"

You can imagine what it was like for his unfortunate parents, our darling aunt and uncle; and she had to go on living. Monye got away somehow and began to work, as did Klare's husband Vilek: he worked for the Jewish community. With him, Klare lacked for nothing. He was a very shrewd operator, and brought home whatever he could.

During one *Aktion,* our uncle happened to visit a neighbor and some SS men came in and asked him for identification. He did not have it on him, since the card was for both him and our aunt. Our uncle wanted to go back to his apartment and get the card, but the Germans did not let him. Our aunt began to implore them, and for that they took her as well. Monye and Vilek were at work. When they got back, Vilek, who arrived first, ran to the assembly point on Sobieska Szalila.

This happened right at the beginning. He went to the Jewish police, and almost managed to bring our aunt to a spot near the little gate, ready to leave — but he did not succeed. Later, Monye brought a German from his workplace but when they got there our aunt and uncle were gone. They had already been loaded into the trains to Bełżec. That was the end of my mother's sister and her husband.

Those who were left were Klare and a small child — a boy — her husband, and Monye. My uncle's sister and her son, moved in with them. Klare was never a great heroine, but she had a very good husband [who] took care of everything.

He engaged in trade even under the Germans. He worked for the Jewish community, and was always traveling around town with horses. They [his group] would requisition furniture from Jews and deliver it to the Germans, so he was able to make a living. He worked until the August *Aktion,* when they stopped stamping the identity cards of the Jewish community workers.

At the last minute he [Vilek] managed to get another job in the well-known company, H.K.P. (Heres, Kraft, Park). He was fired and then got a job working as a locksmith for the SS. (In his earlier job he had also worked as a blacksmith.)

Klare had two identity cards, one from Monye that said she was his housekeeper, and one from Vilek. Meanwhile they were forced to leave their apartment and move into the ghetto. Monye, as a worker for the SS, received a nice apartment on Damarstinowska Street. [It was] on the first floor, right in the corner, across from the Farben factory. [Editor's note: The reference is unclear; it could be to an I.G. Farben branch, or a paint factory.]

At that time we were living on Ordona Street, where Klare, [Vilek] and Monye always visited with us. Vilek would do his trade, and bring everything to Klare. She could gradually have become a landlady. That was when I was smuggling flour from the Christian side, and as it happened, Klare lived near the ghetto gate, near the fence. So when I would come from the Christian quarter with flour [packed against] my belly, I would stop at Klare's place, and then go on to Ordona Street. Monye and his brother-in-law were also regular guests in our home.

After the August *Aktion* it was quiet for a while, until the day the SS ordered an *Appel* [roll call] where all SS workers had to report to their jobs. It was known that people had not returned from many of these gatherings. At best, they were put in the camp. Monye reported to the *Appel* and did not come back. Many who did not report remained alive for the time being. While the *Appel* was being conducted, a group of bandits went into the ghetto and shot [people] and carried out a special *Aktion* against the Jewish men and women who worked for the SS.

They entered Klare's apartment at seven o'clock in the morning, as she was cooking something for her child. They checked her identity card. Poor thing, if she had known, she would have shown them the identity card she shared with Vilek. She believed the SS would allow her to live because she had their identity card, but it just happened that they were looking for them [SS cards]. On that same day the three unfortunate souls fell. Soon, in the afternoon, their clothes were brought back from the sands.

Vilek did not return from work until night time and found four empty walls. He hit his head against the wall, poor man, when he saw the empty little cradle. He had had such a beautiful little boy. In the course of a few hours, he had ceased to be a husband, a father and a brother-in-law. And so, not a trace remained of my dear [aunt]'s family. In that short time everything collapsed.

Vilek moved in with us, and stayed with us until I was put in the camp. He worked with Mechel the whole time and shared the same room with him. We went through several *Aktions* together. His brother was a very quiet young fellow, a person without a drop of bitterness in him. [Vilek] kept him close to his side, and he managed to find him a job in his own workplace.

On one occasion, Vilek went to buy bread in the Christian street. A Ukrainian caught him and arrested him and took everything he had. Then he was taken to the Jewish prison on Weisenhafer Street in the ghetto. From there, they were supposed to take the prisoners to the sands, but when they led them to the trucks, [the prisoners] threw themselves on the SS, and [Vilek] threw himself among the murdered bodies.

I was in the camp during the winter, and Vilek knew I was there. The camp workers came and loaded all the murdered bodies onto sledges, and took them to the Jewish cemetery, where Vilek was given a yellow patch by the foreman and taken into the ghetto. When several of the workers in our barracks escaped, my foreman asked me to supply him with three more people. The first one I took was Vilek. On Sunday it will be exactly a year since that day.

It was already during the most dangerous period. He worked with us on Monday, and in the evening he went back with me into the ghetto. On Tuesday he would have gone [to work], but he knew that my foreman would no longer keep him on, especially because he was asked to stay on Monday and didn't want to. He came back to the camp. At the same time, on Wednesday or Thursday, his brother was shot there, and Vilek most certainly fell when the Jews in the camp were liquidated.

I also want to mention here an incident that involved me and Mr. Krajewski, master of the carpenters' shop on Damarstinowska Street.

As I already noted, during the period before the August *Aktion* until the "W" *Aktion,* I worked for Krajewski in the carpenters' shop at 41 Damarstinowska Street. Pepe's Aunt Messing and her daughter and son-in-law and their two children, lived in the same courtyard. They used to live on Greidinger Street, but when [Jews] had to move out of the Christian streets, they moved in with their parents. The Messings had only that daughter and one son.

Their son-in-law, Tshof, was from Radekiw and under the Polish government had been an official in a timber company. They did very well [financially], but it seems that they did not have a very satisfactory life together. Tshof also worked for Krajewski. He more or less knew about my circumstances. Secondly, through Pepe, he knew that during the Soviet period I had a responsible military post and certainly told Mr. Krajewski about it.

Though I was named Taksel on my identity card, my [supervisor] was aware that I was Stromer not Taksel and that in the Soviet period I was a real mechanic, and [it made no difference to Krajewski.] But then they created an untenable situation. ("They built themselves an attic" is the idiom.)

Once, when I was leaving work, a Ukrainian from Kaminke recognized me even though I was wearing glasses. He went to Krajewski and asked him whether a certain Stromer from Kaminke was working for him. Krajewski showed him the whole list of Jewish workers, and proved that there was no such person working for him. But the other man represented me to him in this way: that he had seen me going out and that I was seeking my fortune under Krajewski's roof.

In any case, Krajewski met the man in a restaurant and asked him not to do anything about this discovery because the man was yelling that he had to destroy me. Anyway, that is how Krajewski presented the whole story to me. At first I was very frightened, so I quickly told Monek Messing, Tshof's brother-in-law, what happened. I got on very well with him.

He told me at once that this was all Tshof's doing because he wanted to blackmail me and had taken Krajewski as his partner. Monek felt that way particularly after I told him that Tshof was a big broker, and told me I to ask Krajewski to take care of the matter. Then he proposed to take care of it for me for a certain sum. That's when Monek said that he would wager his head that this was their [collaborative] work.

By now I was twisting like a worm. I did not know what I should do. I saw that it was blackmail. On Saturday I told Krajewski that I wanted to see the Ukrainian from Kaminke — that I wanted to talk to him. After work on Sunday, Krajewski got drunk. He had an acquaintance, a girlfriend from Kaminke, Krutshenik the shoemaker' daughter, who was also with the firefighters every year. She was a real piece of work.

On Sunday he [Krajewski] told her about.[what had happened] and she just had to tell him that I had been a big *komissar* under the Soviets. When I came in to work early on Monday morning, my Mr. Krajewski was already drunk, or maybe he was still in his Sunday mode — still drunk. Every Sunday he would always get drunk and leave his wife. As soon as I came in, he hurled himself on me. "You bandit!" he screamed at me. "You murderer! I want you to leave my workshop at once! I am not going to hide any communists in my place. Get out, because I am going to call the police!"

Imagine my situation! Tshof heard everything. It appears he regretted starting the whole thing, and I was not able to work for a whole day. Krajewski went off to sleep. But I saw that I could not extricate myself. He took away part of my wages, twenty dollars, and stopped "protecting" me. I don't know if Tshof took part of the money.

I have to point out that Krajewski is a terrible Judeophobe. Every day he verbally abused his few Jewish workers, and all the Jews who worked for him had trouble with him. If anyone occasionally needed something from him, he could not and would not do it for a Jewish worker. Jewish money, Jewish property, furniture — that he would take. If he could have drowned us in a spoonful of water, he would have done it. Getting drunk on Jewish money — that, too, he could do. He was in a good mood when he received a bribe.

His name, too, might as well be obliterated!

With the help of God:
Today is Monday, May 24.

There were fires again at night. I did not see them, but in the morning I heard people talking to each other outside. Bombing and shooting can be heard, but not yet seen. They [the Germans] are running away. If God helps me and I see them running away, then I will think that help is near.

List of Memorials [combined below with other such writing]

I hope to God that He will continue to protect me. This Thursday, it is already three weeks since Streker has not come. He sent messages to say that he would come this week. He may still, perhaps. My new landlord says that he does not want to know anything about me. He does not see me and I do not see him. May God guard me.

If the old landlord comes, I will give him this book to bury, because I am afraid that it may be burned — after all, there is a fire in a different place every night. Meanwhile, up to now, thank God, there has been no fire on Jagonie [Street].

My dearest ones, I think it is clearer now that all the Jews suffered terribly before being murdered. In similar fashion to those friends and acquaintances I listed, all the Jews of Kaminke were killed. Some were shot on Zawada Street and some were taken to that place of torture — to Bełżec. Everyone had horrible experiences. Our Ukrainians from Kaminke had a large part in this, because they egged on the *Kreishauptmann* to make Kaminke free of Jews, and Kaminke became free of Jews earlier than the whole Kaminke region, after the big mass murder on Zawada Street.

[That is] where children and the elderly were thrown into the ditches while still alive and where people were lined up by sevens. [It was where] the first one was shot with a bullet through the heart, and those who stood behind him were thrown into the ditches, one after another, dead or alive. Then they covered the ditches with a little bit of dirt. It was summer time, and the innocent blood boiled. The Earth raised itself up.

They ordered the soil [the mass graves] to be strewn with lime. After the mass murder, the *Kreishauptmann* invited the Governor of the District of Galicia, Dr. [Otto] Wächter, to Kaminke. [He] came with his entourage, and they paraded on the sands in which the Jewish victims lay.

I do not know if at some point, they will order the victims to be cremated as they did in Lemberg, but they do not have any Jews to do the cremation work, like the arsonists in Lemberg. Now, however — for the last two weeks — they have set mines under all the Jewish *Botei Midrash* (Houses of Study). According to what I have heard, they spent a whole day trying to blow up the old synagogue and couldn't — not until they used petrol were they able to set fire to it. Then, I believe, they had to put out the fire.

I do not know what really happened there. I am a prisoner, as you know, and I have not seen Kaminke for 1,066 days. May God help me, so that I will be able to go out and see my *shtetele* [dear little town] as a free person and will not have to shiver with fear.

God can and will help.

Mordche Stromer

I want to tell you more about Bełżec, the most dreadful place, where hundreds of thousands of Jews were killed — because Jews were brought there from Czechoslovakia and Austria and from all of Poland. In Poland there was also another place where Jews were killed: Sobibor was the name of that place. But the main place was Bełżec.

Last year, after work, as we stood near our barracks in Tskouska, [this is possibly one of the factory quarters] a young man came by along the road. He saw me and my comrade standing there — we had yellow patches and numbers on our garments and he realized we were Jews. He approached and asked if any SS were around. I told him there weren't any. Then he spoke to me in Yiddish and told me he was a Jew and that he had come here from [a town] near Chelm. I invited him into our lodgings, and at once prepared food and drink for him. He had been a worker in Bełżec for eight months, [working at] the extermination of Jews, and he told us about it.

This is the authentic person, who was at Bełżec, the greatest place of torture since the creation of the world. Several hundred Jewish men and women worked there. These were his words:

> *When the transports would arrive, all the men and all the women were shaved and ordered to strip. Then, again, a speech was made to inform them that they would all be assigned to work, after bathing. That was in the very first month. After that they didn't make a speech, they only beat them. When they had all undressed, several hundred men and women were driven into a room — 300 people could normally stand in a room like that. But they drove 600–800 people into that room.*
>
> *Small children, if they were alive on arrival, were tossed inside onto the heads of the people standing there. Then the room was closed and the people were suffocated with gas. It was not an easy death. It took more than 15 minutes. There were several of these rooms. Then they took out all the murdered bodies, dragged them, and laid them in ditches of a certain kind. Then they took them out of the ditches, and there were scaffolds of a certain kind. They threw all the murdered bodies onto these scaffolds. There was wood underneath. Everything was soaked in gasoline and set on fire. Only God knows what terrible things were played out there. Mothers with daughters; fathers with sons; husband and wife; couples engaged to be married; grandmothers and grandchildren; infants. People kept hoping until the last minute. They could not believe it. But it was impossible to escape from this.*
>
> *After each Aktion, some of the workers were also packed into the gas chambers, and new people were selected. Money had no*

value because you had to eat what you could get. (I am talking about the workers from there.)

The Jew continued to tell the story.

At the beginning, the workers would have good times: when rich transports arrived with foodstuffs, they could keep it. They did not even look at money, gold, dollars, or diamonds. The girls who worked there sorted through all the objects, ripping open seams, to search for money. Large amounts of property were collected. From time to time a special delegate from Lublin, came and took away all the money — any that had been left [behind] by the local SS.

There were terrible tragedies there. They used to shoot, beat and murder. This was the last road of all our dear loved ones, whom we will never see again.

This man was there until almost the end. By then people were no longer being brought to Bełżec. They loaded them up and drove them to Sobibor, near Chelm. In the railcar he was in there were several strong young people. One night, they jumped out of the little window. The guards shot at them but did not hit [anyone].

The next day we brought him into the ghetto. He was the authentic source, which could convey the most terrible events. He said that as time went on, they became wild. The great Jewish tragedy no longer made an impression on them. They only looked for food. By then, people were arriving naked, and many people died on the way. Many, many children [were murdered this way]. People would go crazy and hurl themselves, one Jew upon another. While they were still in the railcars, before they were unloaded, they would witness various tragedies.

IN THIS WAY HITLER SOLVED THE JEWISH QUESTION.
MAY GOD PUNISH THE GREATEST HAMAN OF THE MODERN AGE!

With God's help
Wednesday, May 31, 1944

Streker's sister just told me that they want me to move out of here tomorrow. Thursday again! I do not know what to do. If I had food I would stay here for a short while on my own, though it is very difficult to be alone in an house where there isn't a living soul — but I would stay. If she would only come from time to time and bring me food, I would stay. But I see that this whole line of thought is foolish. Whatever God gives will be. May God protect and guide me on the right path. I must finish.

Stay healthy, my dear family! It is believable that God will guard me and help me to live to see you — those of you who remain. And I am leaving you this whole book for remembrance, so that you will know that bitter tears are pouring from my eyes. But when I remember that Wednesday when my beloved sister and her two small children lay in deathly terror, [I see that] my current situation is much better. It is only a pity that I have gone through so much up to now, and that I am in this situation now.

I put my hope in God.

I will hand this book over to be hidden somewhere, maybe to be buried.

May God help me.
Your brother,

Mordche Stromer of Kaminke Strumilowa.

With God's help

Friday [June 2]. Today I have to leave this place. I do not know where to go. I have yet to see the new landlord, but he does not want to keep me, even though it is quiet — you do not see any people here.

May God lead me on the right path.

The worst thing is that everybody knows me and I must not show my face. I will have to tie a rag around my face so that I will not be recognized. I am facing a terrible decision. May I be guarded from all evil.

Stay well and happy, you who remain. Remember your loved ones, who suffered much more than I have told you — because that which was suffered cannot be told.

Jagonia, June 2.
Today, a year ago, on the 2nd, I still saw my dear ones.

Moty Stromer

I am going to hand this over to be buried, and I must leave today, on Friday evening.
May God guard me.

[Editor's note: There follow messages in Russian and Polish and an address in English, more or less identical to the note below translated from the Yiddish. Stromer hoped that whoever would find this diary would understand one of these languages and send the manuscript to his sister.]

With the help of God

I am writing these words on the night before I have to leave my place, this attic, where I have been more than — or exactly — 300 days and nights. The days in this place were no brighter than the nights; but what would I like? [I would] like to be able to spend a longer time in this place, or to find one like it. May God help me! Please convey this to my brother Meyer Stromer, or my sister in America Henia Edelstein, to let them know.

Their brother, Mordche Stromer
Kaminke Strumilowa

LIST OF ALL THOSE WHO WERE REMEMBERED [consolidated here]:

I will briefly write about some of our acquaintances, about whose lives I know certain particulars:

The Bari Family. The Baris, with Bronye, were caught in the very first *Aktion*. Mrs Bari sent Bronye to a Christian woman to hide. She was caught on the way. Then her mother ran after her and thought that her child would be given up to her, so she, too, was caught. Bronye was an intelligent, pretty, dutiful child. More than once, she kept our mother company during the difficult time when our parents were left alone, without children. Bari was left, but he was like a crazy person, after what had happened. Later, he and Shmulik were arrested. Their servant, the Blind Kashke, rummaged through all their property and stayed in their apartment. According to our parents, she would cause various troubles, but they could not say anything.

The Klog Family. Moishe Klog, Elia Klog, Tall Itshe Klog (Perele's husband) and Elia's wife and two children were arrested in the very first *Aktion*. The old lady, Chaya-Bine died after they were arrested. Then Perele and her children, Short Itshe's wife, and last of all, Short Itshe, were all captured in an *Aktion*.

The Nimand Lanye-Kohl Family. In the beginning, Lanye, Feyge and her child were taken in an *Aktion*. (Feyge had moved out of Lemberg.) After that, Avrom and Yisroel were killed. Hersh Kigl hid himself and I do not know what happened to him. His father and younger brother were shot during the very first *Aktion*. Elishe Kohl was in Lemberg after people were forced to leave "free Kaminke." I gave him steady support. His sister Rose was arrested in the last *Aktion* and was being taken to Bełżec when she jumped off the train and made it to Zolkwia. She told Lipe about it. I do not know what happened to her and Lipe.

The Plever family. I do not know when they were killed, but none of them survived. Rab escaped to Lemberg. Before the first "contribution" (when the synagogues were held for ransom) he was arrested in the apartment he was staying in. What was happening was that people were held hostage until the contribution was paid and then they were left alone. But they no longer saw the world [they were killed].

The families of Nossin Witlen, the Kornblits, and Moishe Zeigner: No one survived out of that whole crowd. A guy called Suzirowitsh, a Ukrainian who had once worked for Kornblit, beat him [Zeigner] terribly as soon as the Germans came in. I do not know what happened to Fantshe Zeigner. It seems to me that she did not leave with the Soviets — for by then it was too late. Hersh Zeigner, his mother Sarah and his wife Zaze and [their] child and his brother-in-law were arrested in the *Aktion*. Hersh was one of the last who remained to clean up the ghetto.

On the day I entered the camp, the Zeigners left Lemberg for Bisk, and from there they headed for Przemiszlan. Itshe Kohl had family there. From there they had to go to Hungary. Itshe Kohl was at Zlateh's and wanted to see me, but I was in the camp. He was there on a Shabbos and told them that they had to leave in the next few days, but whether they succeeded in saving themselves I do not know, because on that Sunday there was a Liquidation *Aktion* in Przemiślany.

When Itshe Kohl left with Hersh Zeigner, no one from his family was still alive except for the two children: one in the Land of Israel, and Aptshe, who was with the Soviet Army. His mother, father, his sister, and her child [were all dead] and his brother-in-law Dr. Birger had his head cut off in the first *Aktion* — so there was no one. Whether Itshe was able to leave Przemiszlan with Hersh and with Lazer Zeigner, I do not know. We will not find out until after the war.

Lazer Zeigner. His mother, his wife and child and his whole family were no more, long before he came to me in Lemberg. He got a telegram from Washington saying that his brother Robin was in America. But his sister-in-law Salke and his brother Leibish and his parents, Yoshe Lapaukovker, and Mashe Goldberg and all their children were no longer among the living when Lazer was in Lemberg.

Leib Birger. First Regen, then Leib-Shloime and his wife Peshe, were in the camp in Maste Wielka. What happened to them, I do not know.

Menashe Frenkl. Louis-Hersh Zeigner told me that none of his family remained. Old Menashe, poor man, lived at the rabbinate in Kaminke. They were found there in a hideout, several days after the very last *Aktion*. At that time Hersh was "cleaning" the ghetto, and saw how they led out the rabbinate — including Menashe Frenkl. He was stumbling along. They shot them all on Zaboda Street because the transport to Bełżec left several days earlier. After that, all those found hidden were regularly murdered in Kaminke.

The family of Shaye Note Kohl. None of them is alive. Maybe Note's son lives — he succeeded in leaving for Russia with the Soviets.

The Mishel Family. Sumek went to the military in Zloczów and a Ukrainian murdered him. Their mother, and the middle daughter Eshke, were shot in Kaminke during an *Aktion*. Her eldest daughter [was killed] in one of the *Aktions* in Lemberg. After her mother and sister [were murdered], she did not even want to hide and was caught. At that time, Dovke left with Hersh Zeigner for Bisk. I do not know what happened to him. Lole was in Lemberg and certainly fell in one of the last *Aktions*.

Sender Podhoretz. His whole family, his father Shmuel-Kuhos, his mother, his sister Glikele, his elder sister Freyde and her husband and child, (who had married and moved to Szczeric), and Poher's wife with the children (Poher himself was murdered during the Soviet period, in a forest near Kaminke), and the oldest of all the sisters, the wife of Motl, Moshe's son, with her children, have all been exterminated by now.

Sender himself and his wife and one child (because one of his children had already been arrested; he was put in the camp and the little girl was murdered there), and one of his brothers-in-law, from Remenow, wandered up and down near the gate. On the last Tuesday, I believe, they left the ghetto, but that same day he and his brother-in-law were caught and shot. He sent a sister-in-law of his, his wife's sister and her little brother, to a Christian near Lemberg. I do not know if they remain. His father-in-law and mother-in-law, together with all the remaining Jews of Remenow, were murdered by Remenow Christians as soon as the Germans came in.

I want Neshe Barits or Groskopf who is now with her husband in London, and was born in Alshanitse near Zloczów, to learn about the experiences of her parents — if she has the opportunity to read this. I do not know if this book will ever reach the right hands. If it does, she will certainly be informed.

I am writing these words on Tuesday. On this day of the week, Tuesday, I saw my relatives for the last time. On Wednesday, a year ago, began the terrible fire in Lemberg.

I have already mentioned, in connection with Shloime Barits, that I do not know what happened to Leytshe's parents. However, I know that those poor people suffered dreadfully. Neshe's mother used to be a broker in Zloczów for the Christians of Olszanice. That is, she would propose that that they make offers to sell Jews food and various old clothes. That was how she earned a broker's fee, or would receive food from the Christians.

Once someone informed on her, and a few things were taken away, but they extricated themselves. Right at the start there was a calumny against Neshe's brother Avrom — they accused him of supposedly murdering an Olszanice Christian when the Soviets were moving out. We were told about this by Dobzitske. She is from Olszanice, and her second marriage was to Trauvish-Dobzitske. She once lived on Pogodne Street. I am giving her correct address, because during the whole time that we lived in the Bilinkiewtsha we did business with her. She now lives in Dvoiska near Lemberg.

She knew Neshe, and gave over a great deal of information about her parents. She knew me as Shloime's brother. She would call me Fanye Barits. I did not want her to know that Zlateh was my sister, so that she would not talk with her acquaintances about me. Shloime, Sheyve and Zlateh would barter many things with her. She would be given some money, and bring buckwheat, beans, honey, flour, and meat back to us. She would buy things gradually and hold things back, making it almost impossible before one could deal with her.

I cannot give any particulars about the sufferings of Neshe's parents in Zloczów. I know that they turned to Shloime and asked that he support them, but Shloime could not do so at that time. At first, they would send bread, butter and sometimes meat to Shloime in Lemberg. Leytshe would be somewhat afraid of Shloime, when it came to sending something to her mother in return. At that time she could have sent sugar or saccharine or soap. Meanwhile both of them — Shloime and Leytshe — were terribly stingy. This was something that already lay in their nature, not just at that time. Later they moved from Pogodna to Bilinkowska.

It was no longer possible to send [items] from Zloczów; but once, [when we were] still on Pogodna, Brayer the dentist from Zloczów came with Germans in a luxury car. This was right at the start. He bought soap especially for them — they came for soap. Afterwards, a former maid of his came, I think from Bialie Kamien or from Podkamien. Neshe might certainly know who that is. And she brought a message from Leytshe's parents. After that, Leytshe only corresponded with those at home.

Neshe,

Leytshe also knew that you had given birth to a second daughter. That is what Henia, my dear sister, wrote from America. The letter arrived just at the end. Afterwards, when America had entered the war, no news at all came from abroad.

About the family in Rohatyn, Leytshe and Pepe used to write to Tsilke. Her father was arrested in the Soviet period, sentenced and sent as a prisoner to Kherson, near the Black Sea. Whether he is alive is unknown.

I cannot give you a detailed list of those who fell as the first victims of the Ukrainians and Germans. At any rate, they suffered terribly, more terribly than in other regions, because these were very terrible Ukrainians. A maid who worked for Aunt Peshele told Klare, several times, of all the particulars of the family's experiences.

[CONSOLIDATION OF LISTS OF VICTIMS
TO BE REMEMBERED:]

- Dr. Schwartz and his relative, both from Lemberg
- Merindilein Altkoren and Milek Altkoren, both from near the town line. The Altkorens are from Dikiszner. Izzy Lislayfer from Roker who always lived in the factory.
- Hamaides, a young man, a butcher from near the town line.
- Berger or Szapranski from Kristinopol. He married in Lemberg, and had a leather store.
- Fayfer, Lislayfer's brother-in-law.
- Eli Kleynshpirs, a butcher; at one time he was also a coachman. In butcher circles he was called Eli the Doctor. His wife was shot in the place.
- Lipiec, a derma-merchant. He was ashamed that he sold derma in a dairy store.
- Mondik Shtadler, a butcher.
- Botskinder, son of a shoe merchant from Lemberg.
- Yosl Hoinich. He had a sister in America.
- Shamten Noshen, a merchant of roofs.
- Shmerel Kogel, a butcher. He died in the barracks, and we buried him in the garden.
- Shmuel Laupt or Gelber was an art merchant. He was detail oriented. He also died.
- The well-known Dr. Laupt with his brother-in-law, also a doctor. Both of them died in Zborek and were buried in the Jewish cemetery where the ghetto was located. They had been murdered in a factory, across from a slaughterhouse. I don't remember the name of the street.
- Margolis, also a butcher.
- Dr. Teichman. I believe he was from Hoderow or Boleslaw or another town. A friend, a lawyer, brought him, his wife and a one-year-old son to Lemberg during an *Aktion*. When they were getting off the bus, an SS man hit the child over the head with a weapon and killed him in front of his parents. Later, he ran away from our barracks. He was seen

as they led him to the sands [to be killed]. He owned a sulphur factory.

- Bernstein and Lemberger, leather merchants and their son-in-law.
- Sheynbach, a young Hasidic man from Przemyszl or Jaroslaw. His parents were cloth merchants. The man had a say with the German director of the jacket-making department.
- Two brothers, Izzy and Mishke Ekerling or Frank. They and their parents were incarcerated with me in the Jewish prison. The father was sent to Greiding, where he was shot in the camp. The mother, from Wiecbickie, was taken directly to the sands. The two boys lived with me in the barracks. The older brother was a veterinary student, and the younger one a gymnasium student. Their grandfather was a well-known typesetter in Jaroslaw. They have an uncle in Palestine.
- Kotlarski, the younger one, a student. His father had a hardware store near the town line.
- A young friend, Proster, from near the town line. Their home was located past the gas refinery.
- Krenitel, a formerly employed waiter, worked for Zeingahten in Lemberg.
- Izzy Kozel, born in Hungary. A brother-in-law of the Gelber brothers. A butcher.
- The medical doctor, Tabatchnik; a younger doctor studied in Italy, and a son from Volin.
- Kanigel, a father with a 13 year-old boy. I do not have any other information about these two.
- Dovid Fuchs, a youth of 14 or 15. Shapranski was his uncle. His grandfather, I think, had a store in Lemberg.
- Morris or Sternik, a young student, son of a former factory manager at the Kazimierowicz factory, which manufactured salami. Later, he was a shop steward in the Roker canning factory.
- Wander, owner of Koti. Brought in an *Aktion* from Koti to the camp in Lemberg. His wife and children were taken to Bełżec.
- A young, well-known man, Goldfinger from Krakow.

I note here that I am not sure if all the names are correct because people did not always use their real names in the camp. I myself used the name "Taksel." However, I do not have the mental concentration necessary to mention all of the made-up names.

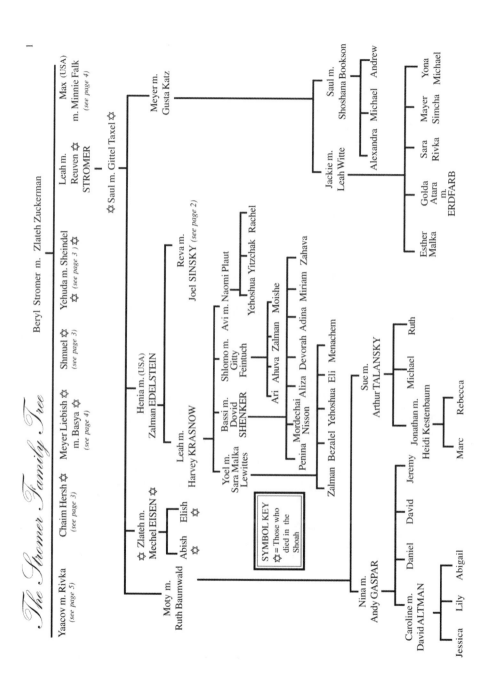

The Stromer Family Tree

Beryl Stromer m. Zlateh Zuckerman

1

Yaacov m. Rivka ✡ *(see page 5)*

Chaim Hersh ✡ *(see page 3)*

Meyer Liebish ✡ m. Basya ✡ *(see page 4)*

Shmuel ✡ *(see page 3)*

Yehuda m. Sheindel ✡ *(see page 3)* ✡

Leah m. Reuven ✡ STROMER

Max (USA) m. Minnie Falk *(see page 4)*

✡ Saul m. Gittel Taxel ✡

Meyer m. Gusta Katz

✡ Zlateh m. Mechel EISEN ✡
Abish ✡ Elish ✡

Henia m. (USA) Zalman EDELSTEIN

Leah m. Harvey KRASNOW

Reva m. Joel SINSKY *(see page 2)*

Moty m. Ruth Baumwald

Yoel m. Sara Malka Lewittes

Bassi m. Dovid SHENKER

Shlomo m. Gitty Feintuch

Avi m. Naomi Plaut
Yehoshua Yitzchak Rachel

Ari Ahuva Zalman Moishe

Penina Mordechai Aliza Devorah Adina Miriam Zahava
Nisson

Zalman Bezalel Yehoshua Eli Menachem

Sue m. Arthur TALANSKY

Jonathan m. Heidi Kestenbaum
Michael Ruth

Marc Rebecca

Nina m. Andy GASPAR

Daniel David Jeremy

Caroline m. David ALTMAN

Jessica Lily Abigail

Jackie m. Leah Witte

Saul m. Shoshana Bookson
Andrew

Esther Malka

Golda Atara m. ERDFARB

Alexandra Michael

Sara Rivka

Mayer Simcha

Yona Michael

SYMBOL KEY
✡ = Those who died in the Shoah

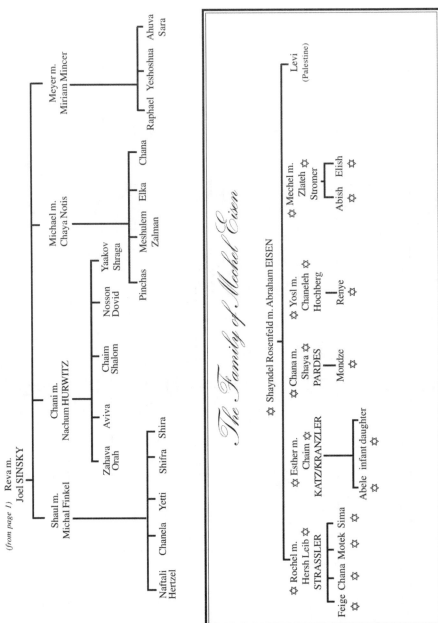

(from page 1) Reva m.
Joel SINSKY

The Family of Mechel Eisen

✡ Shayndel Rosenfeld m. Abraham EISEN

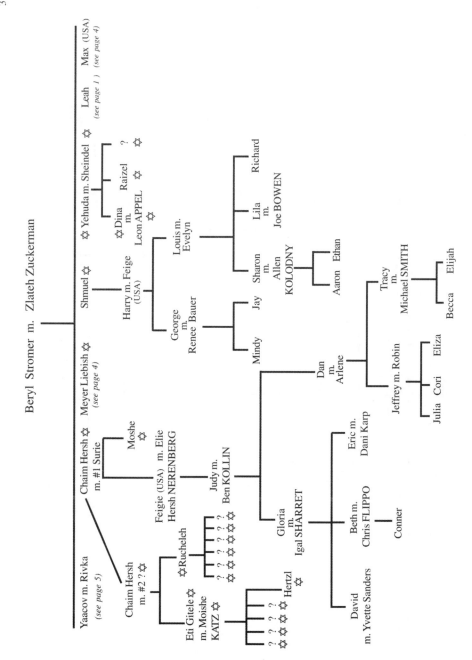

228

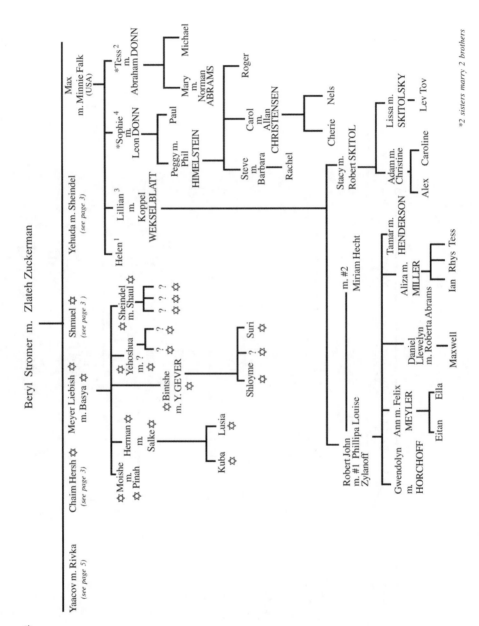

Beryl Stromer m. Zlateh Zuckerman

Yaacov m. Rivka
(see page 5)

Chaim Hersh ✿
(see page 3)

Meyer Liebish ✿
m. Basya ✿

Shmuel ✿
(see page 3)

Yehuda m. Sheindel
(see page 3)

Max
m. Minnie Falk
(USA)

✿ Moishe
✿ m. Pinah

Herman ✿
m.
Salke ✿

✿ Yehoshua
m. ?

✿ Sheindel
m. Shaul ✿

Helen [1]

Lillian [3]
m.
Koppel
WEKSELBLATT

*Sophie [4]
m.
Leon DONN

*Tess [2]
m.
Abraham DONN

Kuba
✿

Lusia
✿

✿ Bintshe
m. Y. GEVER
✿

?   ?
✿   ✿

?   ?   ?
✿   ✿   ✿

Peggy m.
Phil
HIMELSTEIN

Paul

Mary
m.
Norman
ABRAMS

Michael

Shloyme
✿

?
✿

Suri
✿

Steve
m.
Barbara

Carol
m.
Allan
CHRISTENSEN

Roger

Rachel

Cherie   Nels

Robert John
m. #1 Phillipa Louise
Zylanoff

m. #2
Miriam Hecht

Stacy m.
Robert SKITOL

Lissa m.
SKITOLSKY

Lev Tov

Gwendolyn
m.
HORCHOFF

Ann m. Felix
MEYLER

Daniel
Llewelyn
m. Roberta Abrams

Tamar m.
HENDERSON

Aliza m.
MILLER

Adam m.
Christine

Alex   Caroline

Eitan   Ella

Maxwell

Ian   Rhys   Tess

*2 sisters marry 2 brothers

4

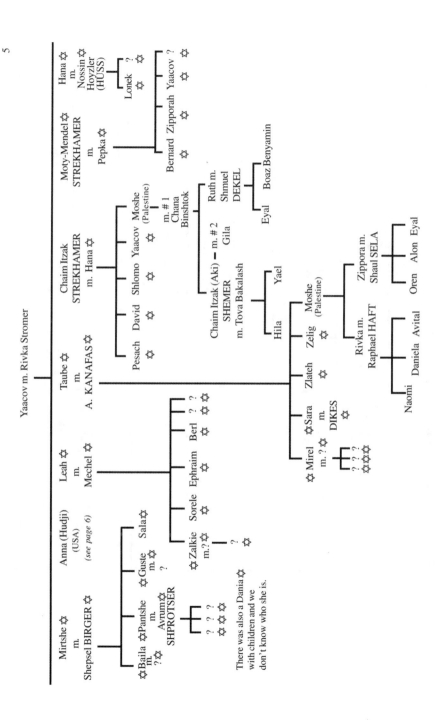

Yaacov m. Rivka Stromer

Mirtshe ✡
m.
Shepsel BIRGER ✡

✡Baila ✡Pantshe ✡Guste Sala✡
m.   m.   m. ✡
?✡   Avrum✡   ?
        SHPROTSER

? ? ?
✡✡✡

There was also a Dania ✡
with children and we
don't know who she is.

Anna (Hudji)
(USA)
(see page 6)

Leah ✡
m.
Mechel ✡

✡Zalkie Sorele Ephraim Berl   ? ?
m.?✡   ✡   ✡   ✡   ✡✡✡
  |
  ?
  ✡

Taube ✡
m.
A. KANAFAS ✡

✡ Mirel   ✡Sara   Zlateh   Zelig   Moshe
m. ? ✡   m.   ✡   ✡   (Palestine)
          DIKES
          ✡

? ? ?   Rivka m.   Zippora m.
✡✡✡✡   Raphael HAFT   Shaul SELA

                                       Naomi Daniela Avital   Oren Alon Eyal

Chaim Itzak
STREKHAMER
m. Hana ✡

Pesach David Shlomo Yaacov Moshe
✡   ✡   ✡   ✡   (Palestine)
                              m. #1
                              Chana
                              Binshtok

Chaim Itzak (Aki) — m. #2
SHEMER   Gila
m. Tova Bakalash

Hila Yael   Ruth m.
                    Shmuel
                    DEKEL

                    Eyal Boaz Benyamin

Moty-Mendel ✡
STREKHAMER
m.
Pepka ✡

Bernard Zipporah Yaacov ?
✡   ✡   ✡

Hana ✡
m.
Nossin ✡
Hoyzler
(HUSS)

Lonek ?
✡   ✡

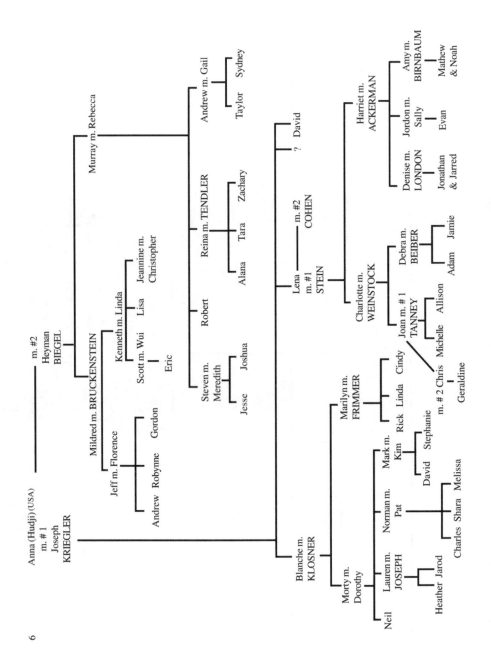

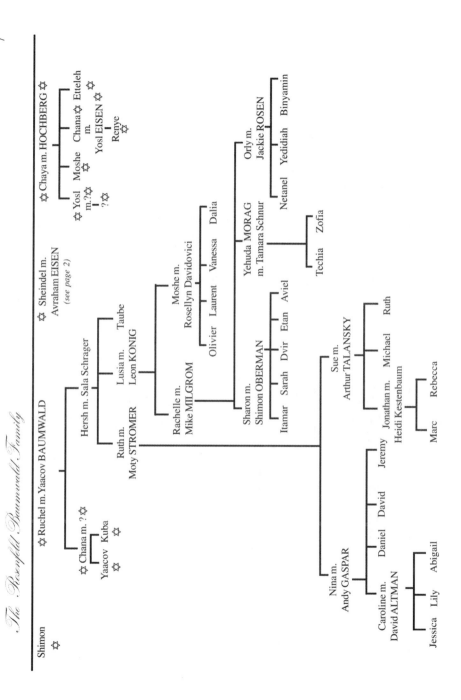

The Rosenfeld Baumwald Family

7

The Vogelfenger/Taxel Family of Narayev

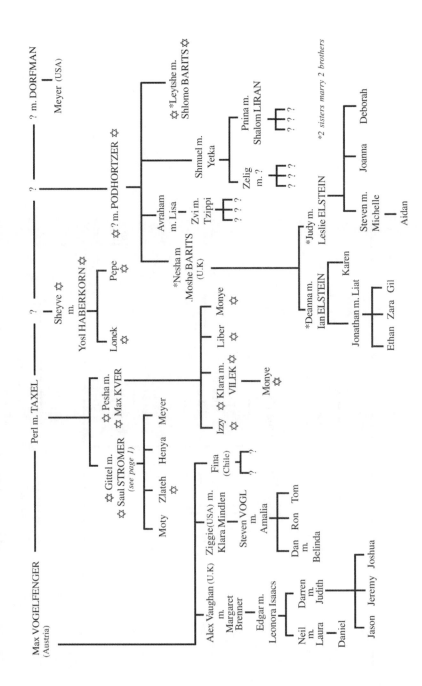

Max VOGELFENGER
(Austria)

? m. DORFMAN
Meyer (USA)

Perl m. TAXEL

Sheyve ✿
m.
Yosl HABERKORN ✿

Lonek ✿   Pepe ✿

? m. PODHORTIZER ✿

✿*Leytshe m.
Shlomo BARITS ✿

Avraham
m. Lisa

Shmuel m.
Yetka

Phina m.
Shalom LIRAN

? ? ?

Zelig
m. ?

? ? ?

Zvi m.
Tzippi

? ? ?

*Nesha m.
Moshe BARITS
(U.K)

*2 sisters marry 2 brothers

*Judy m.
Leslie ELSTEIN

*Deanna m.
Ian ELSTEIN

Steven m.
Michelle

Joanna   Deborah

Aidan

Karen

Jonathan m. Liat

Ethan Zara Gil

✿ Gittel m.
✿ Saul STROMER
(see page 1)

Moty Zlateh Henya Meyer
         ✿

✿ Pesha m.
✿ Max KVER

Izzy ✿   Klara m. ✿
          VILEK ✿

Liber Monye
 ✿   ✿

Monye
 ✿

Fina
(Chile)

? ?

Ziggie(USA) m.
Klara Mindlen

Steven VOGL
m.
Amalia

Dan
m.
Belinda

Ron   Tom

Alex Vaughan (U.K)
m.
Margaret
Brenner

Edgar m.
Leonora Isaacs

Neil
m.
Laura

Darren
m.
Judith

Daniel

Jason Jeremy Joshua

Gittel Stromer and her children: Zlateh, Henia and Moty, 1917

ב״ה

מתכבדים בזה לבקש מאת קרובינו ומיודעינו
לבוא לקחת חבל בשמחתינו, היא יום

חנוכת הבית

אשר תהי׳ אי״ה ביום שבת קודש פ׳ ראה (am 7. August 1926)
בשעה 11 בבקר בביתינו בעיר קאמיאנקא סטר.

ברגשי כבוד

ראובן שטראמער ורעיתו

Chanukat Habayit Invitation, 1926

Stromer Family, 1927.
Standing: Moty, Chaim-Hersh, Reuven, Shmuel, Yehudah
Seated: Yaacov, Leah, Meyer Leibish

Moty, 1930

Stromer children:
Left to right : Meyer, Leah, Zlateh,
Moty, 1927

Shaul Stromer

Moty and Meyer, Kaminke 1930's

Gittel Stromer and Zlateh,
Krynicia Resort, 1934

Moty in the Polish Army, 1932

Podhortzer family 1935. Seated: Zelig and Pnina (Parents)
Standing: Avram, Laiche, Shmuel, Shlomo Boritz, and Nesia (Children)

לחתונת
זלמן עדעלשטיין
עם
העני שטראמער

שתהי' אי"ה בשס"ומצ ביום ז' פ' שופטים א' ברה"ש
אלול ה'רצ"ח (28 אוגוסט 1938) בשעה 1:30 אחה"צ
באולם "יידישער ספארטקלוב" בקמיונקה סט'.
מתכבדים בזה להזמין את כבודכם

יואל עדעלשטיין ורעיתו
אבות החתן סטרעליסק.

שואל שטראמער ורעיתו
אבות הכלה קאמיונקה סט'.

Telegramy: EDELSTEIN–TROMER, Kamionka Str.

Wedding Invitation of
Henia Stromer and
Zalman Edelstein, 1938

Wedding Portrait of
Henia Stromer and
Zalman Edelstein, 1938

Shloime and Leytshe Barits, Zlateh, Abish and Mechel Eisen, Lemberg, 1938

The Eisens : Abish, Mechel, Zlateh, and Elish

Abish Eisen and his Uncle
Moty Stromer

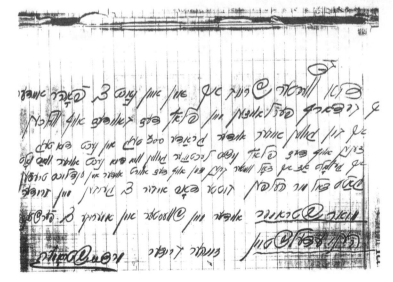

Page from
original diary

Moshe (grandson of Yaacov Stromer)
and Chana Strekhammer, 1949

Rucheli Stromer, daughter of Chaim Hersh
and family

Left to right: Raizel and Dina Stromer (daughters of Yehudah Stromer)
with Leon Appel (Dina's fiancé) in center, Lemberg, 1926

Moty Stromer and friends, 1927

Moty and Meyer Stromer
in front of the family store, 1934

Kamionka-Strumilowa, market day

Kuba and Lusia Stromer,
children of Herman Stromer,
grandchildren of Meyer Leibish

Binshi Stromer Gever and Shaya Gever
and children
(she is the daughter of Meyer Leibish)

Farewell to Zalman, 1938;
Left to right: Mrs. Shayndel
Eisen (Mechel's mother),
Zalman Edelstein,
Henia Stromer Edelstein,
Pepe Haberkorn,
Leytshe Barits, Abish Eisen,
Mechel Eisen, Zlateh Stromer
Eisen, Shaul Stromer

Henia, Gittel and Moty,
in front of store

The Strekers: Rozalie, Helen, and Józef in Jagonia, 1943

Ruth Baumwald and
Moty Stromer
engagement portrait,
Kraków, 1947

Moty, 1947

Hirsch Baumwald, Nina, Sala Baumwald, baby Sue, Ruth, Moty, Antwerp, 1954

Moty, Ruth, Nina and Sue in Knokke, Belgium, 1955

Standing: Meyer Stromer, Zalman and Henia Edelstein, Max Stromer, Reva Edelstein
Seated: Gusta Stromer, Ruth and Moty Stromer, Leah Edelstein,
New York, 1960

Moty, Nina and Sue, Central Park, 1961

Ruth and Moty, 1979

Stromer Family. Standing; Caroline, Andrew and Nina Gaspar, Sue and Arthur
Talansky. Seated: Jeremy Gaspar, Jonathan Talansky, Moty,
Michael Talansky and David Gaspar, 1983

Stromer Family (2001). Standing : Ruthie Talansky, Andrew Gaspar, David Altman, Jonathan Talansky, Heidi Talansky, Arthur Talansky, David Gaspar, Jeremy Gaspar, Daniel Gaspar. Seated : Nina Gaspar, Caroline Altman, baby Jessica Altman, Sue Talansky, Michael Talansky.

Moty's great grandchildren:
Rebecca Talansky, Jessica Altman, Abigail and Lily Altman, Marc Talansky, 2007

Moty Stromer, December, 1992